D0934334

Collective Bargaining in Public Employment

Collective Bargaining in Public Employment

The TVA Experience

Michael L. Brookshire
The University of Tennessee

Michael D. Rogers
Tennessee Valley Authority

Lexington Books
D.C. Heath and Company
Lexington, Massachusetts
Toronto

Library of Congress Cataloging in Publication Data

Brookshire, Michael L
    Collective bargaining in public employment.

    1. Tennessee Valley Authority—Officials and employees. 2. Collective bargaining—Government employees—United States. I. Rogers, Michael D., joint author. II. Title.
HD8005.6.U52T182   331.89'041'35300823   76-53867
ISBN 0-669-01291-2

Published simultaneously in Canada

Printed in the United States of America

International Standard Book Number: 0-669-01291-2

Library of Congress Catalog Card Number: 76-53867

For Kris, Angela, Kristi, and Nikki

Contents

List of Figures and Tables

Figure

Table

Foreword

This volume provides an instructive account of the origins and development of collective bargaining in the Tennessee Valley Authority (TVA) with the construction, production, and maintenance workers and later with the white collar and professional employees. The historical accounts, in chapters 2 and 3, are particularly interesting since TVA management and the leaders of the building trades craft unions who shaped the early policies, agreements, and relationships had wide latitude, a common vision of the TVA mission, and relatively few of the restraints that dominate labor-management relationships in an old government agency.

It was my opportunity early to become acquainted with most of the key figures reported in the narrative: Gordon Freeman, Stanley Rounds, Sam Roper and Marion Hedges, for the crafts; Gordon R. Clapp and E.B. Shultz for TVA; and Otto Beyer and William M. Leiserson, whose broad experience played an influential role, as these pages recount, in shaping the views of TVA decision-makers at the decisive early stage before the 1940 agreement between TVA and the Tennessee Valley Trades and Labor Council. It has also been possible over the years for me to follow at a distance the development of these relationships through various official responsibilities and from a university perspective. The founding fathers were indeed an able and imaginative group, dedicated to the view that responsible collective bargaining could gradually be developed in the TVA to contribute to the public purposes of the new agency, to improve the conditions of the workers and their organizations and for effective management of a public corporation. On all sides these men were conscious of building for a long-term purpose.

This study focuses on major features of the development of the collective relationships; in particular, on the structure and process of bargaining, the arrangements for pay determination, the procedures for impasse resolution and work stoppages, the administration of the agreements, the issues of union security, and the operation of committees for labor-management cooperation. In these features of the relationships, a number of innovative approaches have been designed by the parties over the years, as in the policy to encourage union membership short of a requirement for a union or agency shop and in the procedures to distinguish during the life of an agreement between a walk-off and a strike that is prohibited by statute.

It is easy to share, in general, the favorable view of the performance of collective bargaining in TVA that the authors exude. But one would have liked to have known a bit more of the impact of the relationship on seasonality, annual earnings, productivity, and other measures of comparative performance in TVA construction and power-plant operations. The impact of TVA policies and compensation on private employers in the area would also be a topic of interest. The future course of relationships and policies, in response to challenges from within and from general governmental policies, is a range of issues that grows insistently out of the study. It was not readily perceived, for instance, that the TVA arrangements are inherently incompatible with the structure of federal labor relations under Executive Order 11491, and had the general federal governmental rulings under the Order been applied to TVA, as they were in the fall of 1975, the whole structure of TVA arrangements would have been seriously undermined. (The Executive Order was revised in January 1976 to exclude TVA.)

The TVA experience in industrial relations over the past forty years or more is a fascinating story. It is a tribute to those who designed the policies and institutions. Although the TVA arrangements cannot be readily transferred to ongoing government agencies, individual features of this experience described in this volume are instructive for all those concerned with the difficult issues of industrial relations and collective bargaining in government.

Harvard University   *John T. Dunlop*
3 January 1977

Preface

Many books have been written to describe and analyze the institution of collective bargaining in the private sector of the economy. In recent years, a few books which discuss the nature of collective bargaining in government have also appeared. Yet, a gap has existed in the literature for texts which illuminate the practice and problems of collective bargaining through detailed reference to a particular bargaining setting. This book is an attempt to partially fill that gap with a comprehensive examination of union-management relations in the Tennessee Valley Authority (TVA). The bargaining experience at TVA has long been considered a model for the public sector in this country and a paradigm of sound and stable collective bargaining with all types of employees—blue-collar, white-collar, and professional.

The authors have attempted to provide more than a case study. Important issues of collective bargaining, and particularly of bargaining in government, are discussed in general terms. A second dimension of the book is, then, an analysis of the TVA approach to these issues and problems. A final, important topic is the transferability of efficacious aspects of the TVA experience to other bargaining relationships.

The book is organized to meet these objectives. Chapter 1 presents an overview of the history of public sector bargaining, of TVA's role in that history, and of the special problems of bargaining in government. The next two chapters discuss the historical development of bargaining relationships at TVA. Chapters 4-8 then analyze several important facets of bargaining in the public sector—the structure and process of bargaining, pay determination, impasse resolution, contract administration, and other substantive issues—and the TVA experience with each of these aspects of bargaining. Finally, Chapter 9 draws conclusions and focuses upon the transferability of the TVA experience to other settings.

Research for this book was conducted by the authors for several years. The general literature on collective bargaining was, of course, scrutinized. Hundreds of TVA and union documents were also reviewed, scores of union and management officials were interviewed, and much correspondence was exchanged with national union headquarters, with various federal offices, and with academicians and practitioners of public sector bargaining. As a member of the TVA employee relations staff, one of the authors developed an intimate knowledge of TVA's bargaining relationships. The other researcher, as an outside neutral, witnessed joint bargaining sessions and both union and management caucuses during negotiations. The material presented herein represents the views of the authors and not necessarily those of TVA or of its employee organizations.

Academicians who teach industrial relations will find this book to be a useful supplement for general texts on collective bargaining. Union and management practitioners will also find the book helpful in providing guides for problem solving. As one example, the chapter on pay determination, and the accompanying appendices, presents detailed information on the design and analysis of prevailing wage and benefit surveys.

The authors are indebted to many union and management officials at TVA for their cooperation in our research. In particular, we want to thank Robert J. Betts, Director of Personnel, TVA, for his active support and encouragement of this project. We are also grateful to Professor J. Fred Holly of The University of Tennessee, for his direction of our Ph.D. dissertations and to Mr. Robert C. Krapf, Assistant Chief, Employee Relations Branch, TVA, for his review and helpful comments on earlier drafts. We appreciate also the help from the following leaders of TVA employee organizations: Mr. Reeder A. Carson, Mr. Joseph L. Greene, Mr. W. Charles Harris, Mr. William Lewis, and Mr. Olan R. Long. Finally, we have appreciated the considerable help and understanding of our families during our period of research and writing.

Collective Bargaining in Public Employment

1

The TVA "Model"

In 1937, in a letter to the president of the National Federation of Federal Employees, President Roosevelt stated that the process of collective bargaining as usually understood could not be transplanted into the public service. Only three years later, Roosevelt praised the written agreement signed by the Tennessee Valley Authority and the Tennessee Valley Trades and Labor Council composed of fifteen American Federation of Labor (AFL) craft unions. In referring to this unique agreement in the government sector, he declared that "collective bargaining and efficiency have proceeded hand in hand."[1]

Wide interest in TVA's bargaining experience would continue. President Nixon established a task force to study the federal bargaining experience since 1962, when a framework was created through an executive order for bargaining in the federal government. The study group dispatched a staff member to examine the TVA experience in collective bargaining and union-management cooperation. Also, when the U.S. Postal Service was making its transition to a government corporation, officials of the Post Office visited TVA to study its personnel administration system and particularly its pay determination process. Representatives of various postal employee organizations also studied the labor-management experience in TVA.

The Bonneville Power Administration adopted the basic TVA structure of collective bargaining in dealing with its trades and labor employees. Also, the first "Hoover Commission" studied personnel practices in TVA. It recommendations included a large number of proposals for the federal government which reflected several policies and practices followed by TVA for many years.[2]

Within the past decade, numerous other public agencies have sought guidance from an examination of the labor-management relationships developed in TVA. These organizations include the California State Personnel Board; Manitoba Hydro; the city of Pasadena, California; the city of Milwaukee, Wisconsin; Canada's Preparatory Committees on Collective Bargaining in the Public Service; and the New York State Public Employment Relations Board.

These organizations found that studying labor relations in TVA gave them insight into public sector bargaining with a range of government employees—blue-collar, white-collar, and professional. In fact, a leading expert on white-collar unionism identifies the TVA experience as the outstanding example of collective bargaining between a public employer and unions of its white-collar and professional employees.[3]

Whether information gained from the various inquiries was particularly

1

useful or applicable in specific bargaining settings is generally unreported. Yet, a positive indication was given in 1967 when the chairman of the TVA Board of Directors testified before the Presidential Committee reviewing bargaining in the federal government since the early sixties. Upon hearing testimony concerning the TVA experience in labor-management relations, the Chairman of the Presidential Committee stated that TVA had provided a laboratory for public service labor relations which had been very helpful to his task force and to other departments of the government.

Why has the TVA experience been considered a model for collective bargaining in the public sector and for bargaining with white-collar and professional employees? An obvious reason is that collective bargaining in TVA is the oldest example of continuous meaningful bargaining in the public sector, involving all categories of employees. Bargainers at TVA set precedent as they dealt with the special problems of labor relations in government. This study will focus upon the efficacy of various aspects of collective bargaining at TVA and the possibilities for transferring union-management successes with bargaining at TVA to labor-management practitioners elsewhere.

TVA and Government Unionism

The Federal Level

Public employee unionism at the federal level of government is not a phenomenon of recent origin. One of the earliest groups of federal employees to affiliate with organized labor was the skilled craftsmen working in the shipyards of the United States Navy in the early part of the nineteenth century. Unions representing government employees also existed during the 1880s in the Government Printing Office. Later in the nineteenth century, the National Association of Letter Carriers, one of the earliest affiliates of the AFL, was organized in the United States Postal Service.

The early history of organized labor in the public sector was similar to the early history of unionism in the private sector, since many of the unionized federal workers performed the same types of work as private sector employees. This was true of organized, skilled workers at the Government Printing Office, at the Naval shipyards, and at Army arsenals which became organized. The craftsmen employed by these departments or agencies pursued the same trades and belonged to the same labor organizations as did their immediate counterparts outside of government. The federal civilian employees regarded themselves as machinists, bricklayers, or printers first, and as government employees incidentally; they just happened to work in a government plant.[4] Members of the Letter Carriers Union were a notable exception to this rule, for their work had no direct counterpart in private industry.

A major problem for federal employees in the nineteenth century, and in the early decades of this century, was the inflexibility of their pay determination process. In situations where the pay of federal workers was nominally or actually determined by Congress, the legislative wheels turned slowly and changes in wage scales came infrequently. Of course, the problem was magnified during periods of inflation. After the turn of the century, the Army and Navy began to experiment with more flexible methods of determining wages in arsenals and navy yards. Surveys of prevailing rates were begun to tie the wages of federal workers to those of private sector workers performing similar tasks. However, only a small percentage of federal workers benefited from these procedures. Invariably, the more flexible pay determination procedures instituted in some federal agencies were limited to trades and labor employees and were not extended to white-collar workers in the same installations.

The postal service exhibited all of the problems that plagued federal employees and government workers generally. The attempts of early organizations of postal employees to achieve gains by influencing legislation were met with "gag orders" by the departmental and higher federal officials. Postal employees were ordered not to participate in lobbying activities. They were given no effective means to redress the problems of low wages, of an inflexible pay determination process, and of a pay system which was riddled with inequity because it was not based upon a sound system of classifying jobs.

Furthermore, the pay, hours of work, and working conditions of many postal and other federal employees were determined by their immediate department head and not by law. In many cases, the department head received a lump sum out of which he paid the salaries of those under him. The hiring, promotion, and discharge of employees was often capricious and arbitrary. Political pressure governed the selection, promotion, and retention of large numbers of federal workers, even after civil service protection began for some employees in 1883, and these problems were particularly acute for postal employees.[5]

Postal workers were the first federal employees to join labor unions in significant numbers. Prior to the creation of TVA in 1933, unions of letter carriers and postal clerks were the most active organizations of government employees. Organizational activities in the postal service were first stimulated by the passage of the Lloyd-LaFollette Act of 1912. This statute recognized the right of federal civil servants to form associations for promotion of their own welfare, and it granted federal employees the right to lobby and to petition Congress. Furthermore, the act gave postal employees the right to affiliate with outside labor organizations, provided that these organizations did not assert the right of public employees to strike against the government.

The postal organizations were active in the decades that followed, but their thrust was in lobbying rather than in collective bargaining. They were weakened by internal strife and handicapped by the hostile, antiunion attitudes of most of the Postmasters General whom they faced. By the end of the 1940s, dealings between the department and unions of its employees remained relatively hostile. Any successes in improving benefits and working conditions sprang from lobbying activities.

Many postal clerks suffered from dirty working conditions and poor lighting, political factors remained important in personnel decisions, and workers complained of petty rules, harrassment, and demerit systems.[6] Yet, collective bargaining was considered an ineffective medium for addressing these problems or wage and hour problems. Effective grievance procedures were not available. In contrast, TVA and unions of its blue-collar, white-collar, and professional employees had been developing an effective bargaining relationship for several years.

Outside of the postal service, two unions aimed organizational activities at federal employees specifically. In 1917, the National Federation of Federal Employees (NFFE) was chartered by the AFL to concentrate upon federal workers. This organization reported around 50,000 members in the early 1930s when it withdrew from the AFL because it believed that the federation was not adequately supporting its activities. The AFL promptly founded a rival organization, the American Federation of Government Employees (AFGE), in spite of its historical antipathy to dual unionism. Membership in the AFGE would steadily rise, just as membership in the NFFE would steadily decline. AFGE membership climbed from 25,356 in 1938 to 51,606 in 1954. It was approaching 100,000 in 1962 and had spurted to over 600,000 by the early seventies.[7]

Especially in the early years of TVA's existence, the union members at TVA were quantitatively important to the federal union movement. Union members at TVA were a significant percentage of all union members in the federal government, most notably when total TVA employment climbed toward 42,000 during World War II. .Yet, the real impact of unionism at TVA on government unionism in this country has always been qualitative. As early as the 1940s, TVA bargainers were proving that stable union-management relationships could exist in government, that bargaining could occur over a wide range of subject matter, and that written labor agreements could be executed and administered with no disruption to essential services.

By the decade of the sixties, a wide gap remained between union-management relations at TVA and in the federal government generally—a gap in the framework and scope of bargaining and certainly in the maturity and stability of bargaining relationships. In 1962, only twenty-nine exclusive bargaining units existed in the federal government. Most of these twenty-nine units had long been defined and in operation at TVA, while a few others existed in the Department of Interior.[8] Of course, no framework for establishing bargaining units and certifying unions had been established in the federal government until President John F. Kennedy issued his Executive Order 10988 of January 1962. This presidential order gave most federal employees the right to join and participate in employee organizations. By May 1963, President Kennedy had supplemented the order with a "Code of Fair Labor Practices." Agency management was prohibited from interfering with employees in the exercise of their right to organize, from discriminating because of membership in an employee organization, from refusing to grant recognition or to deal with a qualified organization, and from engaging in reprisals against any employee for having complained or testified under Executive Order 10988.

TVA employees had all of these and other rights and protections as early as 1935, when TVA issued its *Employee Relationship Policy* (ERP). Employees could organize and designate representatives for collective bargaining. They were protected against any restraint, interference, or coercion from members of the staff and from any discrimination because of union membership. These and other rights and safeguards were carried over into the 1940 written agreement with the council of TVA's trades and labor unions and the later agreement with the panel of white-collar and professional unions.

Executive Order 10988 also provided for three types of union recognition. Exclusive recognition required a union to secure a majority vote of approval—with at least 60 percent of the relevant unit voting—to represent all members of the particular unit in collective bargaining. Formal recognition required a union to secure at least a 10 percent vote of approval in a unit and provided consultation rights for the union. Informal recognition could be granted to any other employee group but did not guarantee consultation rights with management.

The latter two forms of recognition, which were heavily pushed by professional groups, made union-management relations and negotiations unnecessarily awkward and complicated. The collective bargaining ability of unions with exclusive recognition was also eroded. TVA, in contrast, had always provided for exclusive recognition only, the form of recognition utilized in the private sector. From the first organizational efforts by craft unions in the 1930s, TVA granted exclusive representation rights to organizations receiving a majority vote of approval in a defined unit, and the organization represented all workers in the unit.

The scope of collective bargaining in the federal government was circumscribed to an extreme degree by Executive Order 10988. In general, an agency was not required to confer with any employee organization over "the mission of the agency, its budget, its organization, and the assignment of its personnel, or the technology of performing its work."[9] Management retained the right to make unilateral decisions over the direction, promotion, transfer, assignment, suspension, demotion, and discharge of employees; maintaining the efficiency of government operations; and determining the methods, means, and personnel by which operations would be conducted. Moreover, the Civil Service Commission (CSC), centralized pay determination procedures, and various other federal laws and regulations, further limited the subject matter of collective bargaining.

The difference in the scope of collective bargaining prescribed by the 1940 agreement between TVA and blue-collar workers and the 1950 agreement with salaried employees is notable. No specific list of management's retained rights was included. Collective bargaining over rates of pay, hours of work, work schedules, classification of positions, grievance systems, and working conditions in general were considered appropriate. TVA's only reservation was that it could not bargain over subject matter beyond its legal authority. However, it shall be shown that TVA had been given, by law, considerable autonomy over personnel matters.

Executive Order 10987, issued along with 10988, required each federal agency to establish an appeals system, or grievance system, for adverse personnel actions, including discharge and suspensions for over thirty days. Advisory arbitration could be included in the system. Section 8 of Executive Order 10988 also allowed for advisory arbitration, but final and binding arbitration of grievances by third parties was not permitted. Furthermore, wage determination, position classification, performance ratings, and reductions in force were excluded from negotiated grievance procedures.

The TVA *Employee Relationship Policy* (ERP) of 1935 provided a grievance system for TVA employees. The 1940 and 1950 written agreements between TVA and unions of its employees also prescribed a grievance system, with final and binding arbitration by an impartial referee as the last step in the handling of any grievance. The subject matter of grievances was not circumscribed to a significant extent.

Finally, Executive Order 10988 prohibited any form of union security arrangement in the federal service, such as union shop or agency shop arrangements common in the private sector. Employees of federal agencies were given the protected right not to join employee organizations, and they were protected from any discrimination for failure to join or to pay dues to a union. TVA has always resisted the inclusion of formal union or agency shop provisions in its contracts, but it had begun to give preference to union members in promotions, transfers, and reductions in force by the early 1940s.

Executive Order 11491, entitled "Labor-Management Relations in the Federal Service," was issued by President Nixon in 1969 to replace Executive Order 10988. The new order was designed to correct major weaknesses of the previous one, and it represented a significant liberalization of the collective bargaining framework in the federal government. For example, a Federal Labor Relations Council was created to oversee the guarantee of organizational rights and to resolve representation disputes within federal agencies. Binding arbitration of grievance disputes by third parties was allowed. The Federal Labor Relations Council could overturn an arbitrator's decision, but an agency head could not. Furthermore, an arm of the Federal Labor Relations Council was empowered to aid in the resolution of bargaining impasses between federal agencies and unions. By the end of the sixties, therefore, the framework for bargaining by other federal agencies was catching up, in some areas, with that of TVA. Yet, in the scope of bargaining, union security, and the overall maturity of collective bargaining relationships, TVA continued to stand out in the federal picture.

State and Local Governments

When the unionization of government workers accelerated in the 1960s, the nature of union-management relations at TVA was also far more advanced than anything which had developed on the state or local levels of government. The American Federation of State, County, and Municipal Employees (AFSCME) had been in existence since the 1930s, but rapid organizational gains by the AFSCME and other unions awaited the passage by state legislatures of at least permissive frameworks for public sector bargaining. Wisconsin made the first move with a 1959 law providing for the recognition of public employee unions and granting some collective bargaining rights to municipal employees within the state. Legislation dealing with public sector labor-management relations in other states began after Executive Order 10988 was issued at the federal level.

By the end of 1967, twelve state laws mandated either a collective bargaining or a meet-and-confer type relationship between various political subdivisions and specific employee groups, such as state or municipal employees, teachers, and firefighters. Twenty-six states had laws either permitting or authorizing some form of collective bargaining for certain employee groups, while five state laws prohibited any form of collective dealing with government employee groups. Twelve state laws denied various governmental units the authority to negotiate with unions representing particular classes of employees.

By the close of the first important decade of government unionism, almost half of the states had statutes mandating either meet-and-confer or collective bargaining relationships where unions of certain public employees had been recognized. Other states had statutes making meet-and-confer or bargaining relationships permissible or very limited statutes concerning only the more basic employee rights, such as the right to join a union. Nine states had no legislation pertaining to the rights of public employees to organize, bargain collectively, or even confer with their employer. Generally speaking, severe problems existed in the lack of effective state machineries for resolving appropriate unit and jurisdictional questions, in the narrow scope of bargaining in most settings, and in the lack of effective grievance and impasse resolution procedures.

Moreover, if the TVA experience stood out in the early development of government union-management relations, it was also prominent in the development of white-collar and professional unionism after the New Deal. By the mid forties, seven white-collar and professional unions and associations at TVA represented almost 5,000 employees. This number was almost one-third as large as the total number of white-collar workers represented by the AFGE. The locals of office employees at TVA actually helped establish their national union, the Office Employees International Union, chartered by the AFL in 1945.

From the 1940s through the 1960s, organizations of TVA engineers, chemists, accountants, and other professionals have been unusually active bargaining entities compared to the few other organizations of similar workers in the public and private sectors. They continue as outstanding examples of professional unions engaging in genuine collective bargaining.

The Seventies

The second decade of widespread union activity by government employees commenced, at the federal level, with an unprecedented amount of unrest and militancy. Among the more publicized incidents which ushered in the decade of the seventies were a prolonged "sick-out" of about one-third of the employees of the Federal Aviation Agency, a strike by sanitation workers in the District of Columbia, and a slowdown in the Government Printing Office. In March 1970, the nation experienced an unprecedented and disruptive postal strike. Prior to the postal strike, the federal government had a remarkably good record of avoiding strikes. Now, it is generally acknowledged that neither the strike sanctions provided by Executive Order 11491 nor those provided by Public Law 330 (the antistrike law applicable to federal employees) are enforceable in the face of large-scale strikes.

Approximately five months after the nationwide postal strike, the president signed into law the Postal Reorganization Act. A quasi-governmental organization was created, and a unique system of union-management relations in the federal sector was also established by this act. Employee-management relations in the postal service were subjected to many of the provisions of the National Labor Relations Act (NLRA), as amended. Specifically, the National Labor Relations Board (NLRB) was empowered to determine appropriate bargaining units, supervise elections, and adjudicate unfair labor practice changes. The Act protected the rights of postal employees to form, join, or assist a labor organization, or to refrain from such activity. These labor-management provisions, plus the 1974 extension of the NLRB's coverage to hospitals, stand as prominent benchmarks in the trend toward convergence of the frameworks for union-management relations between the public sector and the private sector.

The number of federal employees in exclusive bargaining units continued to increase rapidly after 1970. From 1970 to 1974, the percentage of federal employees in exclusive units jumped from forty-eight to fifty-seven. This total increase was made possible by an increase in the percentage of general schedule employees in exclusive units, from 35 to 48 percent; the percentage of wage-grade employees in exclusive units remained at slightly over 80 percent. Furthermore, the percentage of federal employees covered by written agreements rose markedly, from 31 to 49 percent, in this period.[10]

In the seventies, the framework for federal employer-union relations continued to be governed by Executive Order 11491, and thus was still at variance with bargaining in the private sector. Executive Order 11838, a 1975 amendment to Executive Order 11491, did broaden the allowable scope of bargaining in the federal government. It made the scope of grievance procedures in contracts a subject of bargaining, and it weakened the ability of federal agencies to bar or circumscribe negotiations on conditions of employment. The order also established procedures which should lead to the consolidation of small bargaining units into larger units. Yet, these and other amendments to Executive Order 11491 have been more cosmetic than fundamental. They have not forestalled a drive to enact a federal statute prescribing a skeletal structure for unionism and collective bargaining in the federal government more similar to that of the private sector.

The states have been especially active enacting statutes affecting public employer-employee relations in the second decade of significant public sector unionism. By 1975, thirty-three states had designated certain agencies or boards to assume some or all of the responsibilities over state and local government employer-employee relations that are exercised by the NLRB in the private sector. Eight states had provided some sort of right to strike for some state or local employees, or at least had chosen not to prohibit strikes for some of these employees, while many of these and other states had mandated or allowed the binding arbitration of disputes on contract terms.[11]

The scope of allowable subject matter for bargaining is enlarging in many state and local jurisdictions, although bargaining scope is still narrow by private sector standards. In the area of union security, for example, eight states and the District of Columbia had by 1975 allowed their jurisdictions to negotiate agency shop agreements for most categories of public employees. Two other states had mandated that nonunion members pay a service fee to any union granted exclusive recognition to bargain for them.[12]

A possibility exists that federal legislation will be passed to prescribe a framework for union-management relations in state and local governments. One proposal would simply extend the coverage of the NLRA over these jurisdictions. All of the leading proposals would standardize the legal bounds for union-management relations in state and local government and would substantially move the skeletal structure toward that of the private sector. However, a June 1976 Supreme Court decision in *National League of Cities versus Usery* makes the constitutionality of such federal legislation, if passed, doubtful.

All of this rapid change, and potential change, in public sector labor relations means that the TVA experience in union-management relations is more relevant than ever before. At TVA, bargaining units were determined and unions were certified largely by private sector rules. TVA has bargained for decades over a relatively broad scope of subject matter and with great flexibility in fashioning an efficient bargaining structure and in developing, for example, grievance procedures and methods of impasse resolution. As bargainers in other public sector settings begin to enjoy a comparable scope of bargaining and similar flexibility, they will increasingly be able to utilize the substantial body of knowledge produced in the four decades of the TVA experience.

Unique Aspects of Public Sector Bargaining

Despite the transformations in public sector labor relations outlined above, public employees and their organizations continue to be treated differently than private sector employees and unions under public policy and law. One argument for this differential treatment is based upon the premise that the public employer is different from the private employer. The public employer is uniquely sovereign.

Sovereignty has been defined as the "supreme, absolute, and uncontrollable power by which any independent state is governed . . . paramount control of the constitution and frame of government and its administration. . . ."[13] The sovereignty concept has been used by government employers in this country to stop employees from joining unions, then to prevent such unions from affiliating with labor federations, later to justify a refusal to recognize or bargain with public employee unions, and finally to justify a strike ban on public employee groups. No special group of the citizenry, such as a union of government workers, should be able to unduly influence, pressure, or share power with the sovereign government—the supreme overseer of the interests of all.

A second major argument that public policy toward government workers should be different is that public work and public workers are different. Public employment is said to be so essential to society that work stoppages by government workers cannot be allowed. This argument is specious, for if there are services in the economy which society cannot allow to be interrupted, they do not separate out along public sector/private sector lines. A strike of public sector sanitation workers may damage society far less than a strike of private sector steelworkers, or of garbage collectors employed by a private contractor. Furthermore, a prohibition of strikes by public employees does not necessarily insure the continuation of public services. A strike of private sector coal miners might interrupt the flow of electricity from a government-operated utility just as surely as could a strike of those workers employed by the utility.

In general, the differential treatment of public employees does not rest upon a solid foundation. The sovereignty doctrine is not tenable. If government can contract with private firms for services, it can contract with its own employees for their services. If the continuity of some employments is so crucial to society that strike rights in these employments must be limited or withdrawn, then a disparity in public policy between public and private workers is still not justified. Essential services are not necessarily public services, or vice versa.

The most impressive argument made against collective bargaining and a strike right for public employees continues to be that government must oversee and arbitrate the interests of all and cannot fall under the inordinate influence of one special group, its employees. Yet, perhaps our most significant social and economic phenomenon since World War II has been the growth and concentration of special interest group power. Public employees may argue with some justification that their attempts to organize and bargain collectively have been a response to the need of public employees to include their own special interest group in the list of those pressuring government for advantage and favor.

The first and fundamental problem of collective bargaining in the public sector is, therefore, the ongoing conflict over whether public policy should prescribe a different framework for bargaining in this sector than in the private sector. Regardless of the conclusions drawn as to the resolution of the conflict, the parameters for bargaining and the nature and practice of bargaining do differ in the public sector. Specific areas of difference should be explored as "problem areas." They constitute problems either because their existence undermines true collective bargaining or makes it exceedingly difficult or because they are areas of continual philosophical and pragmatic conflict between public management and unions. The latter areas, such as public sector impasse resolution, continue to cloud the bargaining process with ambiguity.

A significant problem in the public service continues to be the proliferation of relatively small bargaining units which often are illogically designed and separated. Prior to Executive Order 10988, and similar orders and statutes formalizing the recognition of unions in some state and local governments, employee groups were granted recognition in a loose and unsystematic manner. Recognition did not entail any bargaining privileges, so federal, state, and local agencies gave little attention to the appropriateness of units. The resulting proliferation of units became a major problem after 1962 when bargaining agents in many government jurisdictions could be granted exclusive bargaining rights or, at least, consultation privileges. Of course, the Executive Order 10988 approach actually intensified the problem of bargaining with a multitude of bargaining agents since a union could consult with management after establishing a meager following of only 10 percent of the members of a unit. By the early seventies, 58 percent of the civilian employees of the Department of the Navy were organized into 536 different bargaining units—a "necklace" hanging "like an albatross around the neck of the Navy."[14] An another example, 90 percent of the public employees of New York State were organized into approximately 3,000 bargaining units.[15]

Collective bargaining between management and a plethora of bargaining agents is difficult in general, but it may be even more difficult in government. With management forced to coordinate its bargaining with the representatives of several units, the bargaining process may become disorderly and drawn out; this may be especially true if the public sector management has little prior experience with the bargaining process in any form. Yet, by law, the particular agency will have a specified deadline for elaborating its budgetary needs.

The federal government began to respond to this problem in 1969 when

Executive Order 11491 mandated that only one bargaining agent be given exclusive recognition to represent one bargaining unit. Recent amendments to this presidential order may hasten the consolidation of the many small units still existing. Such a trend at all government levels can only enhance the orderliness and efficacy of the structure and process of collective bargaining.

Government jurisdictions must also face the bargaining unit issue of whether supervisors should be included in such units. In the private sector, supervisors are generally excluded from coverage since they are considered representatives of management. In the government sector, however, the demands for separate supervisory organizations or for mixed units including both rank and file and supervisory members are increasing, and the experience thus far makes the wisdom of adapting private sector practice to the public sector questionable.[16]

To be meaningful collective bargaining must occur over a reasonably broad range of issues, but the scope of bargaining in the federal government has been severely circumscribed. The narrow scope of bargaining allowed under Executive Order 10988 has been described, and the same listing of management's retained rights was carried over into Executive Order 11491. The allowable scope was widened significantly in the area of grievance procedures and arbitration only. Besides the specific deletions from bargaining scope, Executive Order 11491 prohibited bargaining over subject matter governed by federal law and regulations, including Civil Service Commission (CSC) regulations. These regulations covered much of the major subject matter dealt with by collective bargainers in the private sector.

For example, where Civil Service regulations and Congressional enactments prescribed job classifications and wage levels, collective bargaining could not occur. In 1968, the scope of collective bargaining in these crucial areas began to broaden when the CSC instituted the Coordinated Federal Wage System. The wages of federal workers were tied to the prevailing wage for comparable private sector jobs in the area. Representatives of employee organizations were given a meaningful role at every step in this prevailing wage determination process; Congress gave its approval and reinforced the system by passing Public Law 92-392 on August 19, 1972. However, the system covers only federal blue-collar workers.

The other major example of existing regulations significantly narrowing bargaining scope is the CSC's posture that the selection, promotion, and to some extent, termination of federal employees should be governed solely by an employee's merit, his competence and efficiency, vis-à-vis other employees. Membership and participation in a union are said to have no importance, in themselves, under the merit principle. This principle first disallows the negotiation of union security arrangements, for a federal employer cannot act differently toward an employee who chooses not to join or pay dues to a union. Section 12(c) of Executive Order 11491 reinforces this principle by in effect prohibiting the existence of union security arrangements covering federal workers. The only exception in contract provisions which may enhance the status of a union and which may be negotiated is the checkoff of union dues. Second, the merit principle may remove from the scope of bargaining all other criteria which might be used to guide selection, promotion, transfer, and retention. For example, federal management may refuse to bargain over seniority arrangements, under the presumption that length of service per se is not necessarily positively correlated with competence and ability.[17] Thus, in a number of ways, Executive Order 11491 as amended, and other regulations significantly reduce the scope of bargaining for federal workers—especially for white-collar federal workers.

At the state and local government levels, the scope of bargaining is also circumscribed along similar lines. Although several state statutes now decree that bargaining can occur over wages, hours, and working conditions, Civil Service and other regulations may nevertheless remove important subject matter from the bargaining table. The merit principle continues to affect negotiations over union security and seniority arrangements.

Problems also exist with grievance adjustment procedures in the public sector. In some states grievances may be appealed to the state board which oversees governmental union-management relations, rather than to a neutral umpire. Such a board may not be truly neutral, and its decisions may be affected by political pressures from the government agent involved or from a politically powerful union. Moreover, some types of grievances may be appealed either to such a board or to the state Civil Service Commission. A few states allow an employee to utilize both avenues of appeal, that is, to make a dual appeal. In the private sector, dual appeal through a negotiated grievance procedure and, for example, through the machinery of the NLRB is normally disallowed, for the possibility of dual appeal undermines the primary appeals procedure and shrouds the administration of labor agreements with a great deal of confusion.

The collective bargaining process itself is more difficult and problematic in the public sector. The process is governed as much by politics as by economics. Management's bargaining attitude and tactics may become markedly different in an election year. A greater variety of pressure groups will influence the bargaining stance of public management, and the government employer's posture toward money matters in negotiations may be primarily a function of the anticipated reaction of the electorate to the negotiated results. We might anticipate that public management would be more resistant to wage demands in an election year—unless the political power of public employees can force an opposite response—and where the tax or other adverse ramifications of compensation gains upon the electorate are most visible.

The fact that the executive and legislative branches are separate in federal and state governments further complicates the collective bargaining process. Negotiations are conducted and concluded by agency representatives in the executive branch, but the negotiated package must move into the legislative branch—a purely political arena—for ratification. The legislative branch may refuse to provide necessary funds to make the negotiated agreement effective, and it may refuse to accept a factfinder's or an advisory arbitrator's opinion, which the executive branch has already accepted. Moreover, top agency management has often failed to give its bargaining team adequate authority to negotiate a final agreement. All important aspects of the negotiations must be passed up to top management for review and approval, and the agency head may veto and undercut his negotiators' positions. When these kinds of hindrances prohibit either party to collective bargaining from bringing the process to a final and binding conclusion, the value and credibility of the process is seriously damaged.

Public employee unions have also been guilty of actions which undermine collective bargaining. They can pursue their ends through collective bargaining or through lobbying and will presumably make a rational choice over which vehicle to use. In fact, public employee unions have used both vehicles simultaneously. When unions of government workers are lobbying with the legislative branch and bargaining with agency representatives at the same time, the process of collective bargaining is undermined. The process is also eroded when the unions sign an agreement and then pressure the legislative branch to lump additional benefits on top of the negotiated package.[18]

Impasse resolution is the public sector's most publicized union-management problem area. The right to strike in the private sector places significant pressure upon unions and managements to make concessions in negotiations, for strikes can bring heavy costs to both sides. Effective pressure on both parties to negotiations is the best known mechanism for resolving bargaining impasses with reasonable solutions for all concerned. The mechanism is generally not available in the public sector. Employees of the federal and of most state governments cannot strike. Even if the scope of bargaining were broad, true collective bargaining might be impossible without the availability of effective pressure weapons for both parties. In fact, effective alternatives to full strike rights have not been developed and instituted at a sufficiently fast pace in the public sector—a major reason for a high incidence of mostly extralegal strikes. Man-days idle from public sector strikes have been climbing as a percentage of man-days idle from all strikes since the early sixties, and in 1968 and 1973, public sector man-days idle exceeded 5 percent of total man-days idle from strikes.[19]

Bargaining with White-Collar and Professional Employees

In both the private and public sectors, unionization and collective bargaining differs for white-collar and professional workers versus blue-collar workers. An understanding of these differences is also a necessary foundation for the case study to follow. Traditionally, white-collar work has been characterized as relatively clean and physically nonrigorous, with less time clock pressures and less autocratic work rules than exist for blue-collar work. Fringe benefits, such as paid vacations, have usually come first to white-collar workers. Contact and identification with management has been great. Additionally, a large percentage of white-collar workers have been women who on the average have not viewed their particular job as a stepping-stone in their pursuit of a particular career.[20] Administrators, accountants, engineers, scientists, and similar types of professional workers, when not self-employed, have typically been utilized individually or in small work groups with a high degree of freedom and autonomy on the job. White-collar and professional work, characterized in these ways prior to recent years, was certainly not conducive to unionism. Yet, the union movement has been forced to turn its attention toward the white-collar work force. In 1960, white-collar workers were 43 percent of all workers; by 1985, they will be 53 percent of all workers. During this period, the "professional and technical worker" subgroup of white-collar workers will grow from 11 to 17 percent of total employment.[21] The union movement must organize large numbers of these workers in order to retain significant strength in an increasingly white-collar world of work.

In fact, many unions did not differentiate organizing techniques aimed at white-collar workers from traditional techniques used for blue-collar workers until the late sixties. The new "middle class" approach to white-collar workers features organizers who are more highly educated than ever before and who are more often female. Attacks on management are soft-pedaled during organizing campaigns. Joining a union is characterized as "good business." Even terminology is tailored for the white-collar group: "worker" and shop steward" become "employee" and "business representative."[22]

American Federation of Labor-Congress of Industrial Organizations (AFL-CIO) organizational activities aimed specifically at professionals also changed along similar lines and were coordinated after 1967 by the Council of AFL-CIO Unions for Scientific, Professional, and Cultural Employees (nicknamed SPACE). Organizers emphasized the post-World War II phenomenon of increasing percentages of engineers and other professionals working for large employers, usually in large work groups, with decreasing individual decision-making and autonomy. Narrowing compensation differentials over blue-collar and white-collar groups were also stressed. Considerable effort was expended on attempts to convince professionals that union membership was indeed respectable.[23]

Whether the union movement is developing an adequate capability for organizing white-collars and professionals cannot yet be judged. White-collar union membership as a percentage of all union membership has continued to creep upward in the seventies, reaching 17.4 percent in 1974. However, organizational success with these workers has not been sufficient to prevent the continued percentage decline in union membership. The portion of union members in an increasingly white-collar work force has declined from 23.6 percent in 1960 to 22.6 percent in 1970 to 21.6 percent in 1974.[24]

For white-collar and professional workers who have been organized, collective bargaining has differed in some respects from bargaining between employers and blue-collar workers. First, the organization of the union side for bargaining may vary from the traditional norm. White-collar, and especially professional, "unions" have more often been independent of national unions and federations, and therefore organized on a local or area-wide basis. They have more often been association-like in nature, concerned with welfare and fraternal programs and not with collective bargaining. However, the trend toward national organization and union-like behavior is unmistakeable.

In general, white-collar and professional unions are more open and democratic than are blue-collar unions. They must be, for employees joining these organizations tend to be more concerned about the union's effect upon their economic welfare and their economic and social status vis-à-vis management, their nonunion peers, and blue-collar groups. Professional organizations have also been especially interested in a scope of collective bargaining which is broader than the scope for blue-collar workers.[25] It may include the methods of performing jobs, career development, and even the mission of the organization. Finally, white-collar and professional workers may use available grievance machinery less often than do blue-collar workers, but they may have more solid complaints on the average when they turn to this machinery.

To summarize, unionization and collective bargaining have differed between white-collar and professional versus blue-collar workers, just as they have differed for public sector versus private sector workers. Recognizing these differences, we can proceed to an examination of collective bargaining in a public sector setting involving blue-collar, white-collar, and professional employees.

Notes

1. Sterling D. Spero, *Government as Employer* (New York: Remsen Press, 1948), p. 346.

2. Harry L. Case, *Personnel Policy in a Public Agency* (New York: Harper and Brothers, 1955), p. 113.

3. Leo Troy, "White-Collar Organizations in the Federal Service," *White-Collar Workers,* Albert Blum, ed. (New York: Random House, Inc., 1971), pp. 167-168 and 197-199.

4. Spero, *Government as Employer,* p. 105.

5. Sterling D. Spero, *The Labor Movement in a Government Industry* (New York: Arno Press, Inc., 1971), pp. 32 and 58.

6. Spero, *Government as Employer,* pp. 165-167.

7. John F. Griner, "The American Federation of Government Employees: Fastest Growing Union in the United States," *Collective Bargaining in Government,* J. Joseph Loewenberg and Michael H. Moskow, eds. (Englewood Cliffs,

New Jersey: Prentice-Hall, Inc., 1972), p. 57; and U.S. Civil Service Commission Office of Labor-Management Relations *Union Recognition in the Federal Government* (Washington, D.C.: U.S. Government Printing Office, November, 1974), p. 25.

    8. *The Crisis in Public Employee Relations in the Decade of the Seventies,* Richard J. Murphy and Morris Sackman, eds., Proceedings of a Seminar Conducted by the Public Employee Relations Center (Washington, D.C.: Bureau of National Affairs, Inc., 1970), p. 13.

    9. *Employee-Management Cooperation in the Federal Service,* Executive Order 10988 (January 17, 1962), Section 6(a).

    10. *Union Recognition in the Federal Government,* op, cit., p. 19.

    11. This information is based upon data supplied by the *Government Employee Relations Report* (Washington, D.C.: Bureau of National Affairs, April 14, 1975), No. 51:501.

    12. Raymond N. Palombo, "The Agency Shop in a Public Service Merit System," *Labor Law Journal* (July 1975), p. 414.

    13. Henry Campbell Black, *Black's Law Dictionary,* Fourth Edition (St. Paul, Minnesota: West Publishing Company, 1951), p. 1568.

    14. "Federal Bar Association Labor Law Council Conference Studies First 16 Months' Experience Under E. O. 11491," *Government Employee Relations Report* (Washington, D.C.: Bureau of National Affairs, May 3, 1971), No. 349, A-7.

    15. *1970 Supplement to Report of Task Force on State and Local Government Labor Relations,* Committee on Executive Management and Fiscal Affairs, National Governors' Conference (Chicago, Illinois: Public Personnel Association, 1971), p. 31.

    16. Ibid., pp. 48-49.

    17. I.B. Hellurn and N.D. Bennett, "Public Employee Bargaining and the Merit Principle," *Labor Law Journal* (October 1972), p. 622.

    18. See Moskow, et al., "Lobbying," *Collective Bargaining in Government,* p. 219.

    19. Computed from data in the U.S. Bureau of Labor Statistics, *Handbook of Labor Statistics 1975-Reference Edition* (Washington, D.C.: U.S. Government Printing Office, 1975).

    20. See Everett M. Kassalow, "White-Collar Unionism in the United States," *White-Collar Trade Unions,* Adolf Sturmthal, ed. (London, Illinois: University of Illinois Press, 1966), pp. 355-356.

    21. Rosenthal, Neal H., "United States Economy in 1985, Projected Changes in Occupations," *Monthly Labor Review* (December 1973), pp. 18-20.

    22. See Albert A. Blum, "The Office Employee," *White-Collar Workers,* Albert Blum, ed. (New York: Random House, Inc., 1971), pp. 30-34.

23. Organization brochures from SPACE (the organization has been renamed the Council of AFL-CIO Unions for Professional Employees) have emphasized the names of famous entertainers, scientists, educators, and others who have belonged to or endorsed professional unions.

24. See the U.S. Department of Labor Bureau of Labor Statistics, *Monthly Labor Review* (October 1975), p. 2; and the *Handbook of Labor Statistics 1974*, p. 366.

25. See Archie Kleingartner, "Collective Bargaining Between Salaried Professional and Public Sector Management," *Public Administration Review* (March/ April 1973), pp. 165-168.

2

Bargaining with Blue-Collar Employees

The Creation of TVA

The Tennessee Valley Authority was created as an autonomous government corporation on May 18, 1933. Congress established TVA as part of President Roosevelt's New Deal program and set it up as a regional agency designed to

> improve the navigability and to provide for flood control of the Tennessee River; to provide for reforestation and proper use of marginal lands in the Tennessee Valley; to promote the agricultural and industrial development of said valley; . . . and for other purposes.[1]

As part of the New Deal plan to revitalize the nation's economy, President Roosevelt and the Seventy-third Congress entrusted the TVA Board of Directors with the leadership of a great social experiment. This challenge embraced planned regional conservation and the development of the natural and human resources of the entire Tennessee River watershed, which contained nearly 41,000 square miles of land inhabited at that time by over two million people.[2]

The new approach of vesting the federal government's authority in a regional agency, coupled and in consonance with the spirit and philosophy of the depression-ridden times in which TVA was created, served as part of the heritage which has constituted an important underlying force behind TVA's programs and policies. It is this type of background and heritage that served as the basis for TVA's labor relations policy, helped establish the unique philosophy of both TVA and organized labor, and has continued to influence the course of relationships between labor and TVA.

Although TVA was created as an agency of the federal government, it was established as a "government corporation" and was given many characteristics of a private business firm. The TVA Act provided that the corporation itself would be headed by a three-member Board of Directors, each of whom would be appointed by the president subject to confirmation by the Senate. This Board was clothed with final responsibility for carrying out all provisions of the TVA Act. One provision of the Act was that the Board would not be subject to the terms and provisions of Civil Service laws and that the Board would

> appoint such managers, assistant managers, officers, employees, attorneys, and agents, as are necessary for the transaction of its business, fix their compensation,

define their duties . . . and provide a system of organization to fix responsibility and promote efficiency.[3]

The TVA Act further provided that the corporation would have the legal right to sue and to be sued, have succession in its corporate name, and enter into authorized contracts. Congress created TVA as a regional agency of the government and gave it the flexibility of a private enterprise in order to better accomplish the unique task assigned to it. In his 1933 Message to Congress requesting the creation of TVA, the president asked for "a corporation clothed with the power of government, but possessed of the flexibility and initiative of a private enterprise."[4] Those legislators who wished to endow TVA with such flexibility sought

. . . to write a Bill that would establish a Government Corporation on the same basis of operation as the great industrial corporations of America—the United States Steel Corporation in its efficiency, for instance. To accomplish that efficiency the captain of the team has to have absolute command. It is the only way in which efficiency can be obtained.[5]

As a government corporation TVA also possessed other very important powers conferred upon it by Congress: the right to eminent domain, the right to set rates, general managerial authority, and the right to receive appropriations from Congress.[6] In addition, most of the other functions normally farmed out to various government staff bureaus were made direct responsibilities of TVA. The agency therefore enjoyed a considerable degree of managerial autonomy in making decisions expeditiously.

Although the Act of Congress creating TVA did not specifically provide for a policy of employee relations, it did contain several provisions which have greatly influenced the relationship between TVA and its employees. In an attempt to provide a considerable degree of flexibility to TVA as a corporation, Congress, by not specifying an employee relations policy and by enacting certain related provisions, gave the Board of Directors the discretion to adopt an employee relations policy consistent with current developments on the national industrial scene.[7]

Section 3 of the TVA Act provided, in part, that all contracts requiring the employment of laborers and mechanics should contain a provision that "not less than the prevailing rate of wages for work of a similar nature prevailing in the vicinity shall be paid to such laborers and mechanics."[8] This provision seemed to reflect the assumption that TVA's major building program would probably involve the customary federal practice of calling for bids on any planned construction project and awarding the contract to the lowest bidder. Where such construction work was done directly by TVA, the prevailing rate of wages should be paid in the same manner as though such work had been let by contract.

The Act's provisions relating to prevailing wages were similar to the provisions of the Davis-Bacon Act enacted by Congress just two years before TVA was created. The Davis-Bacon Act, however, applied to prevailing rates for cities, towns, and villages whereas TVA construed the term "vicinity" for purposes of determining prevailing rates in a much broader sense. Both the Davis-Bacon Act and Section 3 of the TVA Act relating to the doctrine of prevailing wages were, and still are, of considerable importance to the building trades unions.

Another provision important to TVA's labor relations policy, which was incorporated into Section 3 of the TVA Act, stated that in the event of a dispute as to what constitutes prevailing wage rates, the question would be referred to the Secretary of Labor for final determination. By designating the Secretary of Labor as the arbiter in such disputes, the authors of the Act evidently contemplated some form of bilateral decision-making with regard to the determination of wage rates. The provision went on to state that in the determination of such prevailing rate or rates, due regard should be given to those rates which have been secured through collective agreements by representatives of employers and employees. Thus, the determination of wages for laborers and mechanics ("trades and labor employees," according to TVA terminology) would be based, to some undefined degree, upon the wages arrived at through collective bargaining elsewhere.[9]

As previously stated, Section 3 provided that the TVA Board would not be subject to the laws and regulations of the Civil Service Commission (CSC) in the appointment of employees. This provision had far-reaching implications for TVA's employee relations policies in general and for its union-management relations specifically. Coupled with the provision relating to the determination of wage rates, it enabled TVA to enter into collective bargaining agreements, the extent and scope of which were comparable to many agreements negotiated in private industry.

The underlying philosophy of Section 3 was based primarily upon the intent of Congress as stipulated in Section 23 of the TVA Act. According to this section, from time to time the president of the United States was to recommend legislation promoting the economic and social well-being of the people living in the Tennessee River basin. The resulting prosperity of these inhabitants would not, according to Section 3, be based on underpaid labor. The ultimate objective of TVA was the improvement of human welfare, and the exploitation of labor in striving to reach such a goal would certainly be in violation of the spirit of the TVA Act and in fact defeat its purpose.

Another important provision of the TVA Act which influenced employee relations was contained in Section 6. This provision established a merit system by stipulating that no political test or qualification would be permitted in the appointment of officials or in the selection of employees. Specifically, it stated that "all such appointments and promotions shall be given and made on the basis of merit and efficiency."[10]   The TVA Board of Directors was charged with the responsibility of formulating and implementing a merit system based on "merit and efficiency." Exemption from various rules and regulations, and the concomitant establishment of an internal merit system, provided TVA with the latitude required for meaningful collective bargaining.

Initial success of TVA's total program was based primarily on its construction activities (needed to meet the provisions of the TVA Act). The type of construction work carried on by TVA is almost identical to that normally performed throughout the construction industry. Even during the early 1930s the AFL had established well-defined patterns of employee organizations in the construction industry, and the construction trade unions, although weak, were the only organizations which represented the interests of TVA construction employees since the very beginning of TVA's work. These construction workers have constituted the majority of TVA's trade and labor work force, their number ranging from about 1,500 to 30,000 since the organization was established. Today this work force numbers about 14,000 employees. The total number of trades and labor employees (construction and operating and maintenance) has ranged from about 5,000 to 35,000; today they number about 20,000.

These trades and labor employees are primarily engaged in one of three separate industries under a single management: construction, power generation and transmission, and chemical manufacturing. Of the 20,000 trades and labor employees, about 14,000 are hourly construction employees. The remaining 6,000 employees represent the trades and labor employees who perform full-time maintenance and operation work in the power and chemical plants and other facilities and who are generally paid annual rates.

In 1933, however, TVA's construction work was just beginning. Its short-range goal at that time was to build nine dams and related facilities to yield a unified system for purposes of flood control, navigation, and electric power. The projected time for completion was twelve years at an estimated cost of $426,000,000 with employment predicted to reach over 12,000 persons.[11]

The first construction project undertaken by TVA was the Cove Creek Dam, which was later named Norris Dam. On June 6, 1933, President Roosevelt transferred the responsibility for the construction of Norris Dam from the Army Engineers to TVA, and the Board of Directors was immediately confronted with the problem of labor relations. The extent of unemployment, particularly in the Tennessee Valley region, was tremendous and work opportunities were extremely scarce. One of the major questions facing the TVA Board was how best to meet the immediate construction requirements, help diminish the high rate of unemployment, and still provide an effective long-range plan to meet the goals dictated by the TVA Act.

In attempting to undertake a construction program of the magnitude envisioned by the TVA Act, the Board of Directors first considered the major policy issue of whether to build dams and other facilities on a low-bid contract basis or to build the necessary structures by "force account" in which case such work would be done directly by TVA. The TVA Board, in accordance with Section 3 of the TVA Act, had the discretion to decide which method of construction it would utilize. In making their decision, the TVA Board members believed that low-bid contract construction, which was then prevalent in the government sector, did not provide for a sound and enduring system of labor-management relations.[12] The Board members also thought that the number of persons employed from the Tennessee Valley region would be much greater if the construction work were done by force account. Another major consideration was that of economy and efficiency. If a force-account system were adopted, a well-trained source of manpower would be readily available for work on similar projects planned in the future.

The Board of Directors consequently decided that it would assume full and direct responsibility for its construction activity and perform its major construction work by force account—a decision which has since prevailed on all major construction projects. In this way, the Board assumed complete responsibility for developing and administering its own labor relations program.

Another important part of TVA's heritage, dating back to the 1920s, is organized labor's support for TVA as reflected in their belief in the public control of water resources, with the services provided from such control available to the people at cost. As early as 1919, the AFL recommended that legislation be enacted providing for government control of water power to provide power at cost.[13] The AFL reported that it opposed the subsidization of privately owned power systems and stated that:

We individually and collectively . . . urge the necessity for a coordinated public development and control of said water resources for the service of the people at cost, giving due regard to the four-fold duty of water for domestic supply, for irrigation, power production and navigation, and to the necessity for flood-water storage and control and to the rights of political subdivisions to the measure of local control in these matters.[14]

The Creation of TVA in 1933 was in line with what the AFL had been recommending for years. Thus organized labor appeared to have at least an ideological commitment to TVA's success. Such a commitment was echoed in a statement made by William Green in a Labor Day speech in 1944: ". . . labor . . . and . . . TVA have transformed into reality many of the dreams of the American Federation of Labor [and] you . . . [TVA employees] have brought labor-management relations to a high pitch of efficiency and success."[15]

Organized labor's support for the concept which TVA exemplified would have a very significant influence on labor-management relations in TVA. Such ideological backing contributed greatly to the active support which organized labor, as represented by the AFL leadership, has given TVA not only during its early years but also throughout its existence.

Organized labor's belief in TVA was also based upon the knowledge that the success of TVA was very important to the economic future of the Tennessee Valley region. TVA represented a powerful force, providing greater opportunities for more stable employment with decent wages and working conditions. If successful, TVA would be a major employer in the region and would have valuable influence on other employers in the area. In the words of one nationally known labor leader:

In the TVA we don't have conflicting interests and a division of spoils to be fought for but rather a common purpose and a common goal to be achieved. We must mobilize our collective intelligence as workers to advance our economic life, not at the expense of the TVA, but rather by understanding that our economic lives are bound up inescapably with the project. If it prospers, we prosper. If it succeeds, we succeed. If it fails, we fail.[16]

Moreover, the TVA Board shared labor's belief in the values that organized labor could contribute to the Tennessee Valley region. They also expressed a belief in the principles of collective bargaining and thought it the best way to communicate with employees and to give them a voice in matters which affected them.

The entire program of TVA represented a willingness on the part of the federal government to assume new responsibilities in dealing with major and long-neglected problems. The Board of Directors and other persons responsible for developing the initial labor relations policy believed that the same type of approach should be made in the field of labor-management relations—an area which had for many years been characterized by disagreement, misunderstanding, strife, and violence.[17]

The Employee Relationship Policy

Although TVA was established as part of the legislative package of emergency measures enacted during Roosevelt's New Deal, it was unlike much of the other legislation passed at that time. TVA was not designed as a temporary unemployment relief measure intended to serve as a substitute for relief payments. TVA was created more on the basis of a permanent public works program designed to make the Tennessee River navigable, to control floods, to produce fertilizer, and to create and distribute electric power at the lowest feasible cost. TVA was to be a long-range project with the ultimate goal of improving the natural and human resources of the Tennessee Valley area. President John F. Kennedy echoed the permanent nature of TVA when he stated that ". . . all the essential roles of TVA remain . . . and new opportunities, new frontiers to explore, are opening up every year. . . . In short, the work of TVA will never be over."[18]

In keeping with the philosophy creating TVA and in consonance with the far-reaching goals established by the TVA Act, the first TVA Board of Directors made the decision to perform its major construction work by force account. In so doing, the Board hoped to avoid the deplorable labor relations and working conditions which had existed at the Boulder Dam development—a project which the Reclamation Bureau of the Department of the Interior contracted on a low-bid basis under the Boulder Canyon Project Act of 1928. Board member David Lilienthal reflected a new, more humanistic approach to labor relations when he stated that "unless TVA's labor policies are just, the whole program is wrong."[19]

Once TVA began its construction program and once the decision was made to assume complete responsibility for its labor policies, the Board of Directors had to formulate a viable system of labor-management relations—or at least develop a basic philosophy and framework from which a sound system could evolve. This endeavor was particularly burdensome during TVA's early years, primarily because of prevailing attitudes with respect to employee and industrial relations in general and with respect to union-management relations in particular. Employers throughout the country, and particularly those in the TVA region, exhibited indifference toward employee-management relations and outright opposition toward unions and collective bargaining. Consequently, organized labor confronted employers with hostility and militancy. TVA, however, wished to develop a system of employee relations based on cooperation and mutual trust.

A further complicating factor was that construction work was almost non-existent in the TVA area, and craft unions were small and very weak. Of course, membership in labor unions throughout the country had been on the decline and unions were relatively weak everywhere, but this was especially true in the South. One result was a lack of experience and expertise in union-management relations in the area. The experience which did exist was based on attitudes more conducive to labor-management unrest and conflict than to the type of cooperative relationships which TVA hoped to achieve.

A negligible amount of collective bargaining experience also existed in the federal service, where it was generally accepted that the presence of the CSC made unionism and collective bargaining unnecessary. Lobbying in Congress by various pressure groups over wages and working conditions was the alternative to collective bargaining in federal employment. Furthermore, collective bargaining was directly associated with the strike weapon. Since no one could ever strike against "the sovereign government," it was generally assumed that negotiations could not be conducted in the federal service. This attitude was reinforced by the traditional view depicting the government employer as master, employee as servant.

An important factor which lessened the effect upon TVA of the prevailing attitudes of union-management relations was the quality leadership of persons selected to be responsible for personnel management in TVA. These men were the true pioneers of TVA's labor relations program. They were directly responsible for the philosophy of union-management relations which developed during the first few years of TVA's history and which constituted the underlying philosophy upon which today's policies exist.

After TVA had begun construction work with its own forces, numerous problems in employee-management relations emerged. The first Chairman of the TVA Board of Directors, Arthur E. Morgan, immediately saw the need for a formal statement of policy which would govern relationships with TVA employees. A formal policy depicting various terms and conditions of employment would help promote consistency and understanding on the part of both TVA management and employees. It would guide supervisors and enable employees to "compare and test the acts of (their) immediate supervisor by the standards therein contained."[20]

The appointment by the TVA Board of Dr. Floyd Reeves as Director of Personnel, whose responsibilities included labor relations and personnel administration, contributed to the spirit and substance of TVA's employee relations policy. His influence, and that of his first appointee, Gordon R. Clapp, helped answer the question of what TVA's basic attitude toward unionism would be.

Clapp in particular played a fundamental role in developing the specific labor relations policies and programs of TVA and also in helping to establish the well-defined philosophy of collective bargaining which began to emerge shortly after his arrival. His entire philosophy of union-management relations was predicted on the principle that employee organizations would react responsibly to an attitude of trust and confidence on the part of management.

Another TVA employee who exhibited a substantial influence on the early development of TVA's union-management relations was Clair C. Killen, Director of the Labor Relations Branch of the Division of Personnel. Prior to his appointment, Mr. Killen had been an international representative of the International Brotherhood of Electrical Workers (IBEW), and his experience with organized labor had a profound impact on TVA's decision to build its labor-management relations program upon the prevailing structure of craft unionism in the construction industry.

TVA personnel managers had no easy task in formulating a policy on employee relations. Even more arduous would be the job of implementing that policy. These problems were compounded by the fact that TVA's projects brought together hundreds of supervisors, engineers, superintendents, foremen, and several thousand blue-collar workers, including skilled craftsmen, laborers, and other unskilled workers. Some of the blue-collar employees were members of trade unions but many were not. All of these employees, from superintendent to unskilled laborer, were of necessity drawn from private industry and from the ranks of the unemployed. In addition to skills and abilities, they brought their prejudices and suspicions.

Underlying Assumptions

From the initial stages of development of an official policy on employee relations, TVA wanted labor's input and participation. Before seeking the views of employees and representatives of organized labor, however, TVA wished to develop the basic assumptions upon which the policy would rest. After many hours of deliberation by staff members of the Personnel Division, the Board of Directors, and outside consultants, the decision was made that "any worthwhile approach to the problem of labor relations either in a Government agency or in a private establishment must rest on certain assumptions."[21] These fundamental assumptions were to be either accepted in toto or not at all; otherwise organized labor would be continually forced to devote most of its attention to a fight for existence. The first assumption was that employees have a certain amount of knowledge about their work, and they have a stake in the enterprise in which they work. Thus, an employer could allow labor unions to serve as mechanisms for the transfer of this knowledge, thereby giving management the benefit of employees' thinking and giving each employee a sense of worth and a sense of participation in his work.

The second assumption, concerning organizational rights, was that government employees were just as responsible and law-abiding as other employees. Therefore, these employees should have the same rights to organize and to be represented in bargaining as employees in the private sector.

The third assumption concerned the more pragmatic question of whether TVA employees should have the right to designate representatives who were not employees of TVA. Although this right for employees in the private sector had been incorporated in the National Industrial Recovery Act (NIRA), TVA was faced with the question of whether this would be sound policy for a public agency. In deciding upon a course of noninterference with employees in their own affairs, TVA made no reservation about employees choosing to be represented by nonemployees; this would be at the discretion of the employees involved, and TVA would deal with their representatives in good faith.

The decision to allow TVA employees to be represented by nonemployees was based not only on prevailing practice in private employment (particularly in the construction industry) but also on the belief that good working relationships between unions and management would depend upon mutual confidence and good faith demonstrated by both groups.

If management could not trust mature employees to select capable and responsible representatives and leaders, it would be hopeless to attempt to establish a relationship of value. On the positive side we recognized that unaffiliated employee groups in their direct contact with management tend to overemphasize the little irritations that are inherent in human relationships. Very frequently these self-contained groups jeopardize broader objectives by their insistence upon making big issues out of little ones. The outside representative frequently understands broader objectives because the issues he is confronted with transcend the minor irritations that develop from day to day. We were prepared to leave the question of representation and outside affiliation entirely in the hands of employees.[22]

These assumptions served as the foundation for TVA's philosophy of labor-management relations, and their complete acceptance by top management was expected to lead to a relationship of cooperation between organized labor and TVA management. The positive acceptance was a unique decision by a government agency during that period of time, when such principles had not yet been fully accepted even by private employers.

Once top management had accepted the basic principles, they turned to the question of appropriate subject matter for bargaining. The applicability of the more fundamental issues of wages, hours, and other terms and conditions of employment were questioned in light of the "sovereignty doctrine" which was then widely accepted by government employers. Wages and other conditions of federal employment were largely determined by Congress and the CSC, but TVA had been granted a substantial degree of flexibility, and many of these employment problems could be solved through collective dealings with employee organizations. Such problems included issues over wages, hours of employment, work rules, selection and placement procedures, training, and other rules and regulations affecting working conditions.

Stages of Development

Having established a basic philosophy toward organized labor and collective bargaining, and on appropriate subject matter for bargaining, TVA set out to develop an official policy statement on labor relations. Rather than unilaterally adopting a management policy regarding conditions of employment and labor relations in general, TVA submitted draft statements to employees and various labor organizations for study and discussion before any formal policy was adopted. For over a year and a half, more than thirty drafts were submitted to exhaustive study and analysis that included numerous conferences held between management and representatives of employee unions at all major work sites.

The official statement of policy governing labor relations, the *Employee Relationship Policy* (ERP), was developed in three stages during the period from 1933 to 1935. The first stage was characterized as a period of unorganized discussions between a few top officials of TVA including Arthur E. Morgan, the Chairman of the TVA Board of Directors, and William M. Leiserson, an outside consultant who was at that time the Chairman of the National Mediation Board. In fact, it was Dr. Leiserson who, after examining TVA's personnel situation, actually recommended the adoption of a formal statement of labor policy.

Morgan then asked Leiserson to prepare a draft of such a policy statement. The draft, received in October 1934, contained a comprehensive statement of principles, administrative organization, and personnel rules and included a long introductory statement setting forth the philosophy of employee-management relations which TVA desired to cultivate. The Leiserson draft served as the underlying framework of TVA's policy and was passed back and forth for revision between Morgan, members of the Personnel Staff, and Leiserson himself.

The second stage of development began around March 1935, and consisted of numerous discussions and revisions of the Leiserson draft. This deliberation included a wider circle of persons than those participating in the first stage and also included high level supervisors in TVA and persons from the Legal Department. During this intermediate stage, Leiserson's influence played a vital role with regard to the inclusion of a fundamental principle involving the sovereignty doctrine. This issue was fully reflected in a statement made by Leiserson in response to Morgan's proposed wording of the introductory paragraph of Leiserson's initial draft:

my most fundamental objection is the principle you state in Paragraph One of Section One that the 'sovereign power cannot be limited except by the Federal Constitution or by an Act of Congress and the President.' Your wording of this paragraph gives the impression that a Government agency cannot limit its power by contract, and that it cannot make a collective contract with its employees through a process of collective bargaining.

This paragraph is, to me, a mistake because it raises doubts as to the legality of collective bargaining when, as a matter of fact, Congress has in several acts not only approved the policy of collective bargaining but has actually adopted the policy of encouraging and promoting collective bargaining.[23]

Leiserson was prepared to end his participation in the development of the policy if Morgan's language regarding the sovereignty principle were kept in the draft of TVA's labor policy. TVA's personnel staff argued that the government could indeed contract with labor and still retain its sovereignty. Morgan finally agreed to change his proposed wording of the first paragraph by adding the statement that "the Government, such as TVA, can, however, set up processes of collective bargaining, of making collective contracts with employees . . . while conforming to national policy and while not ignoring the sovereignty of the Government."[24]

The final stage of development consisted of hearings and conferences conducted between management and groups of employees who were located at various TVA projects. Statements of the tentative policy were distributed to all employees of TVA and also to various labor organizations. Formal hearings and conferences were held at Norris, Knoxville, Chattanooga, Wheeler Dam, Wilson Dam, and Pickwick Dam, where employees and their representatives heard the provisions of the ERP explained. Later they were given the opportunity to present criticisms and recommendations to TVA management. Such participation was adopted to insure thorough employee understanding so essential to effective administration of such a policy. The Chairman of the Board adopted this type of procedure on the recommendation of Leiserson.

The hearings and conferences were held under the leadership of another outside consultant, Otto Beyer, who was at that time Director of Labor Relations for the Federal Coordinator of Transportation. He had previously been instrumental in developing the union-management cooperative program for the Baltimore and Ohio Railroads and for the Canadian National Railroads.

During the hearings, criticisms and recommendations were received not only from TVA employees and their representatives but also from the ranks of management. In fact, a report representing the views of higher supervisory officers of the Engineering and Construction Department made certain suggestions, the adoption of which would have completely destroyed the underlying principles of the proposed policy. Their report stated that the proposed *Employee Relationship Policy* "may lead to serious difficulties in carrying out (their) responsibilities and may result in inefficiency and other abuses; . . . construction costs will tend to increase; . . . employee morale may be lowered instead of raised."[25]

Content and Analysis

The ERP as finally approved incorporated a broad spectrum of issues related to employee-management relations. The statement itself was divided into three different sections: an "Introductory Statement"; a "Policy" section containing twenty-two different provisions; and a "Concluding Statement." The "Introductory Statement" presents a somewhat modified version of the sovereignty principle by stating that TVA is an agency of the sovereign Government of the United States and as such must conform to national policy. The policy statement goes on to say, however, that TVA employees can organize for the purpose of engaging in collective bargaining.

The "Policy" section of the ERP contains the heart of TVA's personnel administration program. It includes five different areas of subject matter: (1) organizational rights and bargaining structure; (2) representational rights; (3) collective bargaining; (4) grievance and dispute statement; and (5) employee-management cooperation.

In the determination of TVA's official policy toward organizational rights of employees, the most important consideration involved their right to be free from management interference. The basic right of noninterference had been established in the private sector by the Railway Labor Act, the NIRA, and by the National Labor Relations Act (NLRA) and to a lesser extent for federal postal employees by the Lloyd-LaFollette Act of 1912. TVA officially recognized such a right as early as October 1933, and incorporated it into the ERP in 1935. The third paragraph of the policy granted to all TVA employees

the right to organize and designate representatives of their own choosing . . . for purposes of collective bargaining and employee-management cooperation. In the exercise of this right they shall be free from any and all restraint, inter-ference, or coercion on the part of the management and supervisory staff.[26]

These statements regarding organizational rights were almost identical to those corresponding to parts of Section 7(a) of the NIRA; they were also similar to the organizational rights guaranteed to employees under the NLRA of July 1935. Furthermore, paragraph 5 guaranteed that there would be no discrimination against representatives of employees nor would employees suffer discrimination because of membership or nonmembership in any labor organization. No formal union security arrangements were included in the policy statement.

An issue subsidiary to the one involving the fundamental organizational right of employees to be free from management interference was the extent to which TVA management might influence the structure of the organizational and representational machinery and still maintain consistency with the noninter-ference principle. This question was important to TVA in its attempt to formu-late a new system of collective bargaining based on employee-management cooperation.

Since TVA was not covered by labor legislation and because craft unions representing TVA employees were weak and poorly organized during the early days of TVA's history, management had an opportunity to choose between various alternative forms of employee representation. Among the choices con-sidered during the formulation period of the ERP were: (1) bona fide craft unions; (2) employee committees of associations and other similar representa-tion plans comparable to the company union arrangement; and (3) joint employee-management councils. The recommendation was made to develop a system of employee representation based on the existing craft union structure and also to promote and strive for a cooperative type of union-management relationship. Specifically, it was proposed that one or more central bodies composed of craft union representatives be created.

The question of appropriate representation concerned the employees' right to select representatives of their own choice without interference from manage-ment. The more significant issues discussed and debated during the formative stages of the ERP were: (1) the right to select a union as bargaining representa-tive; (2) the recognition of the choice of the majority as exclusive bargaining agent; (3) the question of whether to recognize a minority as exclusive bargain-ing agent for such minority; and (4) the method of determining the appropriate bargaining unit.

After the basic principle of the right to organize freely was accepted, little controversy existed over the issue of whether TVA employees should have the right to select a labor organization as their representative for bargaining purposes. Paragraph 6 of the ERP explicitly provides that employees may be represented by an organization, person, or persons. Although some management representatives stressed the disadvantages of adopting the existing system, whereby employees could be represented by outsiders, it was concluded that nothing short of independent trade unions would allow a kind of representation in accordance with the spirit of the Roosevelt administration.

The issue of recognizing organizations to speak for only a minority of a group of workers evoked much controversy. Chairman Morgan tentatively approved for inclusion in the ERP a "minority rule" provision. The provision would have allowed an organization representing a minority of some class of workers to bargain as if it represented a majority of the class, provided that no other organization had more members from the particular class. Rather than to prevent a strong union or other organization from overriding the desires of nonmembers, the TVA proposal was advanced primarily because of the minor extent of organization among TVA employees at that time. Only three craft unions (Electricians, Plumbers, and Masons) then represented a majority of their crafts in TVA's skilled construction force. Leiserson objected strongly to the inclusion of such a minority representation provision, and through much correspondence with Chairman Morgan, convinced him that minority representation was not feasible.

The questions concerning the various criteria used for determining appropriate bargaining units resolved themselves, once the decision was made to accept the established craft union structure as the foundation of collective bargaining. The concept of exclusive jurisdiction expounded by the international craft unions of the AFL was accepted in toto by TVA. Thus, the appropriate unit question concerned only what particular craft represented the work performed by that group of employees.

There was very little discussion of the appropriate unit question during the formulation period of the ERP. One related topic discussed was TVA's desire to provide a supplemental form of overall representation in addition to specific craft jurisdictional lines. Such representation was intended to cross craft jurisdictional boundaries and be agency-wide in scope. The thrust of this arrangement was to provide some kind of machinery for cooperation between the national unions. The Tennessee Valley Workers' Council was established to provide project-wide representation and serve as a vehicle for cooperation between unions.

During 1934, TVA officials were concerned with the general problem of organization and representation. They wished to provide a framework of union-management relations conducive to a more fruitful and harmonious relationship than they believed existed in the private sector. Although most officials had accepted the principle of collective bargaining and agreed that it should be adopted by TVA, Morgan initially rejected the feasibility of bona fide bargaining. This belief is reflected in the chairman's draft of the introductory paragraph of the proposed labor policy:

The Tennessee Valley Authority differs from a private industry in that the management of an industry represents the ownership and can bargain directly with employees as between equals. The TVA is a branch of the sovereign government of the United States. This sovereign power cannot be limited except by act of Congress and the President. It is not proper, therefore, to set up a policy of bargaining between the government and its citizens as though they were two parties of equal sovereign power. The government, deriving its power from the people of the whole nation, must be in final control. The government, or one of its branches, can, however, set up processes of fact finding and policy making which, while not surrendering the sovereignty of the government, can give expression to a sincere desire to establish fair, open, and progressive labor relations.[27]

The initial draft of the labor relations policy submitted by Leiserson to Morgan contained the basic right of employees to organize and to bargain collectively. The Chairman reviewed this draft, but he did not want to commit the Authority to an outright policy of collective bargaining. He therefore changed the wording in several places from "collective bargaining" to "confer collectively." Morgan's views, as well as his proposed introductory paragraph of the TVA labor policy, would have been directly contrary to the official 1934 Board policy of allowing employees to organize and bargain collectively without interference from management.[28]

Officials of TVA's Personnel Department and Leiserson, emphasizing the importance of conforming to the philosophy of the Roosevelt administration and to the NIRA, persuaded the Chairman to modify his proposal to provide for collective bargaining while conforming to national policy.[29]

In conjunction with the Chairman's new position on collective bargaining, Morgan, in a letter to Leiserson, stated:

we are not going to achieve economic democracy at a single step. We are going a long way, and if we make good on this we shall do better than if we had undertaken too much. In some communities where collective bargaining is unknown a job is still something to get from a congressman, and if one is fired all rules and regulations are but excuses for going to one's congressman with complaints, sometimes very persistently. You cannot judge our problems by the mature discipline of a railroad union or the urban solidarity of a clothing workers union. I think we must be allowed a certain amount of tentativeness and reservation and tolerance in developing habits of employee cooperation among groups of people some of whom never heard of collective bargaining except in some vague way as being an evil thing like communism, brought in by foreigners, or as some way to get easy money from the government, as in the C.W.A.

We are trying to develop a different temper on the TVA work from that which commonly exists in labor relations, the temper of people with a common interest trying to work out their relationships in a satisfactory manner. As a matter of fact, our Personnel staff stands between management and other employees, and by the management on the jobs is looked upon as rather hopelessly pro-employee. The personnel service largely occupies the same position as the National Labor Board would in dealing with employee relations on a public job. . . . We have tried in our Personnel Division to furnish a place for non-partisan judicial review, separated from management on the various jobs.[30]

Leiserson's correspondence further indicates his philosophy on how management should approach collective bargaining:

My objection was directed only to any attempt on the part of the management to impose its own views on what is right and best in those matters on the employees. The question of what is right with respect to seniority can only be settled properly when the views of all the parties concerned are adequately considered and ironed out.
. . . I also understand that you are trying to develop a different temper on the TVA work from what commonly exists in labor relations. My comments were primarily intended to warn you that unwittingly you may be bringing that old temper into your labor relations by failing to give sufficient consideration to the views and prejudices of the employees, and failing to make plain that you are providing an avenue for having their ideas given due and thorough consideration in working out common problems.[31]

The early drafts of the proposed employee relations policy contained only very general language pertaining to the bargaining process and the scope of bargaining. Yet, largely due to Leiserson's influence, the final version called for annual bargaining conferences with employee representatives. Rates of pay, labor standards, and working conditions were to be discussed in these conferences.

Leiserson's initial draft of an employee relations statement also contained a procedure for resolving employee complaints and grievances. His suggested procedure for resolving "all disputes between management and employees" included a conference between representatives of the Personnel Department and the employee(s) concerned. Any unresolved issues would then be referred to the TVA Board. Issues pertaining to wages and working conditions and those not governed by applicable federal law would then be appealed to the Secretary of Labor for final resolution. The inclusion of the right to final appeal to the Secretary of Labor would, according to Leiserson, promote real collective bargaining and would be in consonance with the section of the TVA Act which provided for the settlement of prevailing wage disputes.

TVA did not agree with Leiserson's suggestion regarding appeals to the Secretary of Labor, but the desirability of appeals machinery which included recourse beyond TVA management was recognized. Morgan initially agreed to add to the TVA labor policy draft the provision that either party may appeal the decision of the TVA Board of Directors to the National Labor Relations Board (NLRB).

Pressure from professional engineers, supervisors, and management of the Construction Division of TVA, and also the fact that the NLRB's future was then somewhat in doubt, caused the Board to decide not to have the NLRB serve as final arbiter in TVA grievances and disputes. Moreover, it was uncertain as to whether the NLRB could legally accept jurisdiction over such matters. The policy version finally adopted did not incorporate the right of appeal either to the NLRB or to the Secretary of Labor, as suggested by Leiserson, but made the Personnel Department the final arbiter of disputes and grievances.

The grievance and dispute adjustment provisions adopted in the final version of the ERP defined disputes as those growing out of grievances or out of the interpretation or application of the published rules and regulations of the Authority governing labor standards, rates of pay, classification, hours of work, employment conditions, and the like. The employee or his representative, if not satisfied with the disposition of the case after it had been processed through the supervisory channels, could appeal the dispute to the central office of the Personnel Division for investigation and adjustment. In commenting on this proposed version, the General Solicitor of TVA stated that it contained all the vices of grievance procedures adopted under company union plans. He was particularly critical of the provision because it left the settlement of disputes in the hands of management.

The concepts of collective bargaining and employee-management cooperation were generally considered identical during the developmental years of TVA's labor relations. Certainly, Morgan seemed to equate the two concepts. The TVA Chairman believed that cooperation between employees and management was based on the sovereign authority of TVA and the benevolent intentions of its management. This view formed the basis for the ideological conflict between Morgan and Leiserson regarding collective bargaining. The latter believed that true collective bargaining and employee-management cooperation could be attained only between equals, with both parties admitting to their own potential for fallibility and with each having its positions considered by the other. Leiserson stated in a letter to Morgan that if management wished to emphasize cooperation and unity of interest, it would have to deal willingly with employees even on those matters about which it was sure it already had the right answer. In short, Leiserson thought of employee-management cooperation as a joint endeavor between equals. Morgan thought that management was technically best able to judge employment and working conditions and that labor's role was only to criticize or protest the faults of management and not to assume management's functions.

Also significant during the formulation process leading up to the final approval of the ERP were the views on employee-management cooperation expressed by Clair Killen. From early 1934, Killen stressed the fact that TVA's work could be accomplished only through the cooperation and joint efforts of both labor and management. To best attain such cooperation, organized labor would play a fundamental role. Killen believed that it was much easier and more effective to gain the cooperation of men collectively as opposed to individually. The primary task for top-level management would therefore be to obtain a positive acceptance of the philosophy of union-management cooperation by many of TVA's line supervisors.

After the underlying philosophy of union-management cooperation had been accepted by those responsible for writing the final draft of the proposed ERP, the need for specific machinery to implement this type of program was recognized and subjected to discussion and debate. Leiserson suggested that the following paragraph be added to the section on Representation:

Agencies [Committees] for promoting cooperation between management and employees for the welfare of both and for the most effective accomplishment of the purposes of TVA enterprise will be established and maintained.[32]

The Tennessee Valley Workers' Council, already in existence, did not object to the establishment of cooperative machinery, just so long as the cooperative program did not preclude collective bargaining. The Council stated that its spirit was cooperation and that its members wanted to prove that "labor can actually take part in the problems of management and administration in an affirmative, positive way."[33] The Council also wanted to use a cooperative program to aid workers in solving their community problems in the construction camps.

Thus, after much discussion within management and with employee representatives, a guide to the establishment of a union-management cooperative program was presented as a concluding statement to the ERP. A system of cooperative conferences was envisioned and several topics for such conferences were suggested.

Toward a Labor Agreement

Formation of the Council

After the adoption of the ERP in 1935, the next milestone in the history of TVA's labor-management relations was the formation of the Tennessee Valley Trades and Labor Council. This organization was originally made up of representatives from fourteen international craft unions directly affiliated with the American Federation of Labor (AFL). The president, vice president, and secretary of the Council were elected by majority vote of the fourteen craft union representatives. The organization's official name was chosen on February 17, 1937, in Knoxville, Tennessee.

The need for such an organization, designed to represent all TVA trades and labor employees, was apparent to both TVA and the representatives of organized labor once the various unions began negotiating wages and working conditions for their respective members. Over sixteen different crafts, each with many local unions, were involved in construction and/or maintenance work on various TVA projects throughout the region, and negotiating individually with each local or international employee representative presented innumerable problems not only to TVA but also to the union representatives.

Prior to 1935, wage rates were changed by the Board of Directors solely upon recommendations from the Personnel Department. These recommendations were based upon very little input from organized labor. The first actual union and management wage conference was held in January 1936, several months after the formal approval of the ERP. Requests for revised wage rates from twelve different skilled trades were received by the Personnel Department between October 1935 and January 1936. Local unions from throughout the Tennessee Valley and the surrounding area also made proposals for revisions in their wages.

Although requests from employee representatives were no doubt given consideration by the Personnel Department, the main criterion used to determine the wage rate revisions to be recommended to the Board was an extensive survey of prevailing wages made by Clair Killen, Labor Relations Advisor to TVA. The written requests made by various employee representatives contained very little prevailing wage data; that is, documented examples of wage rates being paid for comparable work by other employers in the TVA vicinity. TVA's survey was, nevertheless, supplemented by data on prevailing wages presented during the actual wage conference by a few local unions.

The activities of the first wage conference were reported as being unorganized since they lacked well-defined procedures or standards of operation. Much of the wage conference itself dealt with attempts to establish procedures by which the wage determination process could most effectively be conducted. One of the major problems was the lack of agreed upon spokesmen from organized labor representing TVA employees. Three or four representatives from the same union wished to speak for their respective members. The management committee given the responsibility for representing TVA (the Director of Personnel and representatives from line management) indicated to the unions that they wished to report any proposed wage revisions to a smaller group of labor representatives. The employee representatives were thus forced to consolidate into a smaller group which would represent all trades and labor employees.

During the fall of 1936 several of the craft unions combined their efforts in an attempt to negotiate for their members throughout the TVA area, and they presented to TVA "A General Wage Brief." The wage brief was prepared by Marion Hedges, Research Director of the International Brotherhood of Electrical Workers and was presented on behalf of twelve AFL-affiliated unions. The purpose of the brief was to formally request revisions in the wage rates of trades and labor employees and to offer certain facts and arguments to justify these requests. This is the first time the various international representatives of trades and labor employees officially joined forces to negotiate with TVA.

The cooperating unions believe that our presence here represents an element of growth in employee and Authority relationships. . . . We believe that the cooperating unions are sensitive, that employee relationships between themselves and a government agency are not the same as between employees and private businesses. . . . We also believe that the fact that a number of unions are here cooperating in the presentation of a common brief, is evidence of improved morale and improved employee relationships in the Tennessee Valley Authority.[34]

During negotiations at the second annual wage conference in the fall of 1936, Gordon Clapp, chief spokesman and negotiator for TVA, stated that once the management advisory committee studied the requests from the employee representatives, the committee would make its findings and recommendations to a smaller group of representatives—as opposed to the entire mass of union officials and other employee representatives present at the conference.

You will recall that a year ago in our first annual wage conference, the Advisory Committee on Wages, after having set through the preliminary meeting of the conference and heard the arguments and facts and briefs presented by the labor representative. . . then together with the statistical material collected by the Authority took that material, studied it carefully over a period of about a week or ten days and then reported back to a smaller group which had been selected by the conference delegates. That procedure was developed at that time and found acceptable. . . . As you. . . recall in a conference as large as this, it was the wish of those present a year ago to consolidate their particular groups and speak through their single representative; in other words, a spokesman for each group.[35]

The labor representatives then met in private session to determine the nature of the group to which TVA's Advisory Committee would report its findings.

The representatives [of labor] had a meeting. . . and. . . I was selected as secretary of that group [formed to receive the findings of the Advisory Committee]. At [the] meeting of representatives of crafts affiliated with the American Federation of Labor the following motions were unaminously adopted: (1) We request that each organization [representing TVA employees] have one representative [on] this group. . . (2) That we will not sit in conferences with representatives of groups of organizations not affiliated with the American Federation of Labor. . . .[36]

This group was an ad hoc organization formed to meet TVA's request for labor to better organize itself. Management had made such a request during the first annual wage conference because of the difficulties experienced in trying to deal on an individual basis with each of the many locals as well as with each international union. Such fragmentation was particularly burdensome since many of the requests were on issues of a general nature affecting all trades and labor employees—for example, the number of hours in a workweek when each craft desired a different number of hours.

The informal and temporary labor organization formed during the second annual wage conference in November 1936, was the foundation upon which the Tennessee Valley Trades and Labor Council would be organized. Only three months later the various representatives of the international unions of the AFL representing TVA employees met together in Knoxville, Tennessee, and officially formed the Council.

In addition to the election of the organization's officers and the designation of its name, an Executive Board was formed. The Board was composed of one international representative from each of the fourteen affiliated organizations. The Council itself would represent all TVA trades and labor employees belonging to local unions affiliated with any one of the fourteen AFL international or national unions making up the Executive Board.

Since the local unions representing TVA employees were scattered throughout the Tennessee Valley area and since they often represented TVA employees from a number of different states, the jurisdiction of the Council naturally extended across state boundaries. Most AFL labor councils had been organized on a statewide basis and were subject to state labor federation control. The Tennessee Valley Trades and Labor Council was therefore unique in comparison with other AFL organizations since the Council represented employees from seven different states. In an attempt to alleviate the problem of dual control and overlapping jurisdiction, the Council sought to obtain a charter from the AFL. When the Secretary of the Council, Gordon Freeman, wrote to William Green, then president of the AFL, requesting a charter for the Council, he said:

We are organizing this Council primarily in an attempt to establish satisfactory working hours and conditions in all the Tennessee Valley Authority projects. We believe this can best be accomplished by dealing with TVA as a group rather than individual trades or crafts. This was demonstrated very thoroughly at the November wage conference and we all felt more consideration was given all organizations due to our request for increase in wages being made under one general brief rather than an individual brief for each trade.[37]

In denying the request, Green replied to Freeman stating that:

under the constitution and laws of the AFL, I have no authority to issue a charter to the Tennessee Valley Trades and Labor Council, though I will gladly cooperate with the organization in every way within my power.[38]

It occurs to me that the setting up of an organization to be known as the Tennessee Valley Trades and Labor Council is to say the least quite unusual. It has never been the policy of the American Federation of Labor to organize

and charter organizations of this kind and character. We have always felt that
the City Central Bodies and State Federations of Labor met the requirements
for which an organization such as the Tennessee Valley Trades and Labor Council
would be formed.[39]

The Secretary of the Council then sought the advice of an attorney regarding
whether to attempt to incorporate the Council. Since TVA had recognized the
Council as such, however, the Executive Board decided to continue in operation
without a charter from the AFL and without being incorporated.

International representatives of the unions having members employed by
TVA and representatives of local unions operating throughout the Tennessee
Valley area began meeting as a group in January 1937. The ERP was discussed
and critically evaluated in these meetings. The primary dissatisfactions voiced
about the ERP were: (1) its restrictiveness, (2) its unilateral nature, (3) its
application by certain managers and supervisors, and (4) organized labor's lack
of protection, that is, the union representatives believed the ERP gave them
little voice and therefore that they could not be effective in dealing with TVA
management.

The labor meetings held during 1937 were replete with strong anti-TVA
sentiments regarding its employee relations policies. The first few meetings,
however, were void of any meaningful proposals to improve labor's situation.
International representatives Stanley Rounds, International Association of
Bridge, Structural and Ornamental Iron Workers; Gordon Freeman, International Brotherhood of Electrical Workers; and Samuel Roper, International Association of Plumbers and Steamfitters, were the stabilizing forces throughout
these early meetings. Rounds and Freeman openly recognized that genuine
collective bargaining, as they had known it in the construction industry, did not
exist under the ERP, and each wanted to change the form of their relationship
with TVA. They believed, however, that the time was inappropriate to request
a change in the policy. The reason for this, as stated by Rounds, was that:

it would be a tragic thing for us at this time to open that policy. I know in my
own heart that there are those on the Authority who would be glad to take
away the privileges we now enjoy. I know we should have a change but not at
this time. Unitl the Board and its members have come to an understanding
among themselves, I am of the firm opinion that we should not open the
policy, whatever, at this time.[40]

The international representatives were concerned with the type and quality
of labor relations policies established in TVA and with the role of labor in the
determination of such policies. They were particularly interested in the state
of affairs at TVA because it was generally assumed that other TVA-type organizations would be created throughout the country, and organized labor wanted
to use TVA as a model. TVA was to "set the pace" for labor relations in other

projects soon to be developed. The AFL representatives were also aware of the gains being made by Congress of Industrial Organizations (CIO) unions at that time. TVA's trades and labor employees were considered an important source of union membership, and the international representatives wanted no CIO unions competing with them for those members.

The views of Rounds, Freeman, and Roper regarding the appropriate time to propose changes in the ERP were later accepted by a majority of the labor representatives at a meeting of the Trades and Labor Council held in Knoxville, Tennessee, in 1937. However, there was much discussion and debate at the meeting concerning what could be done to improve the policy. In fact, the Council appointed a Policy Committee to recommend changes in the ERP to be proposed to TVA officials at the appropriate time. Local unions throughout the Tennessee Valley were requested to send recommended changes in the ERP to the Policy Committee, which would then consolidate all proposed changes into one final draft for Council consideration.

Recommending a Labor Contract

Before the Policy Committee formally adopted a revised labor policy—and before the various local labor organizations submitted any proposed changes—the issue of a signed labor agreement was advocated by a member of the Executive Board, O.H. Dye, international representative of the Machinists' Union:

Statements have been made here today that appear to me that Dr. Morgan has made the definite statement that he sees no reason why TVA should not enter into a contract with Labor. Now if that is a fact why worry ourselves on trying to change their policy? Why not instruct this committee to draw up a contract and go after it there at this next conference? I think you should instruct the committee [Policy Committee] to draft a contract which will be approved and then presented at our conference in November along with our new wage scales.[41]

This recommendation produced a series of lengthy discussions in support of the idea and the president of the Council, Samuel Roper, finally agreed to the proposal. The Executive Board of the Council realized that problems of applying the ERP would disappear if a labor agreement could be negotiated. They also believed that a contract recognizing the AFL unions was necessary to keep the CIO unions out.

In a 1938 letter to the Director of Personnel, the Tennessee Valley Trades and Labor Council officially requested a clarification of Section 6 of the TVA Act (the merit and efficiency clause) "in its bearing upon" the signing of an agreement with "the unions formed into the Trades and Labor Council."[42] In November 1938, the Council supplemented the request for clarification of the Act by formally requesting TVA to sign an agreement with the "Tennessee

Valley Trades and Labor Council recognizing the organizations affiliated with the AFL having members employed by TVA as the sole bargaining agent for all employees performing work recognized by the AFL as coming under the several affiliated national and international unions."[43] The letter also asked TVA to agree to a "union shop."

The issue of a signed agreement between TVA and the Council was discussed in depth between the members of the Executive Board of the Council and TVA representatives following the fourth annual wage conference on December 29, 1938. The three major questions explored by the participants were:

1. Can the Authority legally enter into a signed agreement with organized labor under the provisions of the Tennessee Valley Authority Act?
2. What authority is vested in the Tennessee Valley Trades and Labor Council as the negotiating agent for the employees of the Authority acting for the several unions affiliated with the Council?
3. What specific provisions might be contained in a formal agreement between the Authority and the Council?

TVA reported that its legal department believed there would be no legal reason why the Authority could not enter into a signed agreement with organized labor as a form of expressing mutual understandings provided the matters covered by the agreement were within the discretion of the Board as granted by the TVA Act. With regard to the legality of a closed or union shop, it was reported that this seemed clearly illegal since union membership could not reasonably be construed to reflect "merit and efficiency."

The legal question was not whether TVA could sign an agreement with organized labor representing TVA employees; rather the question involved the nature of what TVA could agree to within the confines of the TVA Act. Those areas of interest in which TVA believed that it could lawfully share its authority were those already pledged in the ERP: bargaining over wages and working conditions with those organizations representing a majority of employees in appropriate units; establishment of a procedure to settle employee grievances; and development of a joint cooperative program designed to promote the efficiency, safety, and health of employees.

TVA wanted some assurance that the Council was a properly accredited and responsible agent of TVA's trades and labor employees prior to signing a labor agreement. The Council's president, Samuel Roper, reported that because the Tennessee Valley Trades and Labor Council was an interstate organization, it could not be granted a charter by the AFL but that its status as a negotiating body had been recognized by the international offices of each of the fourteen unions which constituted its membership.

Furthermore, Roper reported that the Building and Construction Trades Department of the AFL officially recognized the Council in a "resolution of confidence" in September 1938. A few of the Council members emphasized that trades and labor employees, by virtue of membership in the local unions chartered by the various internationals, bound themselves voluntarily to the internal law of the internationals through which the Council operated. Only through a signed collective bargaining agreement with the Council, recognizing it as the bargaining agent of employees through membership with affiliated unions, could the Council have control over the local unions.

At the meeting between TVA management representatives and the Executive Board of the Council, the contents of various possible provisions to be incorporated into an agreement were presented for a decision, but the participants concluded that the Council should prepare a draft agreement setting forth all the provisions it believed necessary or desirable. TVA would then study the Council's proposed draft and arrange for another conference. However, no specific commitment to sign an agreement with the Council was made by TVA at that time.

Gordon Clapp, then Director of Personnel, presented the issue of a proposed contract with organized labor to the General Manager of TVA and to the Board of Directors. His significant influence within management, and the persuasiveness of his arguments, contributed greatly to top management's ultimate decision.

On May 25, 1939, the Board of Directors authorized Clapp to begin formal negotiations on the proposed labor agreement with the Tennessee Valley Trades and Labor Council. Otto Beyer, by this time Chairman of the National Mediation Board established under the Railway Labor Act, and for several years after 1934 TVA's regular consultant on labor relations, played an instrumental role in the discussions with the TVA Board and also in the negotiation sessions with the Council. Beyer was particularly helpful in keeping TVA abreast of developments in national policy with regard to collective bargaining. He also played an important role in the early stages of determining the specific content of the proposed agreement by arranging discussions between TVA management representatives and the key men of the Council (Freeman, Roper, and Rounds) and with Marion Hedges, an international representative of the IBEW. Finally, he made extensive analyses of the various drafts of the proposed agreement submitted by organized labor, and he offered suggestions and comments pertaining to the possible ramifications of the proposed language.

Negotiating Basic Principles

The first preliminary draft of a written agreement between TVA and the Tennessee Valley Trades and Labor Council was submitted to TVA by the Council on February 27, 1939. The proposed agreement was presented as being an extension of the ERP. According to Beyer, "the proposed agreement gives a favorable impression in that it. . . is designed to give effect, or, as it were, to implement [the ERP] by committing the organizations signatory to the agreement to many of the features of the policy."[44]

Beyer also pointed out that certain parts of the Council's draft were contradictory to the policies of the ERP. Article I of the proposed agreement, for example, would have resulted in a "membership agreement" with its terms and benefits applying only to the members of the organizations signatory to the agreement. This was an attempt by organized labor to obtain language providing for a closed shop. Beyer emphasized that this type of provision would become a source of many complications and would in fact be contrary to national policy as established by the NLRA and by the Railway Labor Act.

With regard to the settlement of grievances and disputes over the interpretation or application of the terms of the ERP or of the proposed agreement, the Council proposed that a Joint Board of Adjustment be established. This board would be composed of two representatives of the Council and two designated by TVA. If the board failed to resolve the grievance or the dispute, the members of the board would select an impartial person known as a referee to sit with the board as an additional member in the further determination of the case. Beyer agreed with this machinery but suggested that in the event of a deadlock on the board it would be preferable if the parties themselves agreed in advance upon a small panel of individuals who might be called upon to serve as referees.

E.B. Shultz, Chief of the Personnel Relations Division, suggested that if a resolution could not be reached by the Board, an impartial referee would be selected from a panel of five suitable persons. The compensation and expenses of the referee would be jointly paid by TVA and the Council. As a trade-off for agreeing to the Council's proposal to institute a formal grievance procedure culminating in binding arbitration, management proposed adoption of an article dealing with the resolution of jurisdictional disputes between the various unions signatory to the agreement. The proposed language would require the unions to determine jurisdictional boundaries but in the event they were unable to do so, TVA would be able to assign the work to those employees who in its judgment were best qualified to perform the work.

The Council also proposed that joint union-management "cooperative committees" be formed in accordance with union-management cooperative principles underlying the agreement. The purpose of the cooperative committees was to be technical and educational and their functions would not include consideration of subjects which would affect wage agreements already in operation. The committees would confine their recommendations and subjects to such matters as applied only to the advancement of TVA projects and to the welfare of employees and to betterment of public service. Beyer recommended that the subject matter be amplified and made more specific.

The question of labor's right to strike was considered by the Council in one section of the proposed contract. This section stated that the member unions did not waive the right to strike but that they agreed to refrain from stoppage of work during the adjustment of a dispute, or during the life of the agreement. Shultz questioned why the Council believed it necessary to state such a reservation about the right to strike in view of its relative unimportance and because such a declaration would make the Board hesitant to set such a principle as a precedent for national policy. Yet, Clapp questioned whether labor could afford not to mention such a reservation in view of private contracts which included the strike right. Accordingly, TVA proposed that, pending the resolution of disputes or impasses, TVA would not change conditions of employment and the Council would not encourage or sanction employees leaving the service.[45]

One of the more difficult problems in negotiating the labor contract was over the incorporation of a union security clause. Labor had originally hoped for a closed shop provision, but when this was declared illegal by TVA's legal department, the Council sought to include other provisions that would have the same effect. The proposed "membership agreement" was one such effort. TVA did, however, agree to formally acknowledge the advantages of unionism, if that union was affiliated with the Council. TVA's proposed language stated that employee membership in a national union affiliated with the Council is conducive to the furtherance of the purposes of the contract.[46] The intent of such a provision was in fact meaningless as far as the Council's position was concerned, because the language referenced the ERP which guaranteed to employees the right either to join or not to join a union.

Although TVA and the Council agreed to a self-renewing contract which could be reopened after one year upon ninety days' notice by either party, TVA's legal department pushed for a specific method for terminating the contract. However, Director of Personnel Arthur Jandrey did not wish to incorporate a specific method or date for terminating the agreement. He preferred an open-ended agreement and an emphasis on sound methods of impasse resolution to be available when changes were negotiated in the contract. Proposed machinery for resolving disputes included arbitration by the Secretary of Labor on wage disputes, mediation and voluntary arbitration of other negotiation impasses, and binding arbitration to resolve grievances and disputes over interpretation and application of the terms of the agreement.

As a concession to TVA's legal staff, however, Jandrey obtained the Council's official consent to an understanding that if agreement to change the contract could not be reached, either party could elect to terminate the agreement.[47] The understanding was confirmed on July 5, 1940 but was not officially incorporated into the labor contract.

By February 6, 1940, both the Council and TVA were in agreement on a proposed labor agreement. Yet, the Director of Personnel indicated that TVA would not sign the agreement until it was signed by the international presidents of each affiliated union. TVA wanted written confirmation that each international president gave his official approval to the proposed agreement, thereby

authorizing the Tennessee Valley Trades and Labor Council to enter into a
signed contract on behalf of its members and local unions.

By June 28, 1940, the international presidents of sixteen labor unions had
given their official approval authorizing the Tennessee Valley Trades and Labor
Council to enter into the agreement. Shortly thereafter, however, the Council
notified TVA that the President of the International Association of Bridge,
Structural and Ornamental Iron Workers was unwilling for his union to become
a party to the agreement through the Council. Some management personnel
wanted to postpone adoption of the proposed agreement until the Iron Workers
agreed to sign, because they believed that the identity of the Council as a unit
should be preserved. But Arthur Jandrey responded that it would be in the
best interests of TVA to conclude the agreement with those unions which had
approved the contract.

On July 29, 1940, a conference was held with officers of the Council to
discuss the status of a nonsignatory union. The officers assured TVA that such
a union would have no status whatsoever under the agreement, unless it became
a party to the agreement in accordance with the terms of Article IV. Jandrey
then recommended that TVA sign the agreement with the fifteen unions making
up the Council in accordance with the authorization which the TVA Board had
already provided by formal resolution, except that the name of the International
Association of Bridge, Structural, and Ornamental Iron Workers should be
deleted. Thus the *General Agreement* between TVA and the Tennessee Valley
Trades and Labor Council of fifteen international unions was effected on
August 6, 1940.

David Lilienthal of the TVA Board of Directors announced the signing of
the *General Agreement* and highlighted important aspects of the contract and
of the parties' past relationship:

Renewed assurance of intensified labor-management cooperation in the national
defense program of the Tennessee Valley Authority came today as the Tennessee
Valley Authority and the Tennessee Valley Trades and Labor Council announced
jointly that they had signed an agreement between the Authority and its 8,000
employees in the Building and Construction and Metal Trades. The agreement,
formalizing more than six years of amicable labor relations, improves machinery
of conference through formal recognition of the Tennessee Valley Trades and
Labor Council and provides for mediation facilities designed to assure uninterrupted work during the course of negotiations and settlement of disputes. While
disputes are in progress of settlement, the unions agree not to encourage or
sanction strikes.[48]

Bargaining Relationships under the General Agreement

Recognition

The *General Agreement* negotiated in 1940 specifically recognized that both
TVA and the Tennessee Valley Trades and Labor Council endorsed and

subscribed to the entire ERP. In accordance with the Council's objective, the agreement did in fact change the form of collective bargaining between TVA and the unions representing its trades and labor employees by formally establishing a relationship based upon a written and signed labor contract. As an extension of the unilaterally issued ERP, however, the provisions of the *General Agreement* had to be construed and applied in light of its terms and principles. The introductory statement of the ERP continued to serve as the underlying philosophy upon which the total collective bargaining relationship was founded. This statement, considered as a part of the *General Agreement* itself, signified that the parties recognized and accepted the Board of Directors' obligations to carry out the goals established by Congress in the TVA Act. They accepted the responsibility for this in a manner consistent not only with the provisions of that act but also in accordance with all other applicable federal laws and regulations. The Council formally recognized that the public interest in TVA would always be paramount.

According to the provisions of Article I — Preamble, the 1940 *General Agreement* applied only to the fifteen specified AFL unions, each of which included within its membership a majority of the employees eligible to designate such a union as their representative. These unions were to operate and cooperate through the Tennessee Valley Trades and Labor Council.

Article IV established the procedure whereby trades and labor employees in an appropriate bargaining unit might become a party to the contract. A major criterion for recognition of a union was that a majority of such employees signify their intention to conform to the purposes and provisions of the agreement, and that the Council accept each union as a Council member. This provision remains in effect today.

E. B. Schultz, Chief of Personnel Relations, believed that if a union did not "operate and cooperate" through the Council or if a union failed to represent a majority of the employees in a craft or class which it purported to represent, TVA would be free to unilaterally determine all matters and actions applicable to those employees in accordance with the ERP and not with the *General Agreement.*

As of the 1975 revision of the *General Agreement,* sixteen international unions make up the Tennessee Valley Trades and Labor Council. All but the International Brotherhood of Teamsters, Chauffeurs, Warehousemen and Helpers of America are members of the AFL-CIO. Of the remaining fifteen Council members, only the International Association of Machinists and Aerospace Workers is not an affiliate of the Building and Construction Trades Department of the AFL-CIO. The Teamsters were formerly affiliated with the AFL-CIO and the Building and Construction Trades Department.

Although all sixteen international unions have representatives on the Executive Board of the Council, several unions represent only a very small number of TVA employees. (See table 2-1 for the number of employees in each of the labor organizations composing the Tennessee Valley Trades and

Table 2-1

Number of Employees in TVA Trades and Labor Bargaining Units: October 1973

Labor Organization (having agency-wide jurisdiction)	Date Recognized	Number of Employees in Units October 1973 Total
Tennessee Valley Trades and Labor Council. Sixteen craft unions are members of the Council (listed below)		97
International Association of Heat and Frost Insulators and Asbestos Workers	11/12/40	47
International Brotherhood of Painters and Allied Trades	1/36	237
International Brotherhood of Boilermakers, Iron Ship Builders, Blacksmiths, Forgers, and Helpers	1/36	783
Bricklayers, Masons, and Plasterers' International Union of America	1/36	3
United Brotherhood of Carpenters and Joiners of America	1/36	991
International Association of Machinists and Aerospace Workers	1/36	858
International Brotherhood of Electrical Workers	1/36	4374
International Association of Bridge, Structural, and Ornamental Iron Workers of America	1/36	629
International Union of Operating Engineers	1/36	1698
Laborer's International Union of North America	1/36	2495
Operative Pasterers' and Cement Masons' International Association	1/36	92
United Association of Journeymen and Apprentices of the Plumbing and Pipe Fitting Industry of the United States and Canada	1/36	1259
United Slate, Tile and Composition Roofers, Damp and Waterproof Workers Association	11/21/49	8

Table 2-1 — *(Cont.)*

Labor Organization *(having agency-side jurisdiction)*	*Date* *Recognized*	*Number of Employees in Units* *October 1973* *Total*
Sheet Metal Workers' International Association	1/36	230
International Brotherhood of Teamsters, Chauffeurs, Warehousement, and Helpers of America	11/18/36	793
Wood, Wire, and Metal Lathers, International Union	11/12/40	0

Source: Letter, William E. Black, Jr., Administrator of Union-Management Relations, Division of Personnel, Tennessee Valley Authority, to Director, Office of Labor-Management Relations, U.S. Civil Service Commission, January 1974.

Labor Council.) First-line supervisors are included in these bargaining units. In addition to the number of employees represented by the sixteen craft unions, the Tennessee Valley Trades and Labor Council itself represents approximately 100 trades and labor employees (for example, Diver, Reservation Man, and Building Maintenance Mechanic) who are in classifications which are not included in the jurisdiction of any of its sixteen member unions.

The signing of the *General Agreement* itself alleviated some of major problems which organized labor had considered detrimental to its overall relationship with TVA. In addition to formalizing the relationship through official recognition of the Council as bargaining agent for TVA's trades and labor employees, the 1940 contract included several very important provisions which served to form the basis of the TVA and Council relationship. One of labor's major complaints with the relationship before 1940, for example, was the lack of an effective grievance procedure. This source of unrest was resolved by the adoption of a formal grievance procedure which culminated in binding arbitration. Other important provisions negotiated into the 1940 *General Agreement* related to union security, wage determination, impasse resolution, determination of jurisdictional boundaries, and work stoppages and strikes. These issues were highlighted as Articles in the *General Agreement* and other important conditions of employment were included in a second part of the contract and designated Supplementary Schedules. Also, the *General Agreement* was later divided into two contracts, one covering hourly employees and the other applicable to annually paid trades and labor employees. In 1974, the two contracts were changed to reflect construction employment and operating and maintenance work.

Union Security

Although organized labor in TVA was unable to attain the inclusion of contract language establishing the closed or union shop, it did manage to negotiate a statement into the agreement that TVA recognized union membership as being conducive to the furtherance of the purpose and benefits of the contract itself. Also, the contract stated that membership in a national union listed in the agreement and affiliated with the Council should not be discouraged by any TVA supervisor. Regardless of these statements, however, the *General Agreement* was in effect neutral with regard to union membership, because the terms of the ERP were still considered effective. The ERP stated that no employee should be required to join or to refrain from joining any organization or association of employees as a condition of employment, transfer, promotion, or retention in service. This neutral policy reflected prevailing national labor relations principles of private sector law.

Union security continued to be a major issue of concern with the Council, and in 1941 the Council asked for a revision of the *General Agreement* which would provide for a union shop. The Council supported its request by stating that some supervisors continued to discriminate against union members, some employees were dropping out of the unions, and employees who violated negotiated agreements could not be effectively disciplined if TVA practices permitted them to ignore their obligations, TVA's negative response to the request was based on the following reasoning:

1. The TVA Act does not permit making a union membership a necessary condition of employment, promotion, or retention of employment.
2. It would be folly for TVA to risk losing its freedom and flexibility as a government corporation by adopting policies believed to be counter to its basic law.
3. Basic issues on labor organizations and collective bargaining had not been fully clarified in the public service, let alone the issue of union security.
4. Such a move might result in severe criticism by those who have tried to capitalize on the sharp cleavage in public opinion over the question of individual rights.
5. Basically loyal union members are more valuable to the organization in the long run anyway.
6. If it is true that the absence of a union membership provision in the *General Agreement* has made it more difficult to negotiate agreements with private employers containing such provision, it should be possible to dispose of this difficulty by pointing out to such employers the limiting provisions of the TVA Act and the fact that it is a public agency.[49]

As a compromise measure, however, TVA issued a statement to all new employees, part of which stated that TVA believes union membership is conducive to the efficiency and effectiveness of the job and that TVA "looks with favor upon union affiliation as a means of achieving and maintaining the orderly joint contribution of labor and management. . . ."[50]

The union security issue continued to be a major item of concern to the Council throughout the 1940s. The Council was particularly troubled over the divergent policies of the ERP and of the *General Agreement* regarding unionism. This dichotomy was alleviated somewhat by the issuance of a second statement signed by official representatives of TVA and the Council. This statement resulted from a joint union-management committee and recognized the conflicting policies on union membership:

Over a period of years the Authority has gradually developed through its relations with the Tennessee Valley Trades and Labor Council a more and more affirmative position concerning the question of union affiliation, thereby giving emphasis to the underlying meaning of the employee relationship policy as expressed in the concluding statement of that policy rather than to the strictly neutral statement embodied in paragraph 4. This has had the effect of encouraging union membership. . . . Occasional failure on the part of some supervisors properly to interpret and apply joint agreements may result from a lack of understanding of the Authority's pro-union labor policy.[51]

Also, supervisors were charged with the responsibility of giving recognition to individual employees who participated in established labor-management relationships by either joining or actively participating in the union authorized as their exclusive representative. Thus, for the first time TVA recognized union membership as one factor to be considered in evaluating relative merit and efficiency of employees in selections for promotion, transfer, and reductions in force. Such a policy was considered a way of enabling labor organizations to discharge their responsibilities under the *General Agreement* without a closed shop provision.

Despite the efforts made by TVA to come up with a surrogate for the closed shop arrangement, the Council remained dissatisfied over the lack of a definite union security provision. The passage of the Veterans' Preference Act in 1944 only increased their misgivings. That act provided for preference to persons of veteran status in certification for appointment, in reinstatements, in reemployment, and in retention in civilian positions throughout the federal government. The Council recognized that some practices in TVA would have to be different from those followed in private employment, but they also believed that their relationships with TVA had not kept pace with national developments. Specifically, the Veterans' Preference laws were being administered by TVA to the disadvantage of the unions, and TVA was believed to be using the act to circumvent its agreement with organized labor. Some Council representatives also complained that TVA deliberately hired nonunion veterans and nonveterans over union men, and also that the Veterans' Preference Act was applied more rigidly to selection of journeymen than to the selection of supervisors.

A joint union-management committee was delegated the responsibility of generating recommendations on how to resolve the problems related to the union security issue. The members of the committee found that one of the major stumbling blocks to good union-management relations at TVA was the discrepancies existing among the various policy statements then in effect, particularly the conflict between the neutrality of the ERP and the *General Agreement*, and the pro-union joint statement entitled "Procedures for Implementing the Authority's Labor Relations Policy."

The joint committee therefore recommended that the *General Agreement* be revised to include relevant provisions of the ERP and to eliminate such provisions that were inconsistent with subsequent understandings. This recommendation included the incorporation of a new article governing the applicability of the merit and efficiency principle in recognition of union activity. Specifically, the joint committee on union security proposed the following revised language:

Article III—It is recognized and accepted by the parties to this agreement that membership on the part of an employee in a national or international union listed in the Preamble to this agreement and affiliated with the Council and in accord with the recognized jurisdiction of such union is conducive to the furtherance of the purpose of this agreement. Such membership is helpful to labor-management relationships and therefore contributes to the accomplishment of TVA's objectives.

Although not required, union membership is considered to be a positive factor in an appraisal of relative merit and efficiency in selecting for appointment, promotion, transfer, or retention.[52]

In addition to the above recommended language, which provided a basis for giving consideration to union membership in taking personnel actions based on merit and efficiency, one other article and several supplementary schedules were accepted by representatives of the Council and TVA to be included in the revised agreement in order to strengthen union security. These provisions were applied to selections for appointment and promotion, terminations, demotions, suspensions and furloughs, transfers and payroll deductions for union dues and fees. These provisions specified the manner in which the general policy of union preference would be carried out for various types of personnel actions, and each was approved by the TVA Board for inclusion in the *General Agreement* on July 13, 1951.

The provision on union security stated that:

Membership in unions party to this agreement is advantageous to employees and to management, and employees are accordingly encouraged to become and remain members of the appropriate unions. Such membership is a positive factor in appraising relative merit and efficiency. Accordingly, within the limits permitted by applicable laws and Federal regulations, qualified union members are selected and retained in preference to qualified nonunion applicants for employment.[53]

This language has remained unchanged for over twenty-four years and is presently incorporated in the 1975 revisions of the *General Agreement.*

Wage Determination

Certain principles regarding the determination of wages were established by the TVA Act. Section 3 prescribed that not less than the prevailing rate of wages for laborers and mechanics would be paid when such work was done on a contract basis. Where work was performed directly, the prevailing rate of wages was to be paid in the same manner as though such work had been let by contract. The TVA Act also provided that in determining the prevailing rates of pay, due regard should be given to those rates which have been secured through collective agreements by representatives of employers and employees. Any dispute over what constitutes prevailing wages was to be resolved upon appeal to the Secretary of Labor. His decision was to be final. These basic principles of wage determination were incorporated into Article IX of the *General Agreement* of 1940 and have continued to be in effect up to the present time. The agreement also formalized the conference machinery and procedures for determining rates of pay for trades and labor employees which had been followed generally since the adoption of the ERP in 1935.

One of the principal considerations in implementing a prevailing wage system is that of defining the particular area or vicinity from which the wage data will be accumulated. From 1937 to 1947, TVA and the representatives of organized labor on the Tennessee Valley Trades and Labor Council were in basic agreement over the definition of "vicinity" as being the watershed area of the Tennessee River and certain adjacent cities.

For determining the prevailing wages of construction work, five specific cities in the watershed area were surveyed by representatives of the Personnel Department. These areas were: Asheville, North Carolina; Chattanooga and Knoxville, Tennessee; Paducah, Kentucky; and the Tri-Cities area in Alabama. Wage information was also obtained from the following cities which were adjacent to the watershed area: Atlanta, Georgia; Birmingham, Alabama; and Jackson, Memphis and Nashville, Tennessee. Prevailing wage rates in these cities were not given primary consideration but were taken into account since the cities were possible sources of recruitment. The stated purpose for surveying these cities was to determine for each city the union rate that was actually being paid for each class of construction work performed on the Authority's program. Representatives of the Personnel Department obtained information on wage rates from local union representatives and local employers and from projects being constructed in certain areas.

In 1941, the Council and TVA agreed that the definition of the vicinity would be the entire watershed area and the following adjacent urban centers: Atlanta, Birmingham, Memphis, Louisville, Jackson, and Nashville. In 1942, 1945, and 1946, further discussions were held relating to the definition of vicinity but the Council and TVA could not agree on a revised definition. Rather, they stressed the need for improving the methods of collecting and interpreting the data. The parties understood the definition of vicinity to mean that TVA rates would be based primarily on rates found in the watershed area with rates obtained from adjacent centers given secondary consideration. But if TVA performed work in any of the adjacent centers, it would pay the local rate if it was higher than the TVA rate.

The definition of vicinity and the designation of the cities, projects, and plants to be surveyed within the defined vicinity came under attack from the Council in 1947. TVA and the Council agreed to change their definition of vicinity and the revised definition was incorporated into the *General Agreement* as Supplementary Schedule IV entitled Definition of Vicinity and Applicability of TVA Wage Rates. It stated that:

It is agreed that the term "vicinity," as used in Section III of the TVA Act and Article IX of the General Agreement, is interpreted to include (1) the watershed of the Tennessee River, (2) the TVA power service area (in which the TVA owns, operates, or constructs power facilities), and (3) certain adjacent areas and specified urban centers all included within the following boundaries: a line drawn from Birmingham to Atlanta; a line from Atlanta tangent to the eastern boundary of the watershed; the watershed boundary to the northeastern tip of the watershed; a line from the northeastern tip of the watershed to Louisville; and the Ohio and Mississippi Rivers from Louisville to Memphis; the boundary of the power service area from Memphis to the southeastern tip of that area; and a line drawn from the southeastern tip of the power service area to Birmingham.

On all work performed by TVA in the vicinity, as defined above, the TVA wage schedule will apply.

On work performed by TVA outside vicinity, as defined above, the TVA wage schedule or the rates prevailing in the locality of such work if higher will apply except that, should either party believe that use of such schedule or rates is not appropriate for such work, the rates to be used will be subject to negotiation.[54]

Prior to 1947, however, two appeals over the TVA definition of vicinity were made to the Secretary of Labor under the provisions of Section III of the TVA Act. The first such appeal was made in 1943 by the International Association of Bridge, Structural and Ornamental Iron Workers. The union asked the Secretary of Labor to rule that TVA should pay the Knoxville, Tennessee local union rate on TVA work performed in the Knoxville area. The Iron Workers' rate in Knoxville was at that time higher than the vicinity-wide rate offered by TVA. The second case was appealed to the Secretary of Labor in 1946 by a TVA subcontractor (E. J. Electric Corporation) who asked for a finding that the Nashville, Tennessee union rate for electrical workers, rather than the lower vicinity-wide TVA rate, was the proper rate for him to pay on work in the Nashville area.

In both appeals the Secretary of Labor ruled that the definition used by TVA was appropriate. His decision was based on the broad authority contained in the TVA Act and on TVA's established interpretation of Section III of the act. In the Iron Workers' case, the Secretary of Labor rejected the union's contention that the higher Knoxville rate predetermined by the Secretary under the Davis-Bacon Act must prevail. The Secretary stated that it was not unreasonable or arbitrary for TVA to define vicinity in a broader sense than locality or district. In the 1946 case, the Secretary again held that the TVA definition was reasonable. He noted that the TVA Act's language regarding prevailing wages was different from that of the Davis-Bacon Act. The latter required that rates be determined upon the basis of prevailing rates in the city, town, village, or other civil subdivision in which the work was performed.

The definition of vicinity negotiated in 1948 and included in the *General Agreement* with revisions effective June 26, 1949, remains in effect today. The parties do, however, consider actual wage and fringe data from outside the defined vicinity when applicable information is not available within its boundaries. On construction projects performed by TVA outside the defined vicinity, the TVA wage schedule or the rates prevailing in the locality of such work if higher will apply. However, if either the Council or TVA believes the use of such rates is inappropriate for such work, the rates to be used will be subject to negotiation. TVA's application of the term vicinity as defined in the *General Agreement* permits it to pay a uniform wage rate throughout its area of operation, facilitates the transfer of employees between different projects or areas, and eliminates the task of establishing and administering a multitude of local wage schedules. Chapter VI discusses the pay determination process for both trades and labor and salary policy employees in more detail.

Impasse Resolution

TVA and the Council established two procedures for resolving interest disputes: one for wage determination and one for revisions of supplementary schedules. The machinery established for resolving impasses over wages had been instituted by the TVA Act.[55] The machinery created by TVA and the Council for resolving other interest disputes—which was originally negotiated in 1940 and remains in effect today—provides for mediation and voluntary arbitration. For the latter, both parties must agree to submit a dispute to binding arbitration.

These procedures for resolving impasses have served the parties well over the three decades of bargaining and they are discussed in more depth in chapter 7.

Jurisdictional Boundaries

TVA management has always been concerned with the problems caused by jurisdictional disputes. It was able to negotiate a provision for determining jurisdictional boundaries between craft unions in the original 1940 agreement. The primary consideration by TVA in this matter was that TVA should not be responsible for determining jurisdictional boundaries between the various unions representing its trades and labor employees. This responsibility was that of the national and international unions duly authorized to represent the employees.

It was TVA's responsibility, however, to make work assignments, to maintain timely schedules for production, and to meet operating and construction requirements. To achieve this result, TVA decided, in the absence of predetermined jurisdictional agreements or awards between the unions, to make the work assignments to those employees who in its judgment were best qualified to perform the work. Of course, where custom, practice, tradition, previous jurisdictional agreements between certain unions, or decisions or awards by appropriate bodies have been made, TVA would abide by such arrangements. This, basically, has been the agreement between TVA and the Council concerning jurisdictional boundaries ever since 1940. Two clauses in the present *General Agreement* are particularly appropriate:

In the absence of established work boundaries, TVA shall assign the work in accordance with the custom and practice in the vicinity as defined in Supplementary Schedule II. In the absence of custom and practice in the vicinity, TVA shall assign the work to those employees who in its judgment are best qualified to perform the work with due regard to practices of employers outside the vicinity which the disputing union present. If, after work has been assigned on this basis, the unions reach an agreement or if an appropriate body renders a decision or award which conflicts with TVA's assignment of work, TVA agrees to alter its assignment to conform to such agreement except when the period is extended by an agreement between TVA and officers of the Council.

The Council shall notify TVA of jurisdictional agreements or disagreements which affect the assignment of work by TVA.[56]

Work Stoppages and Strikes

As of 1946, federal statutory law mandated criminal penalties for striking, or asserting the right to strike, against the federal government. The Taft-Hartley Act of the next year went on to dictate the discharge of any individual striking against his or her federal employer. Yet, TVA and the Council had already agreed on contract language condemning strikes in the TVA service, and, in a 1951 revision of the *General Agreement,* this language was strengthened.

Prior to the enactment of the 1946 act prohibiting strikes of federal employees, TVA had experienced several work stoppages at its various construction projects. In fact, one of these work stoppages, caused by a jurisdictional dispute, would have to be considered a strike. Generally speaking, however, work stoppages on TVA construction sites involved only a few employees and lasted for relatively short periods of time. In fact, the one strike in this period involved approximately 300 craftsmen and lasted one week. The actions were somewhat characteristic of "wildcat" strikes in private employment and were precipitated for the most part by disputes over work assignments. No strikes or work stoppages have occurred to date as a result of an impasse in negotiations.

The passage of legislation prohibiting strikes against the federal government forced TVA to determine when a stoppage constituted a strike in violation of the law. If a concerted activity were designated by TVA as a strike, management would be obligated to abide by the sanctions provided by federal law. In order to avoid enforcement of penalties prescribed by federal legislation, and to continue to handle violations of the labor contract administratively, TVA found it necessary to distinguish between a "strike" and a "walk-off." TVA officials and Council members have attempted to avoid describing a work stoppage as a strike; both parties strive to make certain that walk-offs do not erupt into concerted activites which are clearly definable as strikes—such as picket lines designed to stop other members from working on the project or actions officially sanctioned by unions.

No specific criteria establishing the difference between a walk-off and a strike have officially been defined by TVA. Ever since legislation prohibited strikes by federal government employees, TVA and the Council have endeavored to resolve all work stoppages within the machinery established in the *General Agreement* or by mutual understanding. TVA's last resort has been to designate walk-offs as strikes.

In addition to the grievance adjustment procedure, jurisdictional dispute resolution procedure, and the impasse resolution machinery established in the *General Agreement* of 1940, TVA and the Council in 1952 agreed on a joint statement regarding employees leaving TVA work in violation of the *General Agreement*. This statement formalized an approach which TVA and the Council had previously utilized in attempting to break walk-offs and to discipline those responsible for initiating the action. This approach involved interviewing those allegedly participating in the work stoppage to find out if they did, in fact, participate and also determining who was primarily responsible for the action.

Of all the work stoppages that have occurred at TVA construction sites, only three have been designated as strikes. The first occurred in July 1939, before the signing of the *General Agreement* and prior to the passage of federal anti-strike legislation. This work stoppage—not officially designated as a strike by TVA at that time—resulted over a jurisdictional dispute between the International Brotherhood of Carpenters and the International Association of Bridge, Structural and Ornamental Iron Workers. Both the general representative and the general president of the Carpenters' union sanctioned the "walk-off" involving about 300 of their members because TVA assigned pile driving work to the Iron Workers. Thus, the action must be considered a strike. It is interesting to note that the jurisdictional dispute was resolved by Samuel Roper, international representative of the International Association of Plumbers and Steamfitters and at that time president of the Tennessee Valley Trades and Labor Council and of the Alabama State Federation of Labor. He was appointed by the president of the AFL, William Green, to resolve the dispute.

The second strike occurred in 1951 and resulted primarily from a jurisdictional dispute between the International Association of Machinists and the Operating Engineers. The Machinists withdrew from the Council over the assignment of certain work to the Operating Engineers, and Machinists throughout TVA failed to report to work for a period of 1 to 1½ days. Picket lines were set up by the Machinists at two work sites, and work stoppages by the members of the International Association of Machinists occurred sporadically until well into 1952. As a result of these walk-offs, over seventy members of the Machinists Union were terminated.

The interview procedures were carried out but the work stoppages continued. TVA then considered the Machinists' actions as constituting a strike against the government of the United States within the meaning of Section 602 of the Independent Offices Appropriations Act of 1952 and of Section 305 of the Labor Management Relations Act of 1947. Penalties for striking against the federal government were fixed by statute, and TVA was obligated to abide by them. All those found to have engaged in a strike were terminated and received no payment of wages previously earned but unpaid as of the date of termination. Also, no annual employee was paid for any annual leave he had accumulated, and all employees were considered ineligible for TVA employment for not less than three years.

The only other work stoppage in TVA's history legally defined as a strike occurred on July 3, 1962, when all of TVA's eighty-four Sheet Metal Workers at the Paradise Steam Plant project failed to report to work because of a jurisdictional dispute with another craft. The employment of these men was held in suspense and arrangements were made to interview each of them, but the union established a picket line before the date set for the interview. The Sheet Metal Workers' local union claimed it had been locked out by TVA. As a result of the ensuing picket line, the entire project covering 2,500 employees was shut down. The picket line continued for about a week before the local union agreed to have its members report for interviews. The joint committee which conducted the interviews concluded that the Sheet Metal Workers were guilty of leaving the job in violation of the *General Agreement,* and those who participated were to be terminated and ineligible for employment for no more than one year. When this decision was made known, the picket line was reestablished.

The failure of the internal TVA-Council machinery to resolve the dispute, and the reestablishment of the picket line, prompted TVA to obtain a temporary restraining order prohibiting the local union involved from further picketing of the Paradise Steam Plant. This order was later replaced by a temporary injunction issued because the federal district court found that the local union and its members had engaged in a strike against TVA.

Since the eighty-four Sheet Metal Workers had been found in violation of Federal Law (5 U.S.C., Section 118), they were terminated from TVA employment. Forty-five of these individuals appealed their termination under the provisions of the grievance adjustment procedure of the *General Agreement.* Twenty-seven of those whose terminations were upheld in the second step of the procedure appealed to the Director of Personnel. Each of their appeals was denied by the Director. The international representative for the Sheet Metal Workers requested that these twenty-seven cases be appealed to arbitration, but the Council refused to support his request.

The Sheet Metal Workers who were terminated in the 1962 strike at the Paradise Steam Plant were considered ineligible for reemployment in TVA until 1966, when the General Counsel of TVA advised the Director of Personnel that Public Law 330 (5 U.S.C., Section 118p, 118q, and 118r) should not be construed as changing the former three-year debarment (under the 1947 Taft-Hartley Act) to a lifetime debarment. Public Law 330 was construed as requiring the termination of an employee who violated it, and as imposing certain criminal sanctions, but not as debarring the violators from reemployment.

The right of appeal from any joint committee's action taken as a result of the interview procedure was prohibited by joint agreement between TVA and the Council. Veterans with more than one year of continuous TVA service, however, have exercised another appeal right in such cases. In 1972, several eligible veterans appealed their terminations over involvement in a work stoppage to the Civil Service Commission. As a result of their appeal, the United States Civil Service Commission Board of Appeals and Review, found the terminations "fatally defective" and recommended that the appellants be restored retroactively to their former positions.

Other work stoppages have occurred, besides those which were formally designated as "strikes," and in all of these cases the interview procedure has been utilized. The most recent use of the interview procedure was.in response to a September 1973 work stoppage by several hundred steamfitters at Browns Ferry, Alabama. Reasons for this particular stoppage will be discussed in chapter 8.

Since a vast majority of TVA's work stoppages over the years have resulted from jurisdictional disputes, it should be pointed out that the establishment of picket lines over jurisdictional problems is in violation of the constitution of the

AFL Building and Construction Trades Department of the AFL-CIO. Specifically, the declaration of policy regarding picketing over jurisdictional disputes states that no local union of any affiliated international union whose general president has signed the policy—sixteen of the total being members of the Tennessee Valley Trades and Labor Council—shall institute or post picket lines for jurisdictional purposes.[57] The policy further states that in the event picket lines are posted for jurisdictional purposes, all other unions are to ignore such pickets pending appropriate disciplinary action by the international president of the local union posting such picket lines. The trouble with this policy is the difficulty of enforcement and also the probability that the picket signs may not convey the message that the picket line is established because of a jurisdictional dispute. However, the policy, coupled with the terms and provisions of the *General Agreement*, has generally assured TVA the cooperation of the international representatives of the Tennessee Valley Trades and Labor Council in attempting to prevent and break work stoppages occurring at TVA's work locations.

Perhaps more important than the building trades' policy on picket lines and strikes over jurisdictional disputes is the fact that the Council considers any work stoppage by TVA's trades and labor employees a violation of Article II of the *General Agreement*. In fact, during the interviews held by the joint committees with employees who had allegedly participated in a work stoppage in violation of the *General Agreement*, union members of the joint committee (international representatives and/or officers of the Council) are often much tougher in questioning those participating in work stoppages than are the management members of the committee. With the support of the international representatives on the Council, TVA has generally been effective in preventing a majority of work stoppages from deteriorating to the point that TVA must designate them as strikes.

The TVA-Council approach to recognition, union security, impasse resolution, pay determination, and to the other substantive issues discussed above reflect the development of the bargaining relationship. In general, a stable relationship between a management committed to the institution of collective bargaining and a highly centralized Council of strong AFL unions developed rapidly and was maintained. The period from 1940 through the early seventies was characterized by some changes in contract language and annual improvements in pay and benefits, but change in the basic nature of the relationship did not occur. In contrast, the development of the collective bargaining relationship between TVA and unions of its white-collar and professional employees was marked by less stability and by pronounced changes in both contract language and in the fundamental nature of union-management relations.

Notes

1. 48 Stat. 58, Public Law No. 17, 73rd Congress, Section 1.

2. Judson King, "The TVA Labor Relations Policy at Work" (Washington D.C.: The National Popular Government League, 1940), p. 9.

3. 48 Stat. 58, Section 3.

4. Herman Finer, *The TVA–Lessons for International Application* (Montreal, Canada: International Labour Office, 1944), p. 110.

5. *Congressional Record,* 66th Congress, 2nd Session, December 1, 1924, pp. 298-299.

6. Prior to the 1959 amendment to the TVA Act, most of the money needed for the construction of dams and steam plants was provided by congressional appropriates. The 1959 amendment authorized TVA to sell bonds and notes in the open market to obtain capital for its power program. Revenues from the power program are used to redeem bonds and also to repay money appropriated to TVA for power functions and for interest on these appropriates.

7. Harry L. Case, *Personnel Policy in a Public Agency* (New York: Harper & Brothers, 1955), p. 44.

8. 48 Stat. 58.

9. TVA interprets the "due regard" clause of Section 3 in such a manner that wage rates arrived at through collective bargaining would be considered the primary criterion for determining the prevailing trades and labor wage rates.

10. 48 Stat. 58, Section 6.

11. King,,"The TVA Labor Relations Policy at Work", p. 9. Primarily as a result of the effects of the World War II expansion, this projection turned out to be far too modest since total employment in 1942 reached 42,000 and by the late 1940s nearly eighteen dams had been constructed.

12. "Labor-Management Relations in TVA," Report of the Joint Committee on Labor-Management Relations, 81st Congress (Washington, D.C.: Government Printing Office, May 12, 1949), p. 8.

13. William Green, president of the American Federation of Labor, speech made at Fontana Dam, Fontana, Tennessee, Labor Day 1944.

14. *Report of Proceedings of the 43rd Annual Convention,* The American Federation of Labor, Portland, Oregon, October 12, 1923.

15. Green, speech made at Fontana Dam, Labor Day 1944.

16. Marion M. Hedges, "Old Man River, and the Life of One Worker," *The Federationist* (November 1937), p. 10.

17. Gordon R. Clapp, "Principles of the TVA Employee Relationship Policy and Their Application," Address before Annual Meeting of the Civil Service Assembly of the United States and Canada, Ottawa, October 6, 1937, reprinted in unpublished TVA document entitled "Material Regarding the Development of the Employee Relationship Policy."

18. Remarks of President John F. Kennedy, Celebration of 30th Anniversary of TVA, Muscle Shoals, Alabama, May 18, 1963.

19. David E. Lilienthal, "The Labor Policies of the Tennessee Valley Authority," Address before the Labor Day Celebration of Detroit and Wayne County Federation of Labor, Detroit, Michigan, September 2, 1935.

20. Letter from Dr. William M. Leiserson, TVA consultant, to Dr. Arthur E. Morgan, Chairman, TVA Board of Directors, September 19, 1934.

21. Gordon R. Clapp, "Principles of the TVA Employment Relationship Policy and Their Application", p. 5.

22. Gordon R. Clapp, "Problems of Union Relations in Public Agencies," *American Economic Review* (March 1943), p. 193.

23. Letter from William M. Leiserson to Arthur E. Morgan, May 9, 1935.

24. Letter from A. E. Morgan to William M. Leiserson, May 15, 1935.

25. Gordon R. Clapp, "Material Regarding the Development of the *Employee Relationship Policy*," unpublished TVA document, February 5, 1938.

26. Board of Directors, Tennessee Valley Authority, *The TVA Employee Relationship Policy,* August 28, 1935, p. 4.

27. "The Formulation of the Employee Relationship Policy," unpublished TVA document, August 1939, p. 39.

28. TVA Memorandum from Charles E. Hoffman, Assistant Secretary to the TVA Board of Directors, to TVA Board of Directors, "Board Action Concerning Labor Relations," July 30, 1934.

29. This proposed revision of the labor policy was included in a letter from A. E. Morgan to W. M. Leiserson, May 15, 1935.

30. Ibid.

31. Letter from William M. Leiserson to Arthur E. Morgan, May 18, 1935.

32. "The Formulation of the Employee Relationship Policy," p. 87.

33. As reported by an "eye-witness," *The Journal of Electrical Workers and Operators,* Vol. 33, No. 9. (September 1934), p. 371.

34. Marion Hedges, "A General Wage Brief Presented by Certain Cooperating Unions Requesting a Revision in the Wage Scale Upward in the Tennessee Valley Authority Development to the Employee Policy Conference Committee," November 18, 1936.

35. Gordon R. Clapp, Second Annual Wage Conference, unpublished TVA document, November 18, 1936.

36. Gordon M. Freeman, Second Annual Wage Conference, unpublished TVA document, November 18, 1936.

37. Letter from Gordon M. Freeman to William Green, February 22, 1937.

38. Letter from William Green to Gordon M. Freeman, February 25, 1937.

39. Letter from William Green to Gordon M. Freeman, March 19, 1937.

40. Freeman, "Proceedings of the Meetings of the Labor Representatives," February 17, 1937.

41. Ibid., May 20, 1937.

42. Letter from the Tennessee Valley Trades and Labor Council (signed by Marion Hedges, G. M. Freeman, Samuel Roper, and Stanley Rounds) to Gordon R. Clapp, Director of Personnel, October 19, 1938.

43. Letter from Tennessee Valley Trades and Labor Council (signed by Samuel Roper, G. M. Freeman, and Stanley Rounds) to Gordon R. Clapp, Director of Personnel, November 2, 1938. Though the Council members were aware that TVA's legal department had expressed the opinion that TVA could not sign an agreement with the Council if it provided for the employment of union members only, the labor committee (Hedges, Roper, Freeman, and Rounds) assigned by the Executive Board of the Council to work on the issue of union security stated that it would be possible to incorporate provisions into an agreement that would bring about the same results. (Letter from Freeman to the Executive Board of Council, January 28, 1938, from Gordon M. Freeman's Personal Files.)

44. Letter from Otto Beyer to Gordon R. Clapp, March 9, 1939.

45. "The Development of the *General Agreement* and Subsequent Reprints, 1940-1958." Article VII of the Council's proposed draft (unpublished TVA document), February 27, 1939.

46. "The Development of the *General Agreement* and Subsequent Reprints, 1940-1948," Article IV of TVA's proposed draft of the labor agreement, June 16, 1939. Such language was retained in the *General Agreement* as approved on August 6, 1940.

47. Letter from Arthur S. Jandrey, Director of Personnel, to Samuel Roper and Gordon M. Freeman of the Tennessee Valley Trades and Labor Council, June 28, 1940.

48. David E. Lilienthal, "News Release on Agreement Between the Tennessee Valley Authority and the Tennessee Valley Trades and Labor Council," in news conference held August 6, 1940.

49. "Summary of Negotiations between TVA and Council with Respect to the Closed Shop and Other Issues Relating to Union Membership," Personnel Correspondence Files, December, 1943.

50. Tennessee Valley Authority, "Employees' Opportunities and Responsibilities Under the Authority's Labor Policy," March 1, 1942.

51. "Procedures for Implementing the Authority's Labor Relations Policy" (joint statement signed by Gordon M. Freeman and James Leahy, the Tennessee Valley Trades and Labor Council, and George Gant and R. F. Bertram, Tennessee Valley Authority), August 20, 1943.

52. TVA Memorandum from Harry L. Case, Director of Personnel, to George F. Gant, General Manager, "Union Security and the General Agreement," May 10, 1950.

53. Tennessee Valley Authority and the Tennessee Valley Trades and Labor Council, *General Agreement* (effective August 6, 1940, revised July 1, 1951), Article III, Sections 2-3, p. 4.

54. The Tennessee Valley Authority and the Tennessee Valley Trades and Labor Council, *General Agreement* (effective August 6, 1940, revised June 26, 1949), Supplementary schedule IV, pp. 32-29.

55. Tennessee Valley Authority and the Tennessee Valley Trades and Labor Council, Article VIII, Section 1, p. 7. It should be noted here that the Secretary of Labor does not actually make the decision on TVA disputes over prevailing wages for laborers and mechanics. In December 1970, the Secretary of Labor issued orders (Secretary of Labor's Order 24-70) which delegated to the Administrator, Work Place Standards Administration, certain functions formerly performed by the Secretary with respect to specific laws and executive orders which included the Tennessee Valley Authority Act. (*Federal Register*, Vol. 36, No. 5, January 8, 1971).

56. Tennessee Valley Authority and the Tennessee Valley Trades and Labor Council, *General Agreement* (effective August 6, 1940, revised July 1, 1951, revised through July 19, 1972), Article VI, Section 3-4, p. 6.

57. "Declaration of Policy Regarding Picketing by Building and Construction Trade Unions for Jurisdictional Disputes," signed by the General Presidents of nineteen international craft unions and by the Executive Council of the Building and Construction Trades Department, AFL, July 24, 1952.

3

Collective Bargaining with White-Collar and Professional Employees

Environment for Bargaining

Both the TVA Act and the *Employee Relationship Policy* (ERP) of 1935 were important factors in the environment for the unionization of TVA's employees, for bargaining relationships would develop within limits set by the Act and the ERP. Many of the parameters applied equally to organizations of all TVA employees, but in several important ways, the bargaining framework was specified differently for organizations of white-collar and professional employees—labeled "salary policy employees" by TVA.

The 1933 Act created a regional planning and development agency, not simply an agency for power generation. This meant that TVA's white-collar and professional work force would be large (both absolutely and as a percentage of the total work force) in contrast to the same work force in an agency with power generation as its single function. The size and stability of this work force at TVA certainly contributed to the unionization of the Authority's white-collar and professional employees and to subsequent collective bargaining. Moreover, TVA's first Board of Directors decided that construction work would be undertaken by force account and not by contracting out its work. Although the immediate result of this decision was the assembling of a large trades and labor work force under TVA's own employ, another ramification was that a large white-collar and professional supporting work force would also exist under TVA's direction.

Section 3 of the TVA Act exempted the government corporation from Civil Service laws and from the regulations of the United States Civil Service Commission. Thus, TVA was granted a flexibility in matters of personnel administration and labor relations which was, and continued to be, unusual in the federal government. The civil service exemption has perhaps been the single most important environmental factor surrounding the development of meaningful collective bargaining between TVA and its employees' unions; bargaining scope was not circumscribed by civil service parameters. However, for approximately two decades, TVA exercised the exemption to a significantly greater extent in its dealings with trades and labor employees than in its dealings with white-collar and professional employees.

Throughout its history, TVA has been forced to fight for its continued exemption from Civil Service laws and regulations. The earliest reviews of TVA's exemption were conducted by the Commission of Inquiry on Public

Service Personnel in 1935 and by a Joint Committee on the Investigation of TVA in 1938. Continued exemption of TVA was recommended, and the Ramspeck Bill of 1940 exempted from civil service coverage TVA and only one other agency.

A major argument which TVA used successfully in pursuing its continued exemption was that TVA's extensive construction and power generation activities made TVA work more comparable to private sector than to public sector work. TVA insisted, therefore, that it needed the greater flexibility of a private employer in fashioning and executing personnel and labor relations policies. It pointed out that the few other agencies which had been exempted from the civil service system, such as the Panama Railroad and the Inland Waterways Commission, had required more flexibility for similar activities of a commercial nature. Of course, this line of argument essentially justified the exemption for trades and labor employees only, and the congressional bodies approving the continued exemption in the early years did have trades and labor employees primarily in mind. For this reason, TVA could at least partially justify keeping its personnel policies for salary policy employees in line with federal practice.

Further major reviews of federal agency exemptions from the civil service were conducted in 1949, 1953, 1955, and the early 1970s, and the continuance of TVA's exemption has been recommended in each case. By the time of the later studies, however, the continued exemption could be justified more easily on the single basis of TVA's record in operating its own personnel and labor relations system effectively.

Two additional provisions contained in Section 3 of the Act would have profound effects upon the disparate development of the relationship between TVA and trades and labor unions and the relationship between TVA and white-collar and professional unions. The Act directed that the compensation of trades and labor employees be tied to prevailing wages for work of similar nature in the vicinity; it added that due regard should be given to wage rates in the vicinity which were determined through collective bargaining. TVA was obligated by law to use the prevailing rate method of compensation determination only for its trades and labor employees or for the blue-collar employees of any contractor. The method of compensation for salary policy employees was not mentioned, except for the general provision that their compensation was not subject to unilateral determination by the Civil Service Commission. Therefore, the Act seemed to delineate, although it did not require, the use of different methods for determining the compensation of trades and labor and white-collar employees.

The other important provision within Section 3 established the Secretary of Labor as the final arbiter of any dispute concerning what constituted the prevailing wage. Again, the provision only applied to trades and labor employees, not to all employees. In negotiation impasses over wage issues, unions of TVA's blue-collar employees were given a clear channel of outside appeal; unions of TVA's white-collar and professional employees were not.

Another provision of the Act would prove troublesome to management and to the organizations representing TVA's professional workers. Section 2(e), combined with Section 3, set the original maximum salary of Board of Directors members at $10,000 and prohibited the salary of any other employee from exceeding this amount. The fixed maximum would be raised only occasionally and would not keep pace with compensation for comparable positions in the nation. At times, this ceiling for the management salary range created significant pressure on the entire salary schedule from above, and made recruitment and retention for certain administrative and professional positions difficult. It also was a factor in stimulating TVA's use of outside consultants when specialized talent was necessary.

The strongly pro-collective bargaining attitude of top management was also a major environmental factor for the development of bargaining relationships at TVA. It was especially important in stimulating the growth of white-collar and professional employee organizations. A neutral or hostile management stance would have retarded salary policy employee organizational activities much more than it would have dampened the activities of AFL craft unions in organizing TVA's blue-collar workers. Management's early, concrete embodiment of its pro-union and pro-collective bargaining attitudes was the *Employee Relationship Policy* of 1935. As has been documented, rights and protections were extended to TVA employees which would not be generally applied to federal employees for almost three decades. For example, the right of all nonmanagement employees to organize and to designate representatives for collective bargaining was recognized and protected.

Paragraph 6 of the ERP would take on great importance as the unionization of salary policy employees evolved. It stated:

The majority of the employees as a whole, or of any professional group or craft, *or other appropriate unit* (emphasis added), shall have the right to determine the organization, person, or persons who shall represent them as a whole, or any such professional group, or craft, or unit.[1]

A great body of precedent existed for the dividing of trades and labor workers into craft units, but much conflict and confusion would come to exist over the "appropriate unit" for white-collar and professional employees. No further elaboration was provided by the ERP.

Most importantly, the ERP carried over and added to the TVA Act's disparate treatment of trades and labor versus salary policy employees. Paragraph 19 of the ERP reaffirmed that the wages of trades and labor workers would be not less than wage rates for comparable types of work in the vicinity.

Paragraph 8 asserted that "In the classification of annually rated positions due regard will be given to standards of classification and rates of pay prevailing in the classified federal service."[2] Therefore, the policy officially established one criterion for determining the compensation of trades and labor employees, and a different criterion for the compensation determination of all other employees.

Developments in collective bargaining between TVA and the Tennessee Valley Trades and Labor Council formed another significant part of the environment for the evolution of collective dealings between TVA and its white-collar and professional unions. The agency became impressed with the centralized bargaining structure of the Trades and Labor Council. The Council served as a single bargaining agent for all trades and labor employees represented by the various craft unions in multistate bargaining units. Because TVA had found the Council structure to be highly satisfactory before serious white-collar organizational activity began, it took an active role in pushing the white-collar and professional groups toward the same type of structure.

TVA and the Council negotiated annually over wages and other terms and conditions of employment and on August 6, 1940, the two parties signed a *General Agreement.* Much precedent was being established for TVA's relationship with the Salary Policy Employee Panel which would develop later. For example, TVA had entered into a written agreement with a group of labor unions; it had agreed to a grievance procedure culminating in binding arbitration by an impartial referee; and, although it had refused a closed shop or union shop contract clause, TVA had agreed to contract language acknowledging the advantages of membership in a union affiliated with the Council. The *General Agreement's* format of a statement of general principles followed by supplementary schedules over specific substantive topics would eventually be adopted in the TVA-Panel relationship. Moreover, the *General Agreement* established an important management stance that no new union of trades and labor employees would be recognized without first being accepted by the Council, and that when any trades and labor union did not operate through the Council, the ERP, and not the *General Agreement*, would be applied to this group of employees.

The early development of the TVA-Trades and Labor Council relationship, in conjunction with the TVA Act's and the ERP's disparate treatment of employees, meant significantly different collective dealings between TVA and the two major divisions of its employees. Between 1937 and 1951, TVA and the Council engaged in annual collective bargaining over a broad range of subject matter. TVA's bargaining with nontrades and labor unions, and later with the Salary Policy Employee Panel, was less regular and stable, and occurred over a limited scope of bargaining. In the least, this disparity adversely affected the ability of white-collar and professional organizations to justify themselves to their actual and potential memberships. Finally, the earlier development of the TVA-Council relationship meant that management negotiators would bring years of collective bargaining experience into the initial negotiations with white-collar and professional groups.

Early Personnel Administration

After the passage of the TVA Act, a handful of management personnel faced the tremendous task of assembly a work force. Not only was a large trades and labor force necessary for the beginning of construction activities but also a large and diverse array of white-collar and professional job slots required attention. The number of salary policy employees grew from forty-five to 5,199 between 1933 and 1936.

TVA had no formalized pay plan for the first few months of its existence. White-collar and professional employees were hired and their salaries were assigned on an ad hoc basis. In the fall of 1933, the Personnel Division began working with the Special Committee on Personnel Classification and Salary Schedules for Emergency Agencies, which had been appointed by the president's Executive Council. The Special Committee was developing a nineteen-grade, one-rate-per-grade salary schedule, and the Personnel Division directed supervisors to complete job descriptions on all salary policy employees so that all positions could be worked into the nineteen-grade system.

In November 1933, President Roosevelt issued Executive Order Number 6440 to bring the salaried positions of "emergency agencies" into the nineteen-grade salary schedule and into close conformance with the classified civil service. TVA was one of the eight agencies listed. However, the Board of Directors had some doubts as to whether the Executive Order actually applied to TVA, because of the salary-fixing discretion given the Board by the TVA Act and because TVA was not really an emergency agency. All salaried positions were nevertheless brought into conformance with the Executive Order by the spring of 1934. In adopting its first salary policy, TVA yielded to the direction of a presidential order and tied its classification and salary system to prevailing federal practice.

Executive Order 6746 issued June 21, 1934, superseded the previous order in applying the nineteen-grade schedule to emergency agencies. All TVA employees were specifically exempted from this emergency agency schedule, but the agency continued its adherence to the schedule and to prevailing federal practice with only minor variations. It cannot be argued, therefore, that TVA was forced into the adoption of a prevailing federal standard for the compensation determination of its salary policy employees. TVA would later defend its adoption of the standard because of the possibility that significant divergence from federal practice might have resulted in the placing of TVA's salaried employees under the Civil Service system. TVA also argued that prevailing rates in the federal service could be easily determined but that, for example, prevailing rates of comparable private sector salary policy positions in the vicinity could not.

TVA faced some difficult problems in developing and administering its classification and salary system. A large number of salary policy employees occupied technical positions with functional responsibilities, but the federal classification structure was developed with little emphasis on these types of positions. TVA also had more administrative levels than were common in the federal government. Trades and labor wages moved with prevailing rates in the vicinity, while salary policy rates could only vary with the rates prevailing in the federal government. The chief of the Civil Service Commission's Personnel Classification Division was hired to consult on these problems in 1934 and 1935, and a personnel classification staff was also assembled.

Several serious defects existed in the first salary policy. For example, only one rate existed in each grade, so a promotion was required for any salary increase in the absence of an across-the-board increase. Management appointed a committee to study the salary policy and the employee service rating systems in May 1935. But TVA only considered substantive changes after similar changes had been made or allowed in federal practice. A salary plan allowing within-grade salary increases was developed only after the 1935 repeal of the Economy Act had provided the possibility of within-grade salary movements for the classified civil service.

While the management committee was discussing salary policy revisions, the ERP was issued. Section 21 of the ERP required that salary schedules be opened for revisions annually; therefore, salary policy employee groups were invited to discuss salary policy changes in the fall of 1935. Meetings of the management committee, and between this committee and employee representatives, continued into 1936. Representatives of at least fourteen small, localized salaried employee groups participated in the meetings. The new salary policy plan which was recommended to the Board of Directors and approved on August 21, 1936 was not a negotiated plan. However, management had significantly utilized the input and feedback of salary policy employee groups in developing this second and rather comprehensive fourteen-page statement of salary policy.

The new plan added an additional grade to the salary schedule and provided three rates—an entrance, a standard, and a maximum—for the first sixteen grades of the twenty-grade structure. Supervisors were to review the service of each salary policy employee semi-annually and to rate his or her performance as unsatisfactory, satisfactory or unusually satisfactory according to enumerated criteria. Annual employees were to automatically advance into the standard rate after approximately one year of satisfactory service. Advancement into the maximum rate could only be accomplished through a difficult process of accruing merit points for highly satisfactory service. The standard rate was designed to be generally equivalent to the middle rate of the salary ranges attached to each grade in the federal classified service, and the maximum rate similarly conformed to maximum rates of classified service salary ranges.

Furthermore, an appeals system was established by the new plan. All ratings were to be reviewed by a Board of Review composed of Personnel Division staff members. An employee aggrieved by a Board of Review decision could appeal through supervisory channels according to the grievance provision of the ERP. A supervisor supporting the employee's position could appeal to an Advisory Board of Appeals consisting of two management and two employee representatives. The Board would hear the case and act in an advisory capacity to the Director of Personnel, whose decision was final.

TVA originally established its hours and overtime policy for annual employees according to federal practice. In 1934, however, the agency diverged from federal practice by allowing supervisors to grant employees compensatory time off for overtime work. This was partially a response to complaints by employee groups that excessive overtime work, with no compensation, was the rule in some departments.[3] TVA also diverged from federal practice in 1936 when it established a maximum work week of thirty-nine to forty hours for inside work and forty-four hours for outside work.

In the early years of World War II, the Board of Directors required employees to work four extra hours per week at no additional pay, notably suspending paragraph 10 of the ERP which by then provided that overtime work would be accumulated as annual leave. Federal law constrained TVA's policies, and it was only able to begin paying overtime for these extra hours worked in December 1942, when Public Law 821 allowed the practice for federal employees. Salary policy positions were divided into flexible schedule and inflexible schedule groups. Because compensatory time off could not be given to employees in the latter group, they became eligible for overtime pay.

TVA voluntarily conformed to prevailing federal practice in its annual leave and sick leave policies for salaried employees. Again, however, TVA learned that it might suddenly be forced to conform to the dictates of Congress and to federal practice. When Congress revised leave regulations for the classified federal service in March 1936, it extended the regulations to encompass wholly owned or controlled government corporations. TVA quickly changed its regulations to comply.

Most areas of personnel administration were handled efficiently. The recruitment and training programs were excellent models for the time period concerned. Employees could take almost any complaint, including termination, to the grievance system established by the ERP. The appeals system for service review ratings has already been noted. Many policies, such as the one governing political activities of employees, were established only after considerable employee input. Employee input was also important in the development of the TVA Retirement System which was established in 1939 after joint investigations and discussions by management and employee representatives. The

system was set up under the Board of Directors representing both management and employees.

The Emergence of Salary Policy Unions

All TVA employees were actually given the right to organize even before the
issuance of the ERP. The Board of Directors stated in July 1934 that employees
had the right to organize and bargain collectively through representatives of
their own choosing and that employees would be free from restraint or interference by management in their exercise of this right. Two local National
Federation of Federal Employees (NFFE) lodges were organized for salary employees in TVA's first few years of existence. However, the primary organizer
of salary policy employees was the American Federation of Government
Employees (AFGE).

In the summer of 1934, many staff members of the Knoxville central
office began to consider three alternative means of organizing: affiliating with
the NFFE, affiliating with the AFGE, or forming an unaffiliated local. The
engineering staff favored the third alternative, but a group of thirty-nine
clerical and administrative employees sought affiliation with the AFGE. In
August 1934, Lodge No. 136 of the Knoxville central office was chartered by
this AFL-affiliated national union. Other AFGE lodges were subsequently
founded at Norris, Chattanooga, New Hope, Alabama, Wilson Dam, and
Pickwick Dam. But the Knoxville lodge, growing to a membership of over 300
clerical and planning department employees, remained the largest and most
active of the loosely connected locals. It was recognized by TVA in 1936 as
the representative of Knoxville salary policy employees.

The AFGE organizations enumerated an eight-point action plan and proceeded vigorously to advance their program. Among the early goals of the
AFGE were union-management cooperation, better educational programs for
employees, the promotion of the interests of members as consumers, the reduction of the work week to five days, and the establishment of a retirement
system.

Both the AFGE and the NFFE participated in the formulation of the ERP.
Included on the special committee which drafted the ERP was the president
of Knoxville AFGE Lodge No. 136. Management discussed a wide range of
subjects affecting salary policy employees with the early locals of white-collar
employees. For example, many employee-management field conferences were
held in 1935 concerning the standardization of hours and of the work week for
annual employees. At a central conference on the same subject in 1936, representatives from nine AFGE lodges, two NFFE lodges, and six other local
organizations of salary policy employees participated.[4]

The Congress of Industrial Organizations (CIO) was founded in 1935. It subsequently established the United Federal Workers of America (UFWA) to compete with the AFL's AFGE in organizational activities aimed at federal employees. Knoxville Lodge No. 136 had become dissatisfied with its national organization, so, in August 1937, it bolted the AFGE and became UFWA Local 24. Six more UFWA locals were quickly established on TVA projects, as the UFWA captured the AFGE's central role in representing salary policy employees. The UFWA found, as had the earlier organizations, that dealings with management were consultative in nature. When UFWA Local 24 suggested seventeen topics for consideration by management in 1937, representatives of the Personnel Division participated with UFWA leaders in a series of "discussion meetings" over some of these topics.

In May 1937, the Tennessee Valley Authority Engineers Association (TVAEA) was formed by a charter group of ninety Knoxville office engineers; another engineering group had already been organized at Pickwick Dam in southwestern Tennessee. By December 1937, the Knoxville group claimed 470 members, and it had formally notified TVA of its intention to represent the interest of engineers. Other associations of engineers were founded at Chattanooga, Tennessee in 1939 and at Kentucky Dam in 1942, but the various associations had no formal ties with each other.

The engineer associations were organized largely to prevent nonengineer groups, such as the UFWA, from obtaining representational rights for TVA professionals (even though nonprofessional, technical employees were admitted into the TVAEA). This purpose originally overshadowed a second purpose of representing members in collective negotiations.

The Knoxville and other TVA Engineers Associations, like other salary policy employee organizations, often participated in discussions with management over personnel policies. They took an especially active role in the formulation of the TVA Retirement System. The engineer groups also resembled the other organizations in being local in nature, rather than valley-wide. Moreover, the process in which all of the groups engaged was definitely one of consultation, as was clearly pointed out to the Knoxville TVAEA by the Director of Personnel:

The procedure followed at the present time by the Personnel Department for informing employees and employee representatives of questions which are to be discussed with employees is notification by bulletin board publications. These notices contain information as to the subjects to be discussed and the time during which employees may indicate an interest in discussing such subjects with management.[5]

Appropriate Units

Paragraph 6 of the ERP, which has already been described, provided for the majority selection of bargaining representatives by employees of a professional group, craft, or other appropriate unit. The rules of bargaining unit determination for TVA's trades and labor employees were already established by the tradition of construction industry craft unionism. But what constituted appropriate bargaining units for TVA's white-collar and professional employees? Little precedent existed. The fact that TVA had such a diverse group of salary policy employees—office workers, professionals, guards, and building service employees—compounded the issue even further.

In the early years, neither management nor the infant salary policy employee groups were quite sure how to approach the problem. The AFGE originally envisioned the organization of all salary policy employees into one bargaining unit even though it accepted recognition for local bargaining units. When the UFWA became the ascendant white-collar organization at TVA, it also moved erratically from attempting the organization of an overall, valley-wide unit to accepting recognition of a limited nature in local areas. By 1941, the first option was eliminated for the UFWA because the TVAEA, the American Federation of Office Employees (AFOE), and other employee organizations were seriously competing with the UFWA for representational rights.

Several organizations tried to organize salary policy employees along departmental lines. TVA quickly realized that jurisdictional overlaps were inevitable, as for example, one union attempted to organize all TVA office workers while another union attempted to organize all the workers, including office workers, in a particular department. Departmental organization was discouraged for this reason and also for the reason that many small TVA operating units and departments might request their own bargaining units. In March 1942, a Chattanooga union requested recognition to represent a Reproduction Unit which contained only fourteen employees. Had TVA allowed bargaining units to be established along these lines, the proliferation of small bargaining units would have become a severe problem.

In the period of confusion between 1936 and 1942, management was forced to develop some general principles regarding appropriate unit determination, which it consistently applied thereafter. Recognition of an employee group would be predicated upon evidence that its membership included a majority of those employees whom it desired to represent. No organization could be recognized if its jurisdictional boundaries with already existing organizations were unclear. Furthermore, in disputes over the appropriate representative for a group of employees, the Personnel Department would assume a quasi-judicial role in resolving the dispute.

A 1942 report from the Director of Personnel to the General Manager elaborated on the stance which TVA was taking in determining appropriate units:

Two basic factors which the Personnel Department has considered in the determination of any appropriate bargaining unit are:

1.   The desires of employees with respect to the type of organization which
they believe will be most effective in facilitating bargaining relationships.
2.   The suitability of a proposed unit for collective bargaining purposes
within the Authority.
These factors are reflected in the following criteria which have been recognized
as pertinent to such determinations:
      a.   The existence of subjects or problems confinable to the unit under
consideration which lend themselves to negotiations.
      b.   Evidence available with respect to the reliability of petitioning organi-
zations to accept and discharge the responsibilities assumed under collective
bargaining agreements.
      c.   Precedents established through tradition or practice with respect to the
recognition of appropriate units . . .[6]

The Director of Personnel also mentioned the department's difficult dual role
of both dealing with employee representatives in negotiations and having to
serve as a judge in representational controversies. When the General Manager
transferred this report to the Board of Directors, he commented that TVA was
literally pioneering in the determination of appropriate bargaining units for
white-collar and professional employees.

By the early forties, therefore, management had developed principles to
apply in determining appropriate units. It was resisting tendencies which
would lead to jurisdictional overlaps, and it had decided to disallow departmental bargaining units. It had also decided to exclude from bargaining units
second-line supervisors and above, and confidential and other employees
closely associated with management.

In 1940, the Public Safety Service Employees' Union (PSSEU), an AFL-
affiliate, began organizational activities at TVA and concentrated exclusively
on TVA's safety officers. The PSSEU approach began a new trend of organization along occupational lines, which proved acceptable to TVA and broke
the stalemate over appropriate unit determination. By limiting its objectives,
the PSSEU was able to organize the majority of employees in one occupational
group. It presented evidence of its majority membership to TVA, and, in
February 1941, it was formally recognized as the representative for safety
service employees. A TVA-wide occupational bargaining unit had thus met the
criteria for appropriateness.

The AFOE also chose to limit its organizational activities to those
employees whose duties closely resembled office operations. After locals had
been formed at several TVA locations, the AFOE succeeded in the important
second step of tying the locals together into a valley-wide Central Council of
Office Employees. Evidence was presented to TVA establishing majority
representation for this valley-wide unit of related occupations, and in February
1942, TVA recognized the Central Council of the AFOE as the bargaining
agent for the unit. Later in the same year, two other unions organized
smaller bargaining units along occupational lines and were recognized by TVA
as bargaining agents for these units: the Chemical Workers' Union and the

Hotel and Restaurant Employees' International Alliance and Bartenders' International League of America.

The TVA Engineers Associations wished to represent all of TVA's professional and subprofessional employees performing technical duties. However, the professional chemists and chemical engineers at Wilson Dam near Muscle Shoals, Alabama had formed their own organization in 1942. The TVA Association of Professional Chemists and Chemical Engineers (TVAAPCChE) was specifically formed to prevent its members from being included in a bargaining unit with nonprofessionals. It presented TVA with evidence of majority representation and convinced the agency that the interests of its members were so closely identical that a separate unit should be established. Therefore, in December 1942, the TVAAPCChE was recognized to bargain for a specific group of TVA professionals, and subprofessionals were excluded from the unit.

TVA Engineers Associations had continued to function relatively independently at various valley-wide locations. In 1942, the President of the Knoxville TVAEA initiated an effort to develop a valley-wide body for the representation of all engineering employees. The other engineer organizations were contacted and several new local units were formed. The federation of units operated informally, but recognition to represent a valley-wide unit was requested early in 1943. Having already recognized the TVAAPCChE unit, TVA agreed on February 15, 1942, to recognize the TVAEA as the bargaining agent for virtually all other professionals and for subprofessionals in technically oriented positions. The TVAEA had first presented evidence that it had organized a clear majority of the 2,160 employees making up this large bargaining unit.

A seventh and final salary policy employee unit was established after a representational election. Both the CIO's UFWA and the Building Service Employees' International Union (BSEIU) of the AFL wished to represent a unit of building service employees. An election was held by the Personnel Department in October 1943, and the victorious BSEIU was immediately certified as the bargaining representative for the unit. Brief definitions of the original seven bargaining units are presented in table 3-1.

The recognition given to these seven organizations was of a very limited, special nature. TVA specified that the organizations could bargain over matters affecting employees in their units only. Since the classification system and salary schedule, the hours of work, and most important personnel policies affected all salary policy employees, TVA would not bargain with any one of the recognized groups on these matters.

Despite this stance toward the scope of collective bargaining, TVA concluded a six-page written agreement with the PSSEU on October 14, 1942. Probably the only previous written agreements between a federal agency and noncraft unions were between the National Labor Relations Board and its

Table 3-1
Abbreviated Definitions of the Seven Original Salary Policy Employee
Bargaining Units

Public Safety Service Employees' Union: The unit includes employees in the Public Safety Service excluding the supervisory levels above first-line supervisors.

American Federation of Office Employees: The unit of general office employees includes noncraft positions, the duties of which are rather closely identified with office operations and related specialized and general clerical functions, such as accounting, editorial, statistical, office procedural, secretarial . . . .

Chemical Workers' Union: The unit is composed of technicians in subprofessional positions who perform laboratory work involving the application of standardized laboratory techniques in the chemical or chemical engineering field, or similar laboratory duties closely related to these fields of work.

Hotel and Restaurant Employees' International Alliance: The unit includes employees engaged primarily in the preparation and serving of foods, beverages, and related consumer services at the Authority's projects.

Building Service Employees' International Union: The unit includes noncraft employees engaged primarily in cleaning and servicing of Authority-operated buildings.

TVA Association of Professional Chemists and Chemical Engineers: The unit involves employees in professional positions involving chemical and chemical engineering, ceramic, and metallurgical work.

TVA Engineers Association: The unit includes employees in professional and subprofessional positions involving engineering, geological, architectural, and closely related activities. The unit excludes employees in professional and subprofessional positions involving chemical, ceramic, and metallurgical work . . . .

Source: TVA Administrative Code, III Union Relations, Recognition, November 29, 1943.

independent unions. The main focuses of the TVA-PSSEU agreement were the formalization of a union-management cooperative program and a delineation of the mechanics of the grievance procedure, the service rating system, transfers, and work scheduling. Further underscoring the circumscribed scope of bargaining was the absence of any specific provisions in the agreement concerning compensation matters. But the agreement did set the important precedent that TVA would enter into written agreements with unions of its salary policy employees.

Formation of the Panel

TVA limited the scope of bargaining with each individual organization primarily because it wished to pressure the seven organizations into forming some sort of centralized structure. In correspondence and meetings with representatives of the salary policy employee groups, management made clear its preference for two overall bargaining units—one for trades and labor employees and one for salary policy employees. Management also took a series of affirmative actions to move the individual units together. In 1939, the Director of Personnel invited representatives of the UFWA, AFGE, and TVAEA to attend a joint meeting. TVA had received numerous requests from these groups to discuss specific policy matters, but for reasons of efficiency, TVA preferred to discuss such matters with representatives of all the groups at the same time. Therefore, the Director of Personnel asked the organizations to discuss the development of a procedure for handling employee problems which would avoid the waste of duplicate conferences and the time involved in coordinating the substance and results of separate meetings.

A procedure was not developed, so TVA tried again to guide the groups together in 1940. Representatives from the UFWA, AFGE, and TVAEA attended a November 25, 1940 conference with management, and they even jointly submitted several requests for policy changes. Management informed these representatives that a Safety Service Employees' local had been formed and that further meaningful discussions would require the new local's presence. An understanding was reached at the conference that the salary policy employee organizations should attempt to work out some sort of coordinated approach for collective bargaining.

At the same time, management was taking action to drive the Safety Service Employees' Local Union toward the other salary policy groups. The local had attempted to establish a loose affiliation with the Trades and Labor Council and to submit proposals to TVA through this Council. However, TVA would not allow this arrangement, pointing out that safety service employees were in nontrades and labor classifications. Management suggested that the union arrange with the AFGE, UFWA, and TVAEA to participate in future joint conferences with management.

Several of the employee organizations were also making their own efforts to consolidate and coordinate activities. By 1941, repeated attempts of the AFGE, UFWA, and NFFE to organize all salary policy employees into one unit had been fruitless. The three groups joined with the TVA Engineers Associations early in 1941, forming the Council of TVA Annual Employees. This federation requested recognition as the bargaining agent for all salary policy employees and asked for the ability to negotiate on general policy matters affecting all of these employees.

TVA denied this request. It observed that some of the Council's affiliates were organized along departmental lines, while others were not. Thus, a potential for overlapping jurisdictions existed within the Council. Management also stated that the AFL-affiliated PSSEU had already been recognized to bargain for one group of salary policy employees and that the PSSEU had not chosen to join the Council.

During 1941, four additional departmental organizations joined the Council and further complicated the potential jurisdictional problems. The AFL-affiliated AFOE also became active. It did not join the Council, and it was formally recognized by TVA early in 1942 to represent a large bargaining unit. In February 1942, the Council protested the AFOE's recognition and again requested recognition to bargain for all salary policy employees. The request was denied. When three other AFL-affiliates were recognized by TVA and when the Knoxville TVAEA withdrew from the Council in subsequent months, the strength of the Council and of its remaining affiliates quickly disappeared.

In February 1942, however, the five AFL-affiliated organizations of TVA's nonprofessional salary policy employees formed a Council. This new grouping of unions requested that it be recognized as the bargaining representative for all salary policy employees, and it renewed its request again in July. Management informed this group that two of its members, the BSEIU and the Hotel and Restaurant Employees, had not yet been formally recognized. TVA also indicated that even if these two unions were recognized, the Council could not be recognized to bargain on matters affecting all salary policy employees, because employees engaged in engineering, chemistry, and related technical activities were not represented.

The group of AFL-affiliates finally established its name as the Tennessee Valley Council of Office, Technical and Service Employees. In November 1942, this Council was recognized as a bargaining agent for the employees in its members' units, but an important condition was attached to recognition. The subject matter of conferences with the Council of AFL-affiliates was restricted to topics affecting only those employees in the units represented through the Council. Because most professional and subprofessional employees in technical positions were not represented by the Council's member unions, classification, salary, and other important matters affecting all salary policy employees would not be allowable topics for collective bargaining.

By the middle of 1943, seven nonoverlapping bargaining units had been established, although the BSEIU had not yet been formally recognized. The two independent units of technical employees and the five units represented by the AFL-affiliates of the Council contained virtually all salary policy employees beneath the second-line supervisory level. The five-member Council repeated its request to bargain on all general policy matters which might affect its members. Management, while continuing its denial of this request, took the final steps to pressure all seven organizations into a highly centralized bargaining structure.

In July 1943, the Director of Personnel suggested in a conference with the Council of AFL-affiliates that a panel be formed to include representatives of all recognized salary policy employee organizations. Bargaining subject matter deemed by TVA to affect all salary policy employees would be handled in negotiations between management and this panel. Moreover, "The Personnel Department would assume responsibility for initiating the establishment of this panel of salary policy employees."[7]

By September 1943, management had refined its stance. It offered the Council and the two independent organizations three alternatives in forming a centralized structure. First, the recognized organizations could make the panel a negotiating body by vesting it with the authority to bargain collectively with management on general policy matters. Second, full negotiating responsibility might not be given to the panel. In such a case, the panel would serve as an advisory body and management would only deal with it informally. Finally, the panel might be a combination advisory and negotiating body. This would be the case if the recognized organizations gave the panel authority to negotiate only on specific matters.

In November 1943, the leaders of the Council, the TVAEA, and the TVAAPCChE jointly informed TVA that the three organizations had combined into a Salary Policy Employee Panel. The Panel had chosen the first form of centralized structure that TVA had suggested, for the Panel was given the authority by its member organizations to negotiate on matters affecting all salary policy employees. Each organization would bargain individually with TVA on matters affecting only its bargaining unit, and the Council would bargain on matters affecting two or more of its five bargaining units.

TVA recognized the Panel on the following day, accepting the scheme for bargaining authority which the Panel members had proposed, but attached two important conditions to recognition. The Panel would have to be capable of negotiating all matters to a conclusion without obtaining specific authorization from the membership of Panel organizations; that is, salary policy employees in bargaining units would not have the prerogative of ratifying agreements. Second, any matters which led to such disagreement among member organizations that the Panel could not effectively negotiate would be unilaterally resolved by TVA. Management's stipulation of the latter condition made obvious its uncertainty about the new organization's cohesiveness.

The formation of the Salary Policy Employee Panel might be described as a "shotgun wedding." TVA had used the incentive of a meaningful bargaining scope to pressure the employee organizations into a central structure. Only after every other alternative for meaningful collective bargaining was closed did the organizations reluctantly accept the structure. The precedential alliance of heterogeneous white-collar and professional organizations would be a loose and uncomfortable one for many years. Whereas the Trades and Labor Council elected officers to speak for all member organizations, the Panel would for two decades speak with the three voices of the Council, the TVAEA, and the TVAAPCChE.

Nevertheless, the management-induced establishment of this bargaining alliance was a remarkable landmark in the history of white-collar and professional unionism. A trend of growing solidarity among the diverse organizations would become unmistakable, even though the centralized structure would be periodically subjected to serious internal shocks. It would also prove to be true that the formation of the Panel was a necessary but not sufficient condition for the emergence of meaningful collective bargaining over a reasonably broad scope of subject matter—a change in the method of salary and fringe benefit determination would be an additional condition for a reasonable bargaining scope.

Bargaining over Restricted Subject Matter

The second formal pay plan, which provided three within-grade salary rates for the first sixteen grades of the twenty-grade salary structure, became effective in January 1937. At least as early as 1940, individuals within management were pointing out serious defects in this classification and salary plan. For example, management personnel observed that three within-grade rates created a few, large steps within each grade and that five within-grade rates creating several steps would be an improvement. It was also pointed out that the standards applied to individuals wishing advancement to the maximum rate of a grade were so rigorous that few people achieved the rate. These early recommendations for salary policy changes are primarily notable because TVA followed several of the recommendations in 1945, only after they had been "negotiated" with the Salary Policy Employee Panel.

After its recognition by TVA in 1943, the Panel presented ten proposals for negotiations. Among these were requests for a 15 percent basic salary increase, the payment of shift differentials, and the use of binding arbitration to resolve grievances. TVA did not negotiate on these matters but suggested a joint study of the classification, compensation, and service rating policies. The Panel agreed to this study and also agreed to resolve the classification and salary policy issues before dealing with any other topics.

The Panel indicated in these extended negotiations that it wished to conclude a written agreement. Management responded that this should wait until the parties had more experience with collective bargaining, and the matter was temporarily dropped. The Panel also continued voicing its desire to replace the prevailing federal standard as the criterion for compensation determination. Management, however, would not consider such a move.

In confidential memoranda, officials of the Personnel Department indicated a great fear that significant deviation from prevailing federal practice would possibly lead to the placing of TVA salary policy employees under the civil service system. The memoranda attempted to justify the adoption of several other of the policy changes being discussed with the Panel on the basis of reasons of efficient personnel administration; they also pointed out that the changes being seriously discussed would not violate the general comparability of the salary policy with federal practice. The confidential communications were apparently aimed at selling top management on the changes being discussed.

They also indicated that the Personnel Department was "negotiating" several policy changes with the Panel that it otherwise might have embraced unilaterally in the absence of a Panel. Indeed, some management personnel had been advocating the adoption of several of these changes for years. In the fall of 1945, management recommended terms for a settlement on a new salary policy, and these terms became the basis for an agreement between the two parties in January 1946.

A special procedure was developed and generally utilized for concluding agreements in the absence of a written contract. The Director of Personnel would send a statement or letter delineating the features of any agreement to the heads of the Council, the TVAEA, and the TVAAPCChE. These individuals would return it signed. Then the agreement would be incorporated into TVA's Administrative Code with a footnote stating that the particular provisions of the Code had been negotiated between TVA and the Salary Policy Employee Panel.

TVA claimed that the 1945 agreement relating to the third formal pay plan represented the first time that a federal agency had ever dealt on a collective bargaining basis with white-collar and professional employees over fundamental personnel policy matters. Although this particular agreement brought about significant changes in the pay plan, a basic salary increase was not made because prevailing federal practice had not changed. Furthermore, TVA included the following proviso in the agreement: "this agreement is subject to modification by the Authority, upon due notice, in order to effect compliance with statutory requirements or with general Federal policy relating to salaries."

Two major changes in the 1945 salary policy revision are notable. The salary grades applicable to the Panel bargaining units were reduced from twelve to seven, thereby eliminating overly refined distinctions between levels of work assignments, classification grades, and employee qualifications. Second, the within-grade salary steps for these first seven grades were increased from three to five. Advancement to progressively higher salary steps was made automatic after either twelve or eighteen months, provided that satisfactory service ratings were achieved.

A separate, significant change in classification policy was also negotiated in 1945. TVA agreed to submit new or revised classification standards for review and concurrence by the Panel organization representing the positions involved. A joint meeting between TVA and the employee organization could follow this review. Unresolved differences would eventually be settled by the Director of Personnel. Furthermore, Panel members could initiate requests for new or revised classification standards.

Yet, the major problem which had been affecting salary policy employees was the wartime inflation that reduced their real wages. TVA had declined to negotiate a general wage increase because federal salary levels had not been raised. When several bills to boost federal pay were introduced in Congress during early 1945, TVA agreed to begin negotiations with the Panel over salary increases. Only after Congress approved a bill to raise federal salaries effective July 1, 1945, did TVA bring the negotiations to a close. The overall percentage pay increase was kept in line with the federal increase (see table 9-2 for TVA negotiated increases), and TVA also agreed to begin paying shift differentials.

TVA continued to tie its salary levels to those prevailing in the classified federal service through 1950. Basic salary adjustments were not made until federal practice changed. From 1946 to 1948, for example, the cost of living steadily climbed. TVA's trades and labor employees had their wages adjusted upward in annual negotiations. Yet the basic compensation of salary policy employees was not changed because, until a federal salary act was passed in 1948, federal salaries had not been revised.

Therefore, collective bargaining over classification and salary matters had minimal meaning. The organizations of salary policy employees had little impact upon increases in pay and benefits. TVA would likely have granted approximately the same basic increases unilaterally. Perhaps TVA would also have unilaterally made several other of the negotiated changes in the pay structure, such as the changes in the number of pay grades and in the number of within-grade rates. The Panel organizations' greatest negotiated gains were probably the automatic within-grade advancements and the organizations' increased ability to influence classification changes.

Two notable policy changes, negotiated by TVA and the Panel in the forties, were outside of the areas of classification and salary policy. In 1946, a negotiated change in the reduction-in-force (RIF) policy gave the salary policy employee organizations their first trace of union security. In an RIF, employees were to be retained on the basis of length of service. Employees with the same length of service in RIF subgroups would be retained according to their relative merit and efficiency, which might include their participation in established union-management relations. When other factors did not allow the differentiation of salary policy employees with equal lengths of service, union members would be retained over nonunion members. Between union members, the member rated most highly by the union would be retained over the less active member. In future years, TVA's requirements for implementing veterans' preference regulations eroded the significance of this union preference in RIF.

Also during the decade of the forties, a union-management cooperative program emerged as a major ancillary process to collective bargaining, and the program reached a high state of development. The only comparable program for white-collar and professional employees in the federal government, and probably in the private sector as well, existed between the National Labor Relations Board and its employees.[8] The cooperative conference program between TVA and its salary policy employee organizations developed concurrently with collective bargaining; the cooperative committee program between TVA and the Trades and Labor Council had developed after collective bargaining. By the late forties, twenty-one local cooperative conferences were in existence, and the parties had formed a Central Joint Cooperative Conference to coordinate these local activities. The two cooperative programs are discussed in chapter 8.

Slow Development of the Bargaining Relationship

The organization of salary policy employees at TVA lagged far behind that of trades and labor employees. The Panel structure developed more slowly than the similar structure for TVA's craft unions. By the end of the 1940s, the Panel structure was still much less developed than the Trades and Labor Council structure in its cohesiveness and efficiency. In contrast to TVA's craft unions, the salary policy employee organizations found that collective bargaining had a narrow scope and consequently a diminished meaning. Why the disparate development of the two bargaining relationships through the 1940s?

An initial factor which made the development of salary policy employee organizations and thus the development of the Panel, a relatively slow and difficult process was the differing understanding of and empathy for unionism by the two major groups of TVA employees. In the largely unorganized southern part of the United States, craft workers in construction trades probably had a greater understanding of unionism than did any other group of workers. More-over, the organized labor movement was geared to attracting the empathy of blue-collar workers. The great majority of TVA's white-collar and professional employees had little, if any, prior contact with unionism. Just as importantly, the organized labor movement had not developed a consistent, specialized approach for organizing white-collar and professional workers. Of course, the development of salary policy employee unionism would have been even less rapid, or perhaps nonexistent, in the absence of a management stance toward unionism which added vital credence to organizational activities aimed at salary policy employees.

A second factor helps to explain the relatively difficult process of welding organizations of salary policy employees into an effective centralized structure for bargaining. The educational backgrounds, attitudes and outlooks, lifestyles, and work assignments of salary policy employees were much more diverse than those of craft employees organized into Trades and Labor Council unions. The salary policy group was, for example, comprised of a largely white male popula-tion of college-educated engineers and other professionals, a predominately female population of clerical workers, and a black population of building service workers. Such heterogeneous groups of employees could only be combined into a centralized bargaining structure with extreme difficulty.

The development of the Trades and Labor Council was also less trouble-some because ample precedent existed for dividing construction craft workers into mutually exclusive bargaining units. The Trades and Labor Council also

enjoyed a reasonable scope of bargaining through its participation in the prevailing wage determination process. White-collar and professional unions, which
were accorded a narrow bargaining scope, faced much greater difficulty in
attracting membership, arousing member interest, and gaining strength. Finally,
many managers who did not oppose the development of blue-collar unions,
had a paternalistic attitude toward white-collar and professional employees.
They believed that salary policy employees simply did not need to be organized,
or, alternatively, that unions of such employees should not deal with management in the aggressive manner common to blue-collar unions.

By the end of the forties, the two bargaining relationships were far apart.
Yet, in the early fifties, the relationship between TVA and the Salary Policy
Employee Panel would begin a slow but steady process of catching up with the
older relationship in its stability, its maturity, and in its meaningfulness.

Bargaining Becomes Meaningful

After its formation in 1943, the Salary Policy Employee Panel repeatedly
requested that TVA enter into a written agreement with the Panel unions. The
request was deferred on the grounds that the Panel structure was too tenuous
and that both parties needed to gain more experience in collective bargaining.
Yet the lack of a written agreement was in itself a source of instability in the
relationship.

Renewing its request for a written contract in 1948, the Panel presented
management with a tentative outline of basic principles and major topics which
might be incorporated into an agreement. Panel spokesmen pointed out that
the union structure had weathered five years. They insisted that the salary
policy employee organizations had gained adequate experience and maturity in
bargaining to justify the formalization of the relationship. TVA indicated that
it would be able and willing to enter into the generalized type of agreement
outlined by the Panel. However, it first wanted guarantees from the Panel on
several topics. Could the Panel provide assurance of the permanence of its
status as the overall bargaining agent for all salary policy employees? Could the
Panel develop the administrative flexibility to admit other employee organizations achieving official recognition and to accommodate changing relationships
among its own organizations? Could the Panel formalize its organizational
status by selecting a single head or secretary, as had the Trades and Labor Council years before?

A series of extended negotiations diverted the parties from the topic of a
written agreement for over a year. During this time, however, management
decided not to resist the development of an agreement covering general principles.
The unions took no steps to provide TVA with the assurances which it had
desired; for example, no effort was made to select a single head or secretary for

the Panel. Nevertheless, the Panel submitted a detailed outline of an agreement in April 1950, and management agreed to participate in a joint committee preparing a final draft. The nature of the grievance procedure to be included in the written agreement became a major issue and slowed the progress of the joint committee. But in the fall of 1950, agreement was reached on a draft proposed by management. The *Articles of Agreement* were then signed and approved by the TVA Board of Directors in December 1950.

Fourteen articles were contained in the fifteen-page document. The majority of the articles simply carried over existing understandings and negotiated agreements. Articles on recognition of the Panel, recognition of bargaining units, rights to organize, and other topics contained no significant new provisions. Article VII on classification and pay reaffirmed the primacy of the prevailing federal standard in these matters. One of the two new and significant items in the agreement extended to promotion and transfer, the preference already given to union members in retention. If all other factors of merit and efficiency were equal in a promotion, transfer, or retention decision, membership and participation in a Panel union would be determining factors in the decision.

The other major negotiated change appearing in the agreement was the grievance procedure delineated in Article VIII. A four-step procedure was prescribed; the grievance moved from the immediate supervisor to the division director to the Director of Personnel. The important change was the fourth step. The Director of Personnel's decision could now be appealed by the Panel to an impartial referee, whose decision would be final and binding. It is notable that the entire Panel had to approve carrying grievances of any union's members to arbitration. The individual union could not utilize the fourth step of the procedure without the concurrence of all the Panel organizations. Thus, the grievance procedure, the basics of which have remained unchanged through the mid-seventies, added an important dimension to the status of the centralized Panel structure. Also notable is the fact that the two major, new provisions in the 1950 *Articles of Agreement* had been incorporated a decade earlier in the *General Agreement*, between TVA and the Trades and Labor Council. The salary policy contract, like the trades and labor agreement, was open-ended. All articles would remain binding upon TVA and the Panel indefinitely unless changed in a joint conference called upon ninety days notice of either party.

The signing of the written agreement was a milestone in the development of the collective bargaining relationship. It added considerable stability to the relationship and credence to the Panel and its member organizations. However, two factors dimmed the significance of this milestone. First, the *Articles of Agreement* incorporated general principles of agreement only. Specific personnel policies and procedures negotiated by the parties would continue to remain outside the written contract in TVA Codes and Instructions. Second, the agreement did nothing to erode the narrow confines of bargaining scope in classification and pay matters. The prevailing federal standard survived intact.

A considerably more important historical benchmark was reached by TVA and the Panel in 1951, when the prevailing federal criterion for classification and pay matters was eliminated. Management was recognizing significant problems arising from the use of this criterion. Especially in a time of inflation, TVA was encountering difficulty in recruiting salary policy employees. Salaries were rising in TVA's recruitment area, but TVA had little flexibility in recruiting since its pay rates were tied to those in the federal classified service. Because wages of TVA's trades and labor employees were tied to the wages in the vicinity, serious pay impact problems were arising between salary policy and trades and labor employees, in situations in which a pay differential should have existed for the former over the latter.

Although management was aware of these problems in 1951, it would not have departed from the prevailing federal standard in the absence of significant pressure from the Panel. Early in 1951, the Panel urged that the prevailing federal standard in the *Articles of Agreement* be changed because TVA salaries were being held below those for comparable positions in relevant labor markets. The Panel suggested that a new salary adjustment plan might be based upon cost of living and productivity standards. By threatening to appeal for a change directly to congressional committees then considering federal pay hikes, the Panel forced TVA to enter into a joint study of alternative criteria upon which salaries might be based.

Confidential reports of management meetings indicate concern still existing that TVA's divergence from federal practice on classification and pay matters would result in the inclusion of salary policy employees in the classified federal service. Yet, the degree of concern had apparently diminished, for management decided to agree upon a divergence if "defensible" new criteria could be found. In March 1951, the joint committee agreed that pay determination would include the consideration of prevailing salary rates in the vicinity. By midsummer, the negotiators had agreed upon the following three criteria, which would be used in determining rates of pay thereafter and which would later be incorporated in the revised *Articles of Agreement:*

1. Prevailing rates for similar work in the vicinity.
2. Trades and labor annual pay rates in TVA, particularly where close working relationships exist between salary policy employees and annual trades and labor employees.
3. The relative difficulty, responsibility, and qualification requirements of jobs.

TVA wanted to place primary emphasis upon the first criterion. This is understandable, because salaries based on prevailing rates were most likely to ease TVA's recruitment and retention problems and were relatively "defensible." The Authority was able to obtain the Panel's agreement that the survey of prevailing salaries would include the federal classified service and some public sector agencies. The Panel would not agree to emphasize the first criterion; indeed, the Panel wished the second criterion to be emphasized in practice. Obviously, the salary policy employee organizations felt that salaries would be pushed higher by underscoring the maintenance of a differential over trades and labor salaries.

Finally, the parties agreed to give the three criteria equal weight in practice. A salary survey of prevailing rates was conducted in the fall of 1951, and salaries were negotiated partially on the basis of the survey data. In November 1951, the Board of Directors approved the negotiated fourth salary policy based upon the three criteria.

How were these criteria put into practice? The third standard of "relative difficulty, responsibility, and qualification" largely related to the classification system and not to the annual across-the-board revision of salary rates. In effect, the criterion meant that the existing classification system would remain intact. Because of the prevailing rate criterion, less pressure would develop to distort the established classification system, and thus to violate the third standard. This pressure existed elsewhere in the federal government. Salary rates changed relatively infrequently in the classified federal service, but federal managers often "adjusted" the classification of employees to remain competitive in relevant labor markets.

The second criterion would be an important one in the early years of the fourth salary policy. Since salary policy employees and trades and labor employees had been compensated under two significantly different criteria prior to 1951, several serious impact problems had arisen. In many cases, the pay differential between trades and labor workers and their salary policy supervisors had been erased. Moreover, a trades and labor position might carry a rate of pay higher than that of the salary policy supervisor.

As the fourth salary policy was being formulated, the negotiators agreed that the second criterion would be relevant for setting salary policy employee pay rates in two major situations: when a salary policy employee had a substantial responsibility for work being performed by a subordinate annual trades and labor employee and when a certain salary class had more responsible work than a certain trades and labor class and positions in the former class were normally filled by promoting employees in the latter class. In these situations, an adequate pay differential would be developed and maintained. The second criterion would become increasingly unimportant after pay rates for both major groups of TVA employees became well-adjusted to prevailing rates in the vicinity.

The prevailing rate criterion constituted the dominant criterion for the annual revision of salary rates from the beginning of the new policy. It became virtually the exclusive criterion as the trades and labor comparison diminished in relevance. The criterion was not easy to translate into practice, even though TVA had considerable experience in using the criterion for blue-collar workers.

As the parties prepared the principles and pragmatics of the first salary survey in the fall of 1951, the definition of "vicinity" for survey purposes became crucial. Management wished to survey a smaller vicinity than was being utilized for the trades and labor survey. However, the end product of negotiations was a broad definition, identical with that used by TVA and the Trades and Labor Council. The vicinity would include the watershed of the Tennessee River, the TVA power service area, and certain nearby urban centers. The parties also had to determine the firms to be surveyed and the key classes of positions to be surveyed. The difficulties inherent in making these determinations and disagreements over the appropriate use and weighting of the data collected would be especially apparent in the early years of the new policy.

The parties realized that the new policy of November 1951 largely eliminated the disparity which had existed in the mechanics of pay determination for trade and labor versus salary policy employees. Pay for both groups would be revised annually in negotiations based upon prevailing rates. The negotiated 11.6 percent average salary increase of 1951 reemphasized to the parties the failings of the old salary plan. Salaries had fallen perceptibly below those for comparable jobs in the vicinity, especially during the rapid wartime inflation. The 1951 salary policy change also marked the first major flexing of muscles by the Panel. Bargaining scope was enlarged to encompass classification and pay matters. A range of pay data would exist over which meaningful collective bargaining could occur. Moreover, the "Prevailing rate in the vicinity" criterion would be utilized in bargaining to govern fringe issues which also could be surveyed. Many practitioners of TVA-Panel bargaining, who had been active before and after the 1951 change, marked 1951 as the beginning of "real" collective bargaining between the two parties. Certainly, the meaning of the bargaining relationship was significantly enhanced.

Solidification of the Panel Structure

For several decades after the formation of the Salary Policy Employee Panel, the centralized bargaining structure was not highly stable. Structural and jurisdictional problems extended even into the seventies. A few jurisdictional disputes occurred between Panel unions and unions of the Trades and Labor Council. In settling these disputes, management seems to have exhibited some paternalistic bias toward the Panel unions. But the most significant jurisdictional and structural disputes occurred among the Panel organizations themselves.

The Single Schedule Controversy

The most prolonged and perhaps the most serious period of intraPanel conflict began with the 1951 negotiations over prevailing practice data obtained in the first salary survey. The TVAAPCChE dissented from the Panel's proposal on salary rates and took no part in the final negotiations leading toward the November agreement. This organization of professionals vigorously objected to having its members' salaries included in the same salary schedule with janitorial, clerical, and all other salary policy employees. The TVAAPCChE felt that its members' salaries were being pulled down by the prevailing rate data for these other employees and that the relevant survey area for its scientists and engineers should be the nation, rather than the region-wide vicinity as defined.

The TVAEA president, whose organization was sympathetic with the TVAAPCChE's complaints, proved unsuccessful in attempting to solve the dispute within the Panel. The TVAAPCChE was thereupon voted out of the Panel and TVA was asked to withdraw its recognition of the dissenting organization. Refusing to consider such a step, TVA repeatedly brought the disputants together until a temporary peace was reached. The TVAAPCChE accepted the results of the 1951 negotiations and was readmitted to the Panel.

A joint committee was appointed soon thereafter to explore the alternatives of a single-schedule salary plan versus a multiple-schedule plan. The TVAAPCChE and TVAEA representatives on this committee were adamant in their insistence upon a change to multiple salary schedules, separating the classification and basic salary determination for their members from those for members of the Council of Office, Technical and Service Employees. In opposition, the AFL-affiliated unions of this Council insisted that the single salary schedule be retained. This stance was only logical, for the lumping of all salaries into one schedule, along with salary determination based upon prevailing rate averages, tended to pull up the salaries of their members. The intraPanel conflict led to the committee's dissolution in August 1952, but management began an independent study of the issue.

The management group recognized significant problems with the single schedule plan.[9] Especially in grade four of the salary schedule, which contained top-level white-collar positions and entry-level professional positions, the salaries of entering professionals were being held down and recruitment problems were resulting. Nevertheless, the management group did not recommend a change to multiple salary schedules, and in the 1953 negotiations, the Panel was almost torn apart once again. The TVAAPCChE and TVAEA and the Council of AFL affiliated unions asked for separate negotiations with TVA but were finally forced by TVA to bargain together.

By 1956, pressures between the professional organizations and the Council had continued to mount, and TVA's recruitment problems due to the single salary schedule had become more acute. TVA thus agreed to appoint a joint

Committee on Classification and Pay to consider alternative multiple-schedule plans. Several plans were proposed during the early deliberations of the committee, and the unions chose to push a plan which divided salary schedules according to union jurisdictions.

Internal management communication indicates that TVA decided to oppose the union jurisdiction plan, which had apparently received the focus of attention in the first months of the Committee's deliberations. Union members of the Committee considered that the union jurisdiction plan would mean direct bargaining between TVA and each individual union for its respective schedule. The unions appeared ready for an effective, if not actual, breakup of the Panel.

Management did not want a revised salary plan to erode the centralized Panel structure to any degree. It feared that the union jurisdiction plan would lead to splinter groups requesting separate schedules. The proposed plan would allow no joint consideration of pay relationships among groups, and the consideration of fringe benefits along with basic pay schedules would be extremely difficult. Therefore, the Division of Personnel began to pressure the Committee toward recommending the adoption of a multiple-schedule plan with schedules divided by related work. The unions were told that collective bargaining would change significantly under a union jurisdiction plan. For example, TVA would deal with individual unions on matters affecting them only, and the scope of bargaining would diminish if the Panel were effectively or actually dissolved.

Representatives of the Council of AFL-CIO affiliated unions prolonged the negotiations by insisting that the single-schedule plan simply needed to be modified. The Council still recognized that prevailing rate averages under a single salary schedule would tend to pull up salaries for lower salaried employees in the schedule. Nevertheless, a five-schedule plan based upon related work was fashioned in the protracted negotiations, and final agreement on this new salary policy was reached in January 1957.

Salary schedule A included classes of positions involving administrative, management-service functions, such as accounting; schedule B covered clerical positions; schedule C encompassed a hodgepodge of building service, safety service, printing, and other functions; schedule D involved professional engineering and scientific functions, and schedule E included subprofessional, technical positions. Management also formally designated those positions in the grades contained in bargaining units (grades one to seven) which would receive an "M" or "management" designation. The positions with "M" designations would be excluded from bargaining units but would remain in the appropriate salary schedule. Those occupying such positions were considered to be management agents with responsibilities of interpreting and applying labor agreements. Not until 1968 did TVA move all positions with "M" designations into a separate, management salary schedule.

The adoption of multiple salary schedules was a necessary move for efficiency reasons. Its added importance was in removing a major internal threat to the continued existence of the Panel. TVA could negotiate with the Panel, but the union or unions with members in a particular schedule could lead the Panel's negotiations over that particular schedule. The greatest barrier that had separated professionals and nonprofessionals within the Panel was eliminated, and the strength and maturity of the centralized union structure could resume their growth.

Problems Within the Council

A second period of structural difficulty occurred in the early sixties and centered on the Council of AFL-CIO affiliated unions. Many PSSEU locals of safety service officers were strung across the Tennessee Valley. Approximately twenty of these locals existed, and they normally contained less than ten members each. The giant of the Council of AFL-CIO affiliates was the Office Employees International Union (OEIU), formerly the American Federation of Office Employees; it found dealing with these numerous locals burdensome. A $15 per month charge was instituted by the Council of AFL-CIO affiliates upon each local within the Council, in addition to the monthly per capita tax upon each affiliated organization.

Most of the PSSEU locals felt that the new tax was more than a simple move to force the amalgamation of the locals into one local with a direct AFL-CIO affiliation. They suspected that pressure was being applied upon them through the Council to affiliate with the OEIU. The locals refused to pay the per local tax and, as directly affiliated AFL-CIO locals, enlisted the aid of the AFL-CIO Regional Director in the summer of 1961. The locals asked TVA if they could withdraw from the Council of AFL-CIO affiliates and assume an independent status on the Panel. TVA's response reinforced its consistent bias toward the highest centralization possible in union bargaining structure. Management informed the locals that the Panel would have to recognize the PSSEU as an independent member. The Council was prepared to block any such recognition of the PSSEU by the Panel. The disgruntled locals still refused to pay the per local tax and, in the fall of 1961, they formed a National Council of PSSEU locals. These locals were then suspended from the Council of AFL-CIO affiliated unions.

TVA was presented with evidence that the new National Council had majority support in the established bargaining unit of public safety officers and building guards. The National Council requested recognition as a bargaining agent independent of the Council of AFL-CIO affiliates and asked that TVA negotiate with it a separate labor agreement. TVA refused these requests, and, since Executive Order 10988 had been issued by this point in the dispute, the PSSEU immediately began to explore its possibilities for regaining recognition and full bargaining rights under the 1962 Kennedy order.

Section II of Executive Order 10988 left the determination of appropriate bargaining units under the authority of individual agencies. In rather ambiguous language, it allowed the Secretary of Labor to appoint an advisory arbitrator when disputes over recognition arose. Moreover, the status of TVA and its employee organizations under the order was itself ambiguous. The agency was thought to be covered, but its *Articles of Agreement* with the Panel, in effect prior to 1962, were excluded from coverage by the Section 15 "savings clause."[10]

Nevertheless, the National PSSEU Council formally appealed its denial of full representation rights to Secretary of Labor Goldberg. TVA took the position that Section II did not apply because the National Council was denied recognition under a contract already in existence when Executive Order 10988 was issued. The PSSEU appeal never received a final determination by the Department of Labor, but TVA and the Panel unions learned from national level OEIU sources that an arbitrator would not be appointed.

Finally, TVA and all the conflicting parties met late in 1962 and the dispute was resolved. The PSSEU locals merged into one Directly Affiliated Local Union #3033 (DALU #3033) and agreed to pay part of the per capita taxes in arrears. The consolidated organization was readmitted into the Council of AFL-CIO affiliates and later regained representation rights. The essentially intraCouncil conflict had ended with the highly centralized union structure intact and with the PSSEU's own centralization as a by-product.

A similar dispute in the early sixties focused upon two locals of the BSEIU. These locals felt that the OEIU-dominated Council of AFL-affiliates did not adequately represent them in bargaining or grievance handling. The locals terminated payments to the Council and were then suspended from the Council. TVA refused to grant the BSEIU separate status on the Panel, and the National BSEIU president pressed the dissident locals to return to the Council. The locals thereupon asked that an arbitrator intervene in the dispute under Executive Order 10988. Both TVA and the National BSEIU president argued that the 10988 framework did not apply to the dispute, and the locals dropped their complaint before the issue was resolved. Resolution of the conflict stimulated all of the BSEIU locals to form a single, valley-wide local, as had the PSSEU, and the single local returned to the Council of AFL-CIO affiliated unions.

Both disputes of the early sixties essentially involved the structure of the Council of AFL-CIO affiliates, rather than the Panel structure. The basic reason for the conflicts would lead to a major change within the Panel structure in 1966. Two of the four small unions, which originally combined with the OEIU into the Council of AFL-affiliates, had disappeared long before the mid-sixties.[11] The two remaining organizations—DALU #3033 and the BSEIU— resisted the dominance of the considerably larger OEIU, a dominance fundamentally grounded in the process of bargaining over salary schedules. The OEIU represented many of its members in bargaining over prevailing rates for salary schedule SC. Yet, all members of the DALU #3033 and the BSEIU were lumped into the hodgepodge schedule SC, and the smaller organizations tended to be overshadowed in bargaining by the larger union.

When the two small organizations expressed a strong desire for independent Panel status in 1965, the OEIU decided to support their wishes and obtained the agreement of the TVAEA and TVAAPCChE to do the same. Separate petitions were presented to TVA by the three organizations within the Council of AFL-CIO affiliates. Each petition reaffirmed the union's majority support in its own bargaining unit and requested that TVA recognize the union as an individual Panel member. In June 1966, the Council of AFL-CIO affiliates officially dissolved itself, and the Panel accepted its three new independent members. TVA recognized this change by accepting the petitions of these unions, and appropriate revisions were made in the *Articles of Agreement.*

Another extremely important step was taken by the Panel in June 1966. A secretary was elected by the five Panel organizations to coordinate Panel activities and to speak for the entire group. Unions of the Trades and Labor Council had always demonstrated their cohesiveness by electing common officers. In June 1966, the Panel organizations reached this important benchmark, indicative of the growing ease with which they accepted and operated within their highly centralized bargaining structure.

The second, logical step in granting DALU #3033 and the BSEIU bargaining independence was to separate salary schedules for their bargaining units from the SC schedule. Before the annual wage negotiations in spring 1967, the Panel agreed to support the separation of two schedules from SC: an SF schedule for the BSEIU bargaining unit of custodial workers and an SG schedule for the DALU #3033 public safety service unit. TVA agreed to this separation, and prevailing pay for key classes of positions in these new schedules was surveyed prior to the negotiations. This move also helped to increase the Panel's stability as a centralized structure for five independent organizations of salary policy employees.

Other Conflicts

Conflicts also arose between the two large, aggressive members of the Panel: the office employees union and the TVA Engineers Association. The most serious dispute began in the summer of 1973, when the OPEIU (the OEIU had by that time changed its name to the Office and Professional Employees International Union) became perturbed with the Engineers Association. It was felt that the TVAEA had been extremely uncooperative when the hodgepodge SC schedule, represented by the OPEIU, was abolished in the process of negotiation and mediation. Because of this lack of cooperation, certain positions in the SC schedule were moved to another schedule considered inferior by individuals in these positions, and the individuals blamed their OPEIU leadership for what they considered a downward movement.

Soon thereafter, the TVAEA requested that TVA upgrade the positions of certain Right-of-Way Inspectors, whom it represented in schedule SE. These inspectors were supervised by Right-of-Way Clearing Agents, who were classified in schedule SA and represented by the OPEIU. Management agreed that the inspectors should be upgraded, but by reclassifying the positions to Right-of-Way Clearing Agents in schedule SA and out of the schedule represented by the TVAEA. The TVAEA promptly filed a grievance to protest this decision, expecting to have the matter resolved by an impartial referee. According to the *Articles of Agreement,* the Panel, and not an individual Panel member, had the prerogative of taking a grievance to arbitration. The OPEIU, still disturbed about the prior incident, blocked the TVAEA's attempt to invoke the last step of the grievance procedure.

Several stormy meetings between the TVAEA and the OPEIU ensured as the controversy over the blocked grievance extended into 1974. A key OPEIU official viewed the ongoing conflict as so serious that it constituted a credible threat to the continued existence of the Panel. In March 1974, the OPEIU international president addressed the valley-wide Cooperative Conference, and at the same time, requested that his union's leaders at TVA attempt to settle the conflict. Subsequently, the OPEIU reversed its stance, which had effectively blocked the TVAEA's grievance from proceeding to an impartial referee.

The two-year conflict between the Panel giants had been a serious one. Yet, in the May 1974 salary negotiations, all of the Panel members worked together in a remarkably smooth manner. No animosity was apparent, and indeed the unions expressed their favor toward the centralized Panel structure. Despite the periodic intraPanel conflicts stretching from the fifties into the early seventies, the period had been marked by a trend of increasing maturity in the Panel structure.

The growth in solidarity among Panel members and in the stability of the centralized organization was unmistakable. Important benchmarks highlighting this trend were the adoption of multiple salary schedules; the centralization of the PSSEU and BSEIU (later the SEIU) and their transition, along with the OPEIU, to independent Panel status; and the Panel's election of a secretary. Moreover, in contrast to the periodic conflicts which occurred, there were instances of close cooperation between unions, and in the early sixties, the TVAEA and TVAAPCChE very nearly agreed to a merger of their two organizations.

The Bargaining Relationship Matures

In the period from the mid-fifties through the mid-seventies, the collective bargaining relationship underwent a significant change. The spirit of mutual respect and cooperation between the parties remained above average. Nevertheless, the relationship became increasingly adversary in nature, as the salary policy employee organizations gained in strength and boldness and as the last traces of paternalism disappeared. Both parties contributed to the changing atmosphere of the relationship, and important determinants of the change can be divided between them.

The basic change involving the employee organizations was a direct and positive function of their own life span and that of the Panel structure. As the organizations and the Panel matured, elected and staff representatives brought increasing experience and confidence to the bargaining table. Their growing professionalism and adeptness in collective bargaining led them to repulse paternalistic attitudes of management. One union leader described the old management attitude as "We know what is best for you," and the emergent union attitude as "We want this no matter what you think is best for us." Paternalism was replaced by the adversary relationship that is collective bargaining.

Second, during this period, the OPEIU and TVAEA created and expanded fulltime, professional staffs. The smaller organizations could not go far in this direction but for example, the SEIU began to receive aid in bargaining from representatives of its international union.[12] The paid representatives had to be aggressive in bargaining; their motivation to press management for concessions was quite different from that of unpaid, elected representatives. They were compelled to deliver results to their memberships which could justify their employment. The memberships had to be shown that TVA was being forced into monetary concessions significantly above what it would have granted in the absence of effective union bargaining.

Especially after 1960, increasing militancy became apparent among federal employees in general and among TVA's salary policy employees. Union leaders at TVA attest to this grass roots change in attitude. They believe that a major reason was the civil rights movement which intensified in the sixties. Minorities appeared to be gaining benefits from militancy, and many salary policy employees began to consider militancy as the only avenue for instituting rapid change. Therefore, direct pressure from the rank-and-file was also forcing the organizations' representatives into a more aggressive stance vis-à-vis management. Intensifying the grass roots pressure was the fact that new, younger salary policy employees were replacing many of TVA's "old timers." Little historical perspective of TVA as an enlightened, model employer was grounded in the new generation of workers. They tended to assume that their unions had to push TVA into reluctantly granting any concession. Aggressive representation was demanded as a necessity.

Later in the period, many bargaining unit employees with long tenure would also become vocal in criticizing TVA's personnel and employee relations policies. They would contend that TVA had lost its lead over the federal service in such policies. It was claimed that salary and benefit levels of the classified federal service had caught up with those at TVA. Also pointed out, as an example, was the fact that Executive Order 11491 gave other federal employees a more effective impasse resolution procedure than was available to the Panel and to its member organizations.

A major factor increasing the strength of the organizations—the improving stability and maturity of their centralized Panel structure—has been analyzed. The bolstered strength of the Panel and of its member unions led to negotiated contract changes which even further advanced the unions' bargaining abilities. Improved union security helped to increase union membership and strength, for example. Also, the final-offer arbitration procedure negotiated in 1972 for salary rate impasse resolution added to the Panel organizations' clout in bargaining.

During the period under discussion, management's acceptance of unionism and collective bargaining continued to be exceptional. Yet its stance toward the Panel unions did change, from a paternalistic disposition to an increasingly aggressive, harder line. Certainly, management's change was partially a response to the increasing maturity and aggressiveness of the Panel and its member organizations. Other reasons for the change in management's posture can also be discerned.

Union representatives, and several management personnel, believe that management was forced to assume a harder line in bargaining after 1959. In that year, TVA began to issue power revenue bonds and switched to self-financing. TVA was forced to pay more attention to costs and had to assure underwriters that rises in labor costs would be kept within reasonable bounds. Several management officials disagree with the contention that self-financing significantly hardened management's attitude. However, the impact of the change to self-financing was essentially felt in conjunction with other determinants of management's changing posture, such as inflation.

After the mid-sixties, serious and persistent inflation pushed TVA's fuel, materials, and other nonlabor costs upward. Environmental concerns and legislation also increased pollution control costs. At the same time that cost pressures were intensifying, the public's adverse reaction to power rate increases seemed to become sharper. Therefore, management developed a harder line in negotiations affecting its labor costs. This was especially true of management in the major operating offices of power and construction.

Furthermore, higher level management personnel, including managers in power and construction, were added to the Salary Policy Negotiating Committee in the 1960s. Managers outside of the Division of Personnel, who were more apt to take a harder line in negotiations, began to exert increasing influence upon management's posture in negotiations. The operating managers began to offer their own proposals in negotiations, so that something could be traded for concessions made to the Panel. Union requests were examined more closely than before, and resistance to salary and monetary fringe benefit increases stiffened.

The nature of the collective bargaining relationship did indeed change from the mid-fifties into the early seventies. The change was gradual rather than sharp, but the rate of change accelerated and became more visible later in the period. It was manifested in a broadening scope of bargaining, in the development of a comprehensive written agreement, in increasingly vocal union criticism of management policies, and in demands for, and the negotiation of, an effective impasse resolution procedure. Each of these manifestations warrants an examination.

Important Contract Changes

Despite its internal problems, the Panel was able to negotiate important policy changes over a broadening range of subject matter. Annual liberalizations in salaries and fringe benefits were, of course, negotiated, but the range of monetary fringe items and nonmonetary items was also increased. Especially in negotiations over matters besides basic salary increases, it became less and less true that negotiated results were those that TVA might have granted unilaterally. In 1954, for example, significant improvements were negotiated in union security—in the status of the union and its attractiveness to potential members. Under the old system, a union member would be given preference in promotion, transfer, or retention, only if all other qualification factors of candidates were precisely the same. Certainly, this was a rare occurrence. The new language had the effect of requiring that union membership and participation always be considered as a positive factor in any promotion, transfer, or retention decision. Management also agreed to instruct supervisors that all employees should be informed of management's favorable attitude toward organizational activities and participation in Panel organizations.

In the same year, management agreed to begin payroll deductions of union dues. The dues check-off, like the other improvements in union security, was indicative of the Panel's growing strength in negotiations. At the same time, these policy changes aided the Panel organizations in increasing their memberships and thus in further adding to their strength.

By the early sixties, other significant agreements had been reached on monetary and nonmonetary matters. TVA had begun to contribute a percentage of each employee's health insurance premium. Insurance contributions, shift differentials, overtime pay, and other fringe items which could be measured were included with basic salaries in the annual survey of prevailing practice. The Panel also increased the pay of workers in a more indirect way by negotiating reductions in the amount of time necessary for within-grade salary increases. As a last example, agreements on prepermanent and permanent tenure were reached. In effect, tenure could be obtained to provide senior employees with preference in retention and reemployment.

Yet, the *Articles of Agreement* only contained the general principles of agreement between the two parties. The expanding multitude of specific

agreements continued to be spread among TVA Codes and Instructions. Therefore, agreement was reached in 1961 that a process should begin of incorporating
all negotiated items into one signed document. The truly general, seldom changed
agreements would be placed in the *Articles of Agreement*; all other items, subject
to frequent negotiation and change, would reside in supplementary agreements.

The process of reviewing and revising existing agreements was exhaustive,
and fall negotiations were begun to supplement the regular spring negotiations
and speed the process. Not until May 1964 were the renewed and reaffirmed
Articles of Agreement and Supplementary Agreements signed. The sixty-six-page
document consisted of seven general articles and nineteen supplementary agreements on specific subject matter. One article contained a forthright statement
that "TVA encourages employees to join the Panel organizations which represent
their positions." This was a new statement enhancing the unions' security, but,
besides some editorial changes, the revised articles contained little that was new.

For example, the procedure for resolving impasses in negotiations over
supplementary agreements was the same as the original procedure prescribed in
1950. A mediator would be appointed. If he could not resolve the dispute, he
would attempt to induce both sides to submit the dispute to final and binding
arbitration. Agreement on arbitration had to come from both sides. If TVA
refused arbitration, the mediator would make recommendations for resolving
the dispute to the TVA Board and to both parties; the procedure would then be
completed. No finality was assured in impasse resolution besides the unilateral
decision of management. Moreover, no impasse resolution procedure was prescribed for negotiation disputes over changes in articles of agreement. Again,
management could make a final, unilateral decision.

The nineteen supplementary agreements covered a wide variety of personnel
policies in great detail: classification, work schedules, pay, selection, tenure,
RIF, grievances, training, and many other policies. The six pages of agreement
governing work schedules are a good example of the detailed language of the
agreement and of the negotiated parameters on personnel policies. Detailed
procedures were spelled out for such subtopics as flexible and inflexible schedules, rest periods, holiday work, time spent in travel, paid meal periods during
overtime, and voluntary exchange of shifts.

The sixty-six-page agreement would remain virtually the same in form
through the mid-seventies with, of course, annual changes in supplementary
agreements covering salary levels and fringe items. The only major substantive
change will be discussed later. Certainly, the comprehensiveness of the renewed
agreement, especially for a public sector setting involving white-collar and professional employees, was a dramatic manifestation of the changing relationship.

Growing Strength and Aggressiveness of Panel

Membership change is a causal factor affecting union strength and bargaining ability; it is quantifiable and relatively easily uncovered. The membership of the Panel's two major organizations increased rapidly in the sixties and early seventies. Enhanced union security may have been a determinant, but the aggressive nature of the two organizations was probably more important. Between 1961 and 1974, the OPEIU increased its membership from 1,737 to 2,554, a rise of 47 percent. Between 1959 and 1974, the TVAEA almost tripled its membership, from 1,670 to 4,200. Certainly this great increase was made possible by the upsurge of hiring for positions in the TVAEA bargaining unit, but the Engineers Association aggressively sought these new employees for membership.

Another quantifiable piece of evidence, indicative of increased restlessness and aggressiveness by union members and leaders, is the change in the number of salary policy employee grievances filed and carried to the last two steps of the grievance procedure. Through the mid-sixties, white-collar and professional employees at TVA, as elsewhere, were extremely reluctant to file and proceed with a grievance. In 1967, the situation changed. A marked upturn occurred in the number of grievances filed and carried to the last two stages of the grievance procedure. Furthermore, TVAEA officials note that professionals in the SO schedule began to file and proceed with grievances. Earlier, the few grievances arising each year had been filed almost exclusively by TVAEA sub-professionals in schedule SE.

Leaders of salary policy employee organizations also shed their caution in openly criticizing management and management policies. In a 1965 issue of the TVAAPCChE's publication *Researchlight*, for example, the organization's president delivered a stinging attack on management because a nationwide labor market was not used to determine prevailing salary levels for professional employees. Criticisms of management also appeared in OPEIU publications and in a 1974 address before the valleywide cooperative conference, the OPEIU national president leveled some sharp charges against management. He claimed that TVA had lost its lead in public employee relations, and he especially criticized management's failure to resolve grievances promptly and the decentralization of personnel administration at TVA.

The fundamental criticism of many union members and leaders was that TVA had lost its status as a leader vis-à-vis the federal service in personnel policies and labor relations. One of the major areas in which TVA was said to have fallen behind was in the implementation of an effective impasse resolution procedure, not terminating with unilateral management action. The TVA-Panel procedure, negotiated in 1950 and extending through the early seventies, has been described. In 1969, Executive Order 11491 prescribed a new and improved procedure for most other federal employees.

The 1969 Executive Order created a Federal Service Impasse Panel (FSIP) under the Federal Labor Relations Council, which was designated to administer the Order. If mediation could not resolve an impasse between a federal agency and a union, either party could request the FSIP to consider the dispute. The

FSIP could or could not become involved and decide on the method of dispute resolution. It had the discretion to order or not to order final and binding arbitration, and its decision could only be appealed to the Federal Labor Relations Council.[13] Just as at TVA, impasses would not necessarily be settled in any other way than by unilateral management action; final and binding arbitration was only a possibility. But at least in the federal service, a third-party agency decided upon the means of dispute resolution, rather than the agency involved in the dispute itself.

Especially after 1967, the Panel and its member organizations knew that their negotiated impasse resolution procedure for supplementary agreements was not viable, and, in effect, meant unilateral resolution of bargaining disputes by management. In the May 1967 salary negotiations, the BSEIU could not reach agreement with TVA on salary rates for its newly created SF schedule. Therefore, the BSEIU asked the Panel to invoke the impasse resolution procedure for disputes over supplementary agreements. Just as in grievances, the entire Panel had to invoke the procedure, although any mediation or arbitration expenses would fall upon the BSEIU. The procedure was invoked by the Panel, for the first time in the history of the relationship.

The procedure's first step was mediation, but the small BSEIU was not ready to bear its share of the costs of a private mediator. Arrangements were therefore made for the Federal Mediation and Conciliation Service (FMCS) to send a mediator, but the mediator could not resolve the dispute. Moreover, the FMCS took the position that its mediator could not appear before the TVA Board of Directors and recommend the means of settling a dispute involving another federal agency. Only one other alternative was available under the negotiated procedure—final and binding arbitration. The Panel requested that TVA submit the dispute to arbitration. Agreement to submit the dispute was required of both parties. TVA refused. The Director of Personnel recommended that management's proposed salaries for schedule SF be adopted by the Board of Directors, and this recommendation was followed. The impasse had terminated with unilateral management action.

This incident was a major spark to rising frustration and discontentment among union members and leaders, especially after Executive Order 11491 improved the impasse resolution procedure for other federal employees. In 1969, the Panel proposed a major change in the *Articles of Agreement and Supplementary Agreements*. According to the proposal, impasses in bargaining over basic salary rates could be taken by *either* party to final-offer arbitration, where an impartial referee would choose between the final offers of the two parties for any disputed salary rates; his decision would be final and binding. The final-offer procedure had first been proposed by the TVAEA, and the OPEIU had agreed to the idea. Furthermore, the Panel proposed that either party could take a bargaining dispute over any other change in articles or supplementary agreements to final and binding arbitration. Despite a strong recommendation from certain top management officials to adopt the Panel's request, TVA moved slowly in considering a change of this nature, and agreement was not reached on all outstanding issues until the spring of 1972. The salary-determination criterion of trades and labor comparisons was eliminated from the labor agreement. Management had feared that an arbitrator would be unable to understand or apply this criterion properly. When impasses occurred over salary rates, either TVA or the Panel could, after mediation, submit the disputed schedule(s) to final-offer arbitration, and the arbitrator's decision would be final and binding. Other disputes over supplementary agreements would be first taken to mediation. Then, either party could take the dispute to an arbitrator, whose decision would be advisory, rather than binding. The lack of an impasse resolution procedure for disputes over changes in articles of agreement remained.

No salary dispute has been taken to final-offer arbitration and only one impasse has been appealed to advisory arbitration under the new procedures. Yet, the adoption of third-party finality for basic salary disputes presented the Panel with the clout which it had lacked in negotiations. The importance of this 1972 change to the collective bargaining relationship was comparable to the significance of the 1951 change to a "prevailing rate in the vicinity" criterion. It was a major stimulus to, and manifestation of, the changing nature of the relationship.

Notes

1. Board of Directors, Tennessee Valley Authority, *The TVA Employee Relationship Policy*, August 28, 1935, Paragraph 6, p. 5.

2. Ibid., Paragraph 8, p. 6.

3. Paul T. David, "Employee-Management Cooperation in the TVA," *Antioch Alumni Bulletin* (November 1936), p. 19.

4. The other organizations were the General Engineering Division Employees, three Hotel and Restaurant Employees locals, the Norris Teachers Federation, and the Pickwick Dam Engineers Association.

5. Letter from Gordon Clapp, Director of Personnel, to George P. Palo, president of the Knoxville TVAEA, July 26, 1937.

6. TVA memorandum from George Gant, Director of Personnel, to Gordon Clapp, General Manager, May 22, 1942.

7. Letter from George Gant, Director of Personnel, to Walter Mitchell, president of the Council, July 31, 1943.

8. Sterling D. Spero, *Government As Employer* (New York: Remsen Press, 1948), p. 365.

9. For example, Harry Case, Director of Personnel, mentioned the problem in his 1955 book *Personnel Policy in a Public Agency* (New York: Harper and Brothers, 1955), p. 79.

10. See *Employee-Management Cooperation in the Federal Service*, Executive Order 10988 (January 17, 1962).

11. When TVA discontinued most cafeteria operations, the OEIU absorbed the remaining members of the Hotel and Restaurant Employees' Union. In the late fifties, the TVAEA absorbed the membership of the International Chemical Workers' Union, apparently because the ICWU had become disinterested in continuing to represent the relatively small number of TVA workers who belonged to the ICWU at that time.

12. Of course, when the Council of AFL-CIO affiliates disbanded, DALU #3033 and the BSEIU lost the staff support which they had shared, to some extent, with the OPEIU.

13. *Labor-Management Relations In the Federal Service*, Executive Order 11491 (October 29, 1969), Sections 5 and 17.

4 Structure of Collective Bargaining

For the purpose of this study, the structure of collective bargaining will be defined as encompassing two major dimensions of a collective bargaining relationship. The first dimension is the organization of the parties for collective bargaining. Topics to be considered under this dimension are, for example, the make-up and representation of bargaining units, relationships among organizations representing different bargaining units, and the selection and composition of union and management negotiating teams.

The second dimension concerns the loci of decision-making power for bargaining within and among the unions, and within management. Included among topics under this dimension are rank-and-file controls over union negotiators, the powers of multiunion bodies and leaders, and the powers of line managers vis-à-vis the personnel staff to influence management's posture in negotiations. The attitudes of the parties, toward collective bargaining and toward each other, might also be included in a broad analysis of structure. However, these attitudes, and changes in these attitudes, have been thoroughly discussed in prior chapters.

The particular bargaining structure existing in any firm or industry may have a profound effect on the nature of union-management relationships in the firm or industry and may in fact be a primary determinant of their success or failure. The importance of efficacious bargaining structure is underscored by a consideration of the adverse effects upon bargaining relationships which can result and have resulted from serious structural problems. For example, an employer might be forced to deal with a large number of bargaining units, several of which might be very small. The inefficiency of separate bargaining with a large number of groups is obvious. An extreme diversity of monetary benefits and personnel policies might be negotiated for a work force, with adverse consequences on morale, productivity, and efficiency. Moreover, each bargaining unit representative might feel compelled to "leapfrog" his unit's wage and benefit package over that of the last compensation package negotiated, perhaps damaging the interests of consumers unjustifiably.

Labor unrest and strike activity can result directly from bargaining structures and processes that perform poorly. A bargaining relationship can be seriously undermined when the constituencies of either party refuse to accept a tentative agreement of the negotiators. The potential problems which can result from suboptimal bargaining structures are numerous. Thus, movement toward an optimal structure and process must be a major goal of every bargaining relationship.

Determination of Bargaining Units

Any analysis of union structure should logically begin with the determination and make-up of bargaining units. It was established in chapter 2 that the determination of appropriate bargaining units for trades and labor employees at TVA was a relatively smooth and unhampered process. The *Employee Relationship Policy* (ERP) of 1935 stated that an appropriate unit could be determined on a craft basis. A majority of employees in a craft were allowed to determine the organization that they wished to represent them, and a means was provided for resolving organizational and jurisdictional disputes.

This policy framework was sufficient to allow a rapid and orderly organization of trades and labor workers, primarily by AFL craft unions. The national or international craft unions simply organized those TVA employees who performed work that traditionally had been considered to fall within their exclusive work jurisdiction. Only one election involving trades and labor employees was ever necessary under the ERP provisions for resolving appropriate unit issues. The Director of Personnel conducted a representational election at the request of the Mine, Mill, and Smelter Workers.

The dispute resolution procedure regarding unit determinations was formalized in the *General Agreement* of 1951 with an additional provision relating to a single criterion for determining an appropriate unit. Article IV of the 1951 revision stated that "units defined by well established standards and practice are recognized as appropriate units." These established standards were those determined by the National Labor Relations Act, as amended in 1947. The 1951 revision also provided for final and binding arbitration of any dispute regarding which organization would represent an appropriate unit.

Under the 1971 revision of the *General Agreement* the Manager of Union-Management Relations is given the authority to conduct an election to determine the authorized representative of a bargaining unit. Both parties to the dispute, however, must agree to hold an election. If the dispute remains unresolved, *either* party may then invoke the services of an arbitrator secured through the Federal Mediation and Conciliation Service. The decision of the arbiter is accepted by all parties to the dispute. No experience with this dispute resolution procedure has yet occurred.

One of the principal reasons that no disputes have occurred over unit determinations or over questions of representation lies in TVA's acceptance of the doctrine of exclusive jurisdiction. Under this concept the AFL established definite job territories for each affiliated national union. Each such union received a charter from the AFL granting it exclusive jurisdiction over specific areas of work and no two unions of the AFL were given jurisdiction over the same work operations. Each union controls its assigned work jurisdiction either by obtaining recognition as the source of manpower for employees engaged in work involving that particular craft or by obtaining the affiliation of employees assigned to the work.[1]

Under the doctrine of exclusive jurisdiction, the individual worker has no direct influence nor does he express any preference in the selection of a particular union. Thus the AFL, and the international representatives assigned to represent a particular craft on the Tennessee Valley Trades and Labor Council, actually determined the union to which the individual employees would belong. After the particular areas of work were created, the union having exclusive jurisdiction over that work automatically represented the employees engaged in that operation. The question of whether to join a union was left to the trades and labor employees, but after TVA accepted the doctrine of exclusive jurisdiction, questions of representation and unit determination became largely moot. This is not meant to imply that TVA's trades and labor workers resisted or disliked the division of bargaining units along traditional craft lines. The craft workers did not oppose the scheme for establishing bargaining units, primarily because of the fundamental nature of crafts and craft unionism which affected their attitudes.

Members of crafts consider their work to require special skills. They take pride in working autonomously with a minimum of supervision. Even authoritarian relationships have an egalitarian flavor. Foremen are members of the same craft as their subordinate craftsmen, and a foreman's authority is normally derived from his skill in the field.[2] More importantly, members of crafts tend to identify with a particular occupation or trade rather than with a given employer. The well-defined work traits and traditions which become associated with particular crafts give their members common bonds. Thus, it is not surprising that TVA's craft workers easily attached their loyalties to the particular AFL unions which traditionally had represented their job territory. Membership in such a union reinforced their special identity and pride in their skill. It also normally meant that entry into the apprenticeship program necessary for acquiring the appropriate skill level of the craft could be subjected to more formalized control.

In summary, the determination of appropriate bargaining units for trades and labor employees was not difficult. TVA provided a policy framework for making unit determinations. Aided by the traditions of AFL craft unionism, a clear basis for dividing bargaining units was easily found, and the employees involved did not object to the scheme of dividing bargaining units which was utilized.

The policy framework of the ERP applied equally to unit determination for salary policy employees, but in all other respects, the two experiences stand in stark contrast. Appropriate bargaining units for TVA's white-collar and professional employees were determined in a void of precedent and with great difficulty, as was documented in chapter 3. By 1942 the Personnel Department had developed criteria for the subsequent determination of white-collar and professional bargaining units. The desires of employees and the suitability of units for bargaining would be given major consideration. Additionally, precedents in unit determination, especially National Labor Relations Board precedents, would be guiding factors. Under the 1942 criteria, salary policy employee bargaining units were fashioned along occupational, valleywide lines. The Director of Personnel resolved all unit determination and jurisdictional issues.

Centralized Bargaining Structures

Given the make-up of bargaining units in a union-management relationship, the structure for bargaining may assume an array of forms. Unions representing workers in particular bargaining units may bargain separately with a common employer at each work location. Or the national union may bargain separately for a contract covering all work locations. Alternatively, the unions may join together in bargaining with a common employer at either local or national levels. Finally, the unions may face a multi employer group in bargaining. The critical issues of bargaining structure which have received attention in the last few decades have largely involved the possibilities for structural arrangements that present themselves once bargaining units are determined. Particularly important issues to be considered now are centralization versus decentralization in bargaining structures, and responsibility versus democracy in bargaining structures. The issues will be considered first in general terms, so that a framework will be available for evaluating particular bargaining structures in this case study and in other settings.

Few students of industrial relations would argue with the contention that the most significant trend in union bargaining structures from the thirties to the sixties lay in the centralization of such structures. This centralization was both vertical and horizontal. It was vertical in the sense that decision-making power was transferred upward from the local union level to the national union level. It was also horizontal because independent unions, at local, intermediate, and national levels, joined together in various formal and informal ways to bargain with common employers. Employer centralization for bargaining likewise occurred; horizontal centralization was the most visible and was manifested in the growth of multi employer bargaining structures. Practitioners of collective bargaining and academicians have also noted the reaction of many union members and local union leaders against the degree of structural centralization which has been evolving on the union side. The reaction probably began among the craft workers of industrial unions in the mid-fifties and spread to other groups of workers.

Two reasons for union centralization have received the most treatment in the literature: the need to preserve and expand leverage in bargaining as structural changes occurred in industrial organization, and the need to bargain successfully over increasingly complex issues. For example, as product markets became national in scope, business firms began to produce for a nationwide market from plants that were often scattered across the country. If locals of the same or different national unions bargained for separate labor contracts at each plant location, the strike threat and bargaining clout of each local might be ineffective. The company might be able to weather even a long strike at one plant by shifting production to other plants. Therefore, vertical centralization became necessary within unions, so that bargaining at the national level for all plants would make the strike threat effective. Horizontal centralization among local and national unions was also directed toward the same end.[3]

Horizontal centralization in the last two decades has largely been a union response to another significant change in industrial organization, the diversification of business firms and the conglomerate merger movement. Assume that a business firm produces many unrelated product lines and bargains separately with several different unions, each representing the production workers of one product line. How can any one union threaten the firm with serious harm from a strike when the firm can continue normal production and sales in its other product lines? In these cases, unions realized the necessity of pushing for common expiration dates on their contracts and of cooperating closely in bargaining, so that the firm would face meaningful pressure from a united front of its employees' organizations.

Another often mentioned reason for union centralization, especially of the vertical type, is the changed nature of bargaining issues. After World War II, a sharply increasing percentage of total compensation began to come to workers in the form of fringe benefits. Local unions bargaining over fringes found insurance, pension, and other issues increasingly complicated. Expertise in such matters tended to reside at national union levels, and decision-making power began to flow upward for this reason. Bargaining over these issues at higher levels also became preferable for actuarial and administrative purposes.[4]

The management of many private firms and public agencies have also found that dealing with horizontally centralized union structures has major advantages. One is efficiency. Collective bargaining that is conducted separately with a large number of unions expends a great deal of management's time and monetary resources in the bargaining process itself.

Management may also find that a great advantage of bargaining with a centralized union structure lies in the uniformity of negotiated results. Unions that represent relatively heterogeneous groups of workers will not likely bargain through a central structure for uniform basic pay levels or basic pay increases, but they might bargain centrally for uniform negotiated results on fringe benefit issues, grievance procedures, seniority and union security provisions, and some work rules. These negotiated results would not vary by the relative strength of the unions, nor would they vary locally by the relative strength of particular union locals if the centralized bargaining was being conducted above the local level.

Morale and thus productivity may be enhanced because bitterness is not engendered among employees due to widely different fringe benefits and work rules. Those responsible for personnel administration can more efficiently communicate negotiated provisions to the various line managers of employees, and the provisions are more likely to be uniformly applied. In particular, first- and second-line supervisors can more easily be trained in the administration of negotiated results. Transfers of these individuals to the supervision of employees in another bargaining unit does not require extensive retraining in contract administration. Neither are employees transferring among bargaining units uncertain that significantly different contract provisions may be applied to them.

The benefits of horizontally centralized union structures, which are realized by employers, may also be realized by society. For example, centralized bargaining should involve less people hours of management time and monetary resources. This should translate into lower unit costs for any given volume of output, if all other things remain the same (the "ceteris paribus" assumption commonly made by economists). If centralization and uniform negotiated outcomes mean net positive morale effects, and productivity increases, then, ceteris paribus, unit costs will be lower for any given volume of output. Lower unit costs may be passed on to consumers in lower prices, or extra services, depending upon the market power of the employer, the profit or nonprofit status of the employer, and perhaps other variables. Moreover, industrial peace might be more likely as unions centralize horizontally for bargaining. If negotiated results are more uniform, rank-and-file discontent arising from comparisons with negotiated results of other unions, which bargain with the same employer, may be less likely to occur. Productivity slowdowns and strikes which damage the public's interests would be less probable.

On the other hand, uniform contract provisions resulting from centralized bargaining can have undesirable consequences, especially when the uniform provisions apply to diverse occupations and work locations. For example, certain work rules may best be negotiated on a decentralized basis where differentiated contract terms are needed to reflect particular occupational or locational circumstances. Otherwise, negative morale effects may decrease labor productivity and increase labor unrest, to the detriment of both management and society.

Many of those opposing the combination of unions into horizontally centralized structures believe that unions centralize mainly to increase their leverage in bargaining. The unions are able to collude in pushing their average wages and fringe benefits further above competitive labor market levels than would occur in the absence of centralization. Unit labor costs are higher, ceteris paribus, than they would be without centralization. If prices tend toward unit costs levels, then prices paid by consumers of the firm's goods or services will be higher than otherwise. This may mean employment decreases in the particular firm. Displaced workers might shift to other labor markets and depress the wages of workers in those markets—workers who, along with other consumers, are paying the higher prices for the original firm's goods or services.

Even if average compensation levels are pushed higher than otherwise by union centralization, the adverse theoretical results espoused by opponents of centralization do not necessarily follow. Higher-than-otherwise wage levels might bring morale-induced productivity increases sufficient to prevent any rise in unit labor costs. Furthermore, if the firm engaged in bargaining has significant market power, the prices which it charges may have little relationship to unit cost levels.

Perhaps the strongest argument for centralized bargaining structures is made by knowledgeable academicians and practitioners who have seen both centralized and decentralized bargaining in action. They observe that supercompetitive compensation increases are often more likely where several unions bargain individually with management. Each union attempts to "leapfrog" its negotiated settlement over that of the last union involved in negotiations.[5] Also, it may be less easy for the public and government to learn about, and respond to, inordinate compensation gains reached in decentralized negotiations.

Does the centralization of union bargaining structures result in social benefits greater than, equal to, or less than social costs? Theoretical arguments already presented can be used to support either a positive or a negative social evaluation, and empirical evidence is sufficiently mixed that we cannot yet reach a conclusion on empirical grounds. However, the final private and social evaluation of centralized bargaining structures will primarily rest on grounds other than those discussed so far. Conclusions on both centralized union and management structures will depend upon how well these structures accommodate adequate degrees of both responsibility and democracy simultaneously. In the trade-off of responsibility versus democracy lay the greatest strengths and the greatest weakness of centralized bargaining structures.

Responsibility Versus Democracy

Responsibility in bargaining structures means that negotiators should have the authority to bring bargaining to a final and binding conclusion. They should not have their positions undercut or repudiated by their constituencies. Responsibility also infers that bargaining structures should enable negotiators to consider the impacts of their actions and negotiated results upon society.

Both horizontally and vertically centralized structures tend to insulate union negotiators from direct observation and pressure by the rank-and-file union members. This means that the bargaining process may be less long and complicated than otherwise. The union negotiators need spend less of their time in the purely political activities associated with convincing the rank-and-file that they are being well represented in bargaining. More time can be spent in moving the negotiations toward a satisfactory conclusion. The authority to make final decisions on contract terms may also have flowed vertically or horizontally to the union negotiators, so that the final position of these negotiators cannot be repudiated by the rank-and-file. Moreover, social responsibility tends to spring more easily from centralized as opposed to decentralized bargaining. Centralizing bargaining makes the results of negotiations more visible, and both government and the public are more able to influence the negotiators toward results that are considered socially reasonable. The "leapfrogging" of one union's demands over those of another, and the high rate of wage inflation which may result, is also avoided in horizontally centralized bargaining.

Many examples of the irresponsibility flowing from decentralized bargaining have been cited in the literature. The leapfrogging demands of craft unions in the fragmented bargaining of the construction industry are important examples.[6] It is argued later in this book that the TVA collective bargaining experience has constituted an important model of the responsibility which may result from the use of centralized bargaining structures.

Management bargaining structures must also be responsible. The existence of responsibility in these structures relates primarily to the authority level of those who are involved in negotiations within the management hierarchy. If low-level managers perform the negotiating function, perhaps on a decentralized basis, they may be vulnerable to upper management's rejection of a tentative agreement. Therefore, the management bargaining structure must be one in which negotiators can communicate with, and enjoy the confidence of, top management and boards of directors. The vertical centralization of decision-making power regarding management positions during negotiations may thus be necessary to insure the exercise of responsibility.

Especially in public sector bargaining, management structures have often not been responsible in this sense. Management negotiators have seen their positions repudiated from above; the discretion given them in the management bargaining structure has not been great or well-defined. Furthermore, management responsibility is weakened in the United States political system vis-à-vis a parliamentary system, where executive and legislative decision-making are largely combined. Public sector management may find its bargaining agreements repudiated in a legislative body when, for example, funds necessary to enforce the agreement are not made available. In fact, legislatures have rejected negotiated settlements on a number of occasions.[7]

The other dimension of the important trade-off in bargaining structures is democracy. The degree of democracy embodied in a union or management bargaining structure is the relative ability of constituencies to control or influence the positions taken by negotiators. Democracy is more accurately defined broadly as constituent control over representatives in all aspects of union-management relations, because many controls apply to more than collective bargaining itself.

The term is often not applied to the management bargaining structure. This is a mistake, for management negotiators certainly have constituents. The basic constituency of negotiators in the private sector would be the stockholders; theoretically, the public would be the basic constituency of public sector negotiators. Realistically, neither group can be given effective, direct input into the positions taken by management negotiators before and during negotiations. Yet, another important constituency should and can be given reasonable democratic controls. Let us assume that staff employee relations officers perform the negotiating function. Line management should be represented on the negotiating team and should have a meaningful role in formulating management's positions. Tangible benefits can result from building this type of democracy into the bargaining structure: line management is more likely to support the negotiated results and these results are more likely to be administered consistently in all operating divisions and departments. Also, top management may be less likely to repudiate negotiated results which have been influenced by a broad spectrum of management, so both democracy and responsibility would accrue to the management structure.

The degree of democracy in union bargaining structures has long been an important analytical issue. Indeed, bargaining is not "collective" if rank-and-file workers have insignificant controls and checks over their representatives. Workers would not be greatly served by a union which fought arbitrary treatment by employers, but which substituted its own uncontrollable bureaucracy over members. Moreover, when the rank-and-file feel impotent in controlling their representatives, social damage can result and take the form of contract rejections, legal and illegal strikes, or low morale and productivity. The greatest potential drawback of structural centralization on the union side is the possibility that centralized structures embody an unacceptably low degree of democracy.

Two major methods of controlling union leaders may be open to rank-and-file union members: the election control and the referendum control. Certainly, the election control of workers loses potency where bargaining structures are either vertically or horizontally centralized, for any given group of workers constitutes a smaller portion of the total constituency of elected union leaders and negotiators. The referendum control—the right of union members to approve or reject the tentative agreements of negotiators through a referendum vote— therefore assumes great importance as a means of insuring adequate democracy in centralized union structures.

The right to a referendum means that union negotiators must heed the wishes of the rank-and-file regardless of the clout of the particular group of union members in the union election process. The referendum right also provides union members with a direct comment on negotiations, whereas many issues may be involved in a union election. If approximately one-half of all union members in this country now have referendum rights,[8] why not simply guarantee such rights to all union members?

The primary reason is that the referendum issue is important in the responsibility of bargaining structures, as well as in their democracy. Rejections of tentative agreements by constituencies reflect a use of democratic control, but they also undermine collective bargaining and may lead to work stoppages which damage the public interest. In fact, recent studies have indicated an alarmingly high rate of contract rejections by union members exercising their referendum rights.[9] In a significant number of collective bargaining situations, union negotiators were being undercut, the credibility of these negotiators in future bargaining was being damaged, and the ability of the bargaining process to peacefully culminate in jointly determined results was being eroded.

Thus, a trade-off exists in the responsibility versus the democracy of bargaining structures. The structural arrangement for bargaining in union-management relationships should allow the simultaneous existence of adequate degrees of both responsibility and democracy. Certainly the bargaining structure in this case-study and in other union-management settings must be examined closely with regard to this trade-off, for the overall evaluation of the efficacy of a bargaining structure, especially of a centralized structure, may critically depend upon our judgment in this area. Where the responsibility or democracy of structural arrangement are judged deficient, structural changes or procedural changes in election, referendum, or other controls may be necessary.

Trades and Labor Council Structure

The factors affecting the evolution of both centralized union structures for collective bargaining at TVA were generally the same. These factors took shape as the structure for bargaining with trades and labor unions developed, and they largely spilled over to influence the formation of the Salary Policy Employee Panel. In the formative period for the structural arrangement of both relationships, the outstanding constant was the attitude of TVA management.

During the period from 1933 to 1940, TVA proceeded in carrying out its broad mandate of improving the navigability of the Tennessee River, controlling floods, producing and transmitting electric power, and improving the natural and human resources of the entire region. The construction of dams was the primary activity of the period. Eight major dams were started, and four were completed before 1940. To accomplish the broad set of its tasks, TVA began the employment, on a procurement basis, of thousands of construction workers each year. The nature of construction work has changed over the years, with current concentration on the building of nuclear plants, for example, but the breadth of functional operations has not been significantly diminished. Management has continually realized therefore that the enormous scale of force-account construction work, coupled with maintenance and operating work, demands an organized system of labor relations designed to make a positive contribution to the overall efficiency and productivity of the organization.

The geographical scope of TVA operations has also been relatively broad. The total area of operations covers portions of seven states, and construction projects have been undertaken at numerous locations, usually many miles from a major town or city. With this functional and geographical breadth of operations in mind, management decided that TVA's effective performance required centralized control over the bilateral determination of employment policy. Policy matters handled through local, decentralized negotiations, with possibly hundreds of small unions throughout the TVA region, could result in confusion, inconsistency of policy, and administrative chaos, to say nothing of expense.

Management also pressured unions of its employees toward structural centralization because of its attitude on union responsibility. TVA's early encouragement of unionism and collective bargaining was grounded in the premise that it would be dealing with responsible unions. Originally, the social aspect of the term "responsibility" was stressed; responsible union representatives should take positions which tend to promote efficiency and economy of operations so that TVA could fulfill its overall responsibilities to society. Yet, TVA quickly came to demand responsibility from its unions in the sense that union negotiators should have the authority to bind their constituents. TVA management felt that both the vertical and the horizontal centralization of union structures promoted responsibility. The entire history of management dealings with unions of its employees supports this contention, for TVA both influenced the horizontal consolidation of its unions and also attempted to deal with union representatives located as high as possible in the union hierarchy.

Whereas unions representing TVA's salary policy employees agreed to horizontal centralization only under conditions of extreme management pressure, international representatives of the major trades and labor unions concurred in management's general attitude. They shared a concern for the problems inherent in excessive fragmentation and in highly decentralized bargaining with a proliferation of local bargaining units. They also assured management that the trades and labor unions, bargaining through a centralized structure, could be responsible and still effectively represent rank-and-file union members.

The environment for bargaining probably also influenced the union leaders into a centralization scheme. The union movement was very weak in the TVA vicinity during the thirties, and AFL unions and their locals found any organizational scheme attractive that might increase their leverage in bargaining. They were similarly influenced by the depressed economic conditions which pervaded the nation. In fact, during such depressed economic circumstances, various unions have often decided to negotiate with a contractor as a group or to follow a pattern set by a joint bargaining committee or council. In better times, the stronger local unions tend to bargain for themselves, since they believe that their bargaining strength would be weakened by negotiating as a group with other unions.[10]

Another factor affected the movement of trades and labor unions toward a responsible and a centralized structure for bargaining. In order to attain this type of union-management relationship, a conflict between the authority of the international representatives organizing and representing TVA construction employees and that of various officials of State Federations of Labor in the seven-state TVA area had to be resolved, as well as conflicts between the international representatives and the many local union officials functioning within the TVA area.

State labor federations have always been considered an important arm of the central American Federation of Labor itself. During the 1930s when TVA's employees were organizing into craft unions, state federations of the AFL were responsible for organizing the work within their respective states; they also served as a lobbying force in their state legislatures. Although the AFL's state federations having jurisdiction within the seven states of TVA's area of construction operations were relatively weak in membership, as well as in lobbying effectiveness, their roles within the AFL structure, and their relationship with local craft unions within their respective states, had been well established by 1937 when the Trades and Labor Council was officially organized. Since the statewide labor organizations were responsible for conducting organizational drives on a state-wide basis, they were in an intermediary position between the local craft unions and the national and/or international unions.[11] The traditional role played by the state federations having jurisdiction over union members working for TVA, particularly the Alabama and Tennessee federations, had a significant effect on the collective bargaining structure established by the international unions representing TVA's trades and labor employees.

Seven state federations had an interest in the TVA construction operations being conducted in their state. These federations were officially responsible for organizing TVA employees who resided within the boundaries of their respective states. The international representatives of craft unions representing the varied work at TVA construction sites, and not directly affiliated with the state federations, were also attempting to organize TVA employees. These latter representatives conducted their organizing activities independently of the state federations having traditional responsibility for organizing the workers in their states. This dual responsibility gave rise to a conflict between the leaders of the state federations and those international representatives seeking to organize and to represent TVA employees. The international representatives were in effect undermining the authority and responsibility of the various state federation officials, because once the Trades and Labor Council was formed, its jurisdiction would have to be on a regional basis to be effective, and thus its responsibilities would necessarily cross state lines. The conflicting relationship between the Council and the state federations was particularly apparent in Tennessee and Alabama where most of TVA construction work was being performed; these states also made up TVA's primary labor markets.

After Samuel Roper, international representative of the Plumbers' Union and first president of the Tennessee Valley Trades and Labor Council, had been elected president of the Alabama State Federation of Labor, AFL, this conflict was somewhat alleviated. The problem of overlapping jurisdiction nevertheless remained a thorn in the intraunion relationship between the state federation officials and the various international representatives of the unions having jurisdiction over TVA's trades and labor employees.

In an attempt to alleviate this problem of dual control, and for other reasons, officers of the council sought, unsuccessfully, to obtain a charter from the president of the American Federation of Labor. As a counter measure to the lack of a charter, the Council members believed that the only effective way to solve the problem was to have the presidents of the various international unions sign a written labor agreement with TVA. This would place the TVA-Council relationship above the control and authority of the state federations. Perhaps even more importantly, however, it would create Council supremacy over the various local unions within the TVA area. The Council members believed this latter advantage to be the only effective way to achieve valleywide wage scales and generally uniform conditions of employment.

The supremacy of the Council over the various local unions, and its ability to achieve uniformity in negotiated results, was clearly established in the late 1930s when the Carpenters' local union of Chattanooga, Tennessee decided to hold out for more than the wage rate negotiated with TVA by their international representative. The representatives of the Chattanooga local appealed the issue to the Secretary of Labor but the Council members reported to the Secretary that no dispute existed over the wage rate. The Carpenters' international representative on the Council reportedly told the Chattanooga Building Trades Council that the local unions would have to make a sacrifice in order to help the cause of all carpenters throughout the valley.

The signing of the *General Agreement* did indeed place the authority of the Trades and Labor Council above that of the state federations of labor and of the various local unions or building trades councils which represented TVA trades and labor employees. This feature of the bargaining structure was an important one. It provided for an enlarged scope of bargaining covering all trades and labor employees whose union (or whose work was subject to jurisdiction of a member union) was included as a member of the Council, while at the same time maintaining the craft concept and thus leaving the local unions as well as the international unions completely intact. Although the relationship between national union representatives and leaders of salary policy employee unions at TVA differs from the trades and labor experience, the experience of the Trades and Labor Council vis-à-vis state federations of labor did set a precedent for the salary policy employee experience. The way was paved for valleywide unions of TVA's salary policy employees to form, centralize, and enter into a written labor agreement without coming into conflict with state federations of labor.

Since its establishment in 1937, the Trades and Labor Council has served as the bargaining agent for TVA's employees in the trades and labor classifications. The Council is made up of local unions of the international unions which are signatory to the *General Agreement* and have members working for TVA, and international representatives assigned by their unions to TVA. For administrative purposes the Council members created an Executive Board which had responsibility for conducting the affairs of the Council. The Board itself is composed of the duly authorized international representatives from each of the unions recognized in Article I of the *General Agreement.* The number of members on the Executive Board has changed since 1937 depending on the number of unions recognized in Article I.

Each member union of the Council represents those trades and labor employees who perform work of the type traditionally performed by members of that particular craft union. The trades and labor employees of TVA who are members, or eligible to become members of a craft union, are not individually members of the Council. They either belong to various member local unions operating within each TVA work location, or they belong to other local unions throughout the country and work as "travelers" out of locals in the TVA area. Thus, the international representatives on the Executive Board of the Council represent all trades and labor employees within their respective unions' work jurisdictions.

The members of the Executive Board annually elect three officers of the Council: a president, vice president, and secretary. In actual negotiations, the president serves as spokesman for the Council on matters of general application and represents the Council's interest in other matters with TVA occurring outside negotiations. On matters affecting each union separately—wages, for example—the particular international representative of that union speaks for his union's membership and the decision to accept or reject TVA's "final offer" on wages is his alone, not that of the Council or of the Council's president.

During negotiations the international representatives who are members of the Executive Board have the final authority to commit their unions and union members employed by TVA to a final settlement. The rank and file membership does not vote to ratify the wage scales or other conditions of employment negotiated by TVA and the Executive Board of the Council. Throughout negotiations each international representative is advised and consulted by a number of delegates from the various local unions having members employed by TVA, but, as will become even more clear in the following chapter on the process of bargaining, decision-making power resides with the international union representatives.

The system by which local delegates are selected has varied over time since 1940, and also according to the particular international union involved. A majority of the unions send either the local business manager from the various locals throughout the TVA area or other delegates elected by the local membership or appointed by the business manager. The business agents (or managers) of each local union representing trades and labor unions throughout the TVA vicinity are elected by vote of the rank-and-file membership of that local.[12]

The union structure is highly centralized vertically, as well as horizontally, for decision-making power emanates from agents of the international union. The high degree of centralization has brought efficiency in the negotiation and administration of labor contracts. It has resulted in the exercise of responsibility by the unions in negotiations, for positions taken by international representatives cannot be repudiated by rank-and-file union members. Social responsibility has also come from TVA's bargaining with the Trades and Labor Council. No strikes have resulted from contract negotiations, and average wage increases for trades and labor workers have appeared reasonable in social terms (see table 9-2 for the schedule of negotiated wage increases).

The Achilles heel in this highly centralized union structure certainly lies in the degree of democracy which is embodied in it. Historically, local unions of the building trades have been able to preserve a considerable degree of autonomy in conducting their own affairs. Local unions of the AFL-CIO building trades have traditionally negotiated the provisions of collective bargaining contracts, as well as enforced these provisions. At TVA, however, the international representatives of the unions representing trades and labor employees assume a more central role in negotiations and contract administration than local unions having jurisdiction over TVA work since the *General Agreement* is with the international unions themselves and not with particular local unions or with groups of local unions.

Because the unions' bargaining structure is so highly centralized, it lacks certain democratic aspects apparent in the construction industry as a whole. Rank-and-file members of international unions in the Tennessee Valley Trades and Labor Council, who are employed by TVA at the time wages are negotiated or at other times when the agreement is being revised, neither have the right of contract ratification nor do these trades and labor employees actually choose their representatives who sit on the Executive Board of the Tennessee Valley Trades and Labor Council and who represent their interests in negotiations with TVA. Also, at any one particular time most of the local unions affiliated with the Council are composed of members who are employed by TVA but who retain active membership in the local union. In these cases, the locally elected officials who serve as delegates during negotiations, and who are supposed to represent the desires and needs of its TVA union members, may not have been the chosen representatives of the local union members working for TVA at that time.

Some annual employees do belong to local unions made up of only TVA employees. They do elect their own local representatives, but they still have no voting rights to elect their representatives on the Trades and Labor Council. These representatives are appointed by the international unions themselves. Thus, the two most important and most prevalent methods for rank-and-file members to put pressure on union officials—ratification by the rank-and-file of union policies and agreements and election of union leaders with decision-making power in dealings with management—are either not available or of slight significance to TVA employees in trades and labor classifications.

One student of labor relations who conducted an earlier study of the TVA experience criticized this aspect of the labor relations program as a significant weakness of the TVA experience. Specifically, John Crispo charged that TVA and the Council participated in "deal bargaining" rather than collective bargaining.[13] This concept refers to a bargaining relationship where management and the union(s) representing its employees become so powerful that they tend to "make deals" with each other rather than truly representing the interests of their constituencies. Crispo uses the term to refer to a situation where agreements may be reached which do not reflect the views and wishes of the majority of the union members affected. The implication here is that the trades and labor employees either do not participate or that their voice is so ineffective as to be meaningless. The danger, of course, is that the price of adhering to the centralized union structure could prove extremely high and take the form of employee discontent, poor work attitudes, spotty production, more work stoppages, and other forms of overt dissatisfaction.[14]

Members of some of the Trades and Labor Council unions have more influence over their Council representatives than do members of other unions. Union members tend to elicit more response from their international representatives, for example, where the fraction of TVA membership to the total membership of the international union is relatively significant. Also, union members classified in annual positions can exert more influence over their representatives than can employees classified in construction and temporary maintenance and operating work.

In general, however, the means for trades and labor employees to influence the negotiation and administration of the collective bargaining agreement are neither direct nor powerful. The ability to influence international representatives on the Trades and Labor Council, by voting and participating in international union conventions, is certainly indirect. The most significant control available to the local union members lies in their ability to elect local officers and representatives, and this is only important to the extent that these local officials exercise meaningful power in the collective bargaining relationship.

Prior to 1974, the powers of these local officers, vis-à-vis the powers of international union representatives on the Executive Committee of the Council, were extremely limited. In 1974, the written agreements for construction employment and for operating and maintenance employment were separated. More significantly, the contractual powers and prerogatives of local union officers were largely eroded. For example, the old contract said that Trades and Labor Council members were required to invite local union representatives to participate in the annual wage conference; the revised construction contract states that these locally chosen representatives "may" be invited to participate.

The old contract also provided that management consult with local union officers over such matters as the assignment of employees to work involving dual classifications, the hiring of workers when construction operations are begun in new locations, and the recall of workers after temporary interruptions of work. The 1974 contract revisions for construction work transferred these prerogatives away from local union officials to the Council representative of the union involved.[15] Similar changes, eroding rank-and-file controls, were also made in the contract revisions for annual and hourly operating and maintenance employment. The major remaining prerogative of local union representatives involves their dealings with management during the first two steps of grievance adjustment. Yet, the international representative takes over any representation of a union member at the third step of appeal. Furthermore, appeal cannot be made to an impartial referee without the consent of both the international representative and the Trades and Labor Council as a whole (grievance adjustment will be more fully discussed in chapter 8).

After these contract changes were made, rank-and-file frustrations over the lack of democratic controls became exceedingly visible. A number of annual and hourly operating and maintenance employees hired a law firm to present their complaints to TVA. In petitioning TVA, these workers claimed that the majority of operating and maintenance employees wished TVA to hold an election, so that they might withdraw support of the Trades and Labor Council as their representative. Barring this, they requested that serious reforms be made to improve democratic control within the centralized union structure.[16]

The group of workers threatened action in federal court, or under Executive Order 11491, if TVA took no action to alleviate their lack of controls over representatives and over positions taken in negotiations. TVA did not take any of the actions requested. Thereupon, the workers involved brought suit in federal court, but the court claimed that it had no jurisdiction to act in the matter. At present the issue has not been resolved. Perhaps structural or procedural changes will be necessary to make democratic controls adequate. Certainly, this aspect of the TVA experience has already illustrated significant problems which may develop in highly centralized union structures.[17]

Salary Policy Employee Panel Structure

It has been established that the centralization of unions of salary policy employees was forced, and enforced, by management. Only after the unions had weathered many years of conflict and accommodation within the structure did they begin to feel comfortable in centralized bargaining and to voluntarily accept its continuance. Of course, in few other bargaining settings have such diverse groups and interests been involved in a centralization, either voluntarily or involuntarily.

The Salary Policy Employee Panel is officially composed of a secretary and one representative from each of the five member organizations. An official Panel representative may be a professional staff member of a Panel union or more often, a TVA employee selected as president or Panel representative of a member union. All of the official Panel representatives are employed or selected by TVA employees in the bargaining unit they represent. In negotiations and union-management relations, other elected leaders and staff members of the Panel unions may join their official representatives in working within the Panel. International union officers and representatives sometimes play a role in negotiations and other union-management matters, but the Panel is primarily a creature of the salaried employee bargaining units at TVA, and not of international unions.

Each member union, through its representative(s), exercises control over the Panel's position on salaries and any other matters affecting its bargaining unit only. Yet, on almost all fringe benefit and nonmonetary contract items, the unions' positions must be developed and espoused by the Panel as a single entity. Therefore, the Panel members work closely in developing their bargaining stance, and the secretary speaks for the entire group. The Panel also acts as one entity in taking grievances to an impartial referee, in participating in union-management committees and conferences, and in other matters.

The member unions differ in their ties to international unions and labor federations. The Office and Professional Employees (OPEIU) and Building Service Employees (SEIU) are affiliated with international unions which are, in turn, affiliated with the AFL-CIO. The Safety Service Employees DALU #3033 is a directly affiliated local union of the AFL-CIO. The TVAEA and TVAAPCChE are not now affiliated with any national or international union or federation. Consideration has been given by the TVAEA to affiliation with an AFL-CIO union that would guarantee only loose ties between the national and TVA area organizations. The Marine Engineers Beneficial Association was one of the national unions considered. Yet, a merger or affiliation with a national union has never occurred. The TVAEA was a charter member of the Engineers and Scientists of America federation in 1952, before withdrawing in 1957. It was a founder of the Council of Engineers and Scientists Organizations in the late sixties, but it later withdrew from this federation also.[18]

Together, the Panel members represent approximately 87 percent of salary policy employees; except for about one hundred nonmanagement employees, those not represented are in the management schedule. Approximately 90 percent of the represented employees are union members. The membership size of the individual Panel members is another significant factor differentiating the salary policy employee organizations. The TVAEA has 4,000 members and the OPEIU has approximately 2,500 members; in contrast, the other three organizations have 275 members or less.[19] These drastically different sizes underscore the main advantage of the Panel to its members. Especially the leaders of the three smaller organizations believe that the collective power of the Panel members is vital in dealings with TVA. They admit that their small size would give them little leverage in separate bargaining with the Authority. They also benefit from the professional staffs of the larger organizations, who are valuable in preparing the Panel's positions on matters affecting all salary policy employees. At the same time, each of the two larger organizations also gains leverage from the combined memberships of the other four organizations.

Management has found that dealing with the centralized union structure, instead of the alternative of separate dealings with five unions, is highly efficient and economical. Responsibility springs from the Panel structure, for the members of Panel unions are contractually precluded from voting upon, and possibly rejecting, the agreements reached by their negotiators. Moreover, the exercise of social responsibility has emanated from this centralized bargaining. No Panel member has engaged in strike activity, and average basic salary increases have not been inordinately high (see table 9-2). For example, from 1962 through the mid-1960s, the Kennedy-Johnson guidepost for noninflationary wage and salary increases was 3.2 percent per year, and between 1962 and 1967, the average of basic salary increases for salary policy employees was 3.4 percent.

Bargaining structure is, of course, only one factor which may affect negotiated results. Yet it is doubtful that TVA would have demonstrated a consistent bias for the centralized Panel structure if inordinately high compensation increases were a probable result. This is especially true since TVA utility rate increases, caused by any type of cost increases, have been met by increasingly hostile public reaction.

Again, the potential weakness of the structure lies in the absence of referendum rights for the rank-and-file union members. This right was contractually precluded by a 1952 change in the *Articles of Agreement*, which stated, "The organizations comprising the Panel recognize that they must clothe their representatives with sufficient authority to negotiate for the membership." If the democracy of Panel unions is adequate, then other controls must compensate for the lack of referendum rights.

For each Panel union, the hierarchical levels between the rank-and-file and their negotiators have been few, even though three of the unions are affiliated with international unions and/or the AFL-CIO. The election process had been an effective control device for the union members over officials of their own union. Members of the TVAAPCChE probably enjoy the most democracy because they are all professionals and demand effective controls over their leadership, because their union is small in size, and because they are all in one location. Every ten rank-and-file members elect one representative, and the representatives sit with the popularly elected officers on the Board of Directors. This body each year selects the Executive Committee, but the Executive Committee only has two less members than the Board of Directors. The Executive Committee determines positions in bargaining, and the president and president-elect, also annually elected, directly participate in bargaining.

The other organizations decentralize their elections, at least to some extent, among the major work locations of their members. For example, the OPEIU at TVA has four locals which annually elect officers. The president and vice president of each local constitute eight of the nine members on the union's Executive Board. The ninth is the valleywide president, who is annually elected in a valleywide vote. Furthermore, a Full Council of delegates, elected by the locals on a per capita basis, convenes once a year. The Full Council is all powerful, and the Executive Board acts, and participates in bargaining, in its absence. The valleywide president heads the bargaining team, along with the professional staff members.

Executive bodies and negotiating teams of the other organizations are elected and constituted similarly. However, DALU #3033 elects its officers for staggered two-year terms, and the SEIU elects officers every three years. The smaller unions send fewer representatives from their executive body to actually participate in bargaining and to espouse the executive body's positions.

The Panel is a centralized bargaining structure extending over each of the five organizations and adding another hierarchical level. Yet, representatives of each union participating in the Panel's activities are responsible to their union local(s) at TVA, rather than to an international union or federation at another hierarchical level. This is also true of the professional staff members employed by the OPEIU and TVAEA. International union representatives may occasionally play some role in bargaining, and in activities associated with the administration and interpretation of the labor agreement. However, the Panel structure is responsive to controls from below, and not from above.

The lack of referendum rights for the rank-and-file is, therefore, offset to a significant degree by these other factors. Certainly, the white-collar and professional rank-and-file have not overtly expressed any discontent that their controls over leaders and negotiated positions are inadequate. Neither have serious morale problems emerged from other ramifications of the centralized structure, such as the uniformity of negotiated results, especially since separate salary schedules were created. Ironically, the Panel structure, which developed so slowly and with such difficulty, may now be more sound and stable in overall terms than is the older union structure, which evolved with relative ease and enjoyed great stability for so long.

Reinforcements for Centralized Bargaining

It should lastly be mentioned that, regardless of the attitude of union members and leaders at TVA toward the centralized structure in which they are involved, several similar features of both the trades and labor and salary policy employee written agreements provide a continued reinforcement to the maintenance of the high degree of structural centralization which now exists. The first reinforcement involves the prescribed procedure by which a union representing some group of TVA workers can come under the coverage of the relevant labor agreement. The reinforcement exists in all written agreements between TVA and the two centralized bargaining structures, but perhaps the reinforcement can best be illuminated by focusing upon provisions of the trades and labor agreement.

The *General Agreements*, written and revised by TVA and the Trades and Labor Council since 1940, have specified a procedure to be followed by employees constituting an appropriate bargaining unit in order to become a party to the agreement. This provision mandated compliance with four separate conditions: (1) that the "appropriate bargaining agent" of trades and labor employees apply to the Council and to TVA through a national or international union affiliated with the American Federation of Labor; (2) that such group of employees must signify their intention to conform to the purposes and provisions of the agreement; (3) that a majority of employees in an appropriate unit designate such national or international union as their representative; and (4) that the Council agree to accept such union as a member before it could become a party to the agreement.[20] This procedure is still in effect today except that recognition was given to the merger of the AFL and CIO in 1955 by requiring the employees to apply for membership in the Council through a union affiliated with the AFL-CIO.

When the *General Agreement* was officially approved by the international presidents of the fifteen unions delineated in Article I of the 1940 agreement, thereby authorizing the Tennessee Valley Trades and Labor Council to enter into the agreement and in effect sanctioning the existence of the Council itself, the International Association of Bridge, Structural and Ornamental Iron Workers refused to sign the agreement. The charter of the Iron Workers' international union at that time prohibited signing a collective bargaining agreement which did not contain a closed-shop provision. The Council had requested that the agreement contain a union-shop arrangement but TVA declined to agree to such a provision because it would not be in keeping with the TVA Act.

As a result of the Iron Workers' refusal to sign the agreement, and at the insistence by TVA that the Council adopt guidelines covering nonsignatory unions, the Council proclaimed that "any such nonsignatory organization is not eligible to participate in deliberations or actions on matters arriving out of the interpretation or application of the agreement." Thus, such unions, although they may have been members of the Council, could not participate with the Council in negotiation sessions. TVA would have to negotiate separately with any union which did not sign the *General Agreement* but which was officially recognized as a duly authorized representative. (The International Association of Bridge, Structural and Ornamental Iron Workers signed the agreement with TVA on June 25, 1951.)

On June 5, 1951, the International Association of Machinists (IAM), an original member of the Council and signatory to the *General Agreement* of 1940, withdrew from the Council because of a jurisdictional dispute with the Operating Engineers. Article I of the *General Agreement*, with revisions effective June 26, 1949, stated that the unions recognized as the accredited representatives of TVA trades and labor employees must act through the Council. This indicates that a union not affiliated with the Council cannot be recognized as an accredited representative under the provisions of the *General Agreement*. TVA, as well as the Machinists, interpreted the language in this way, and the union was not considered as being signatory to the *General Agreement* since it had disassociated itself from the Council.

The next year the Machinists submitted an application for reaffiliation with the Council and also agreed to comply with all established agreements and decisions made regarding the jurisdictional dispute. On June 23, 1952, the IAM, having become a member of the Council once again, signed the *General Agreement* and became a party to its terms and provisions.

It has likewise been true that, by contract terms and past practice, a union of salary policy employees *must* either become or remain a member of the Salary Policy Employee Panel to be covered under the provisions of the existing labor agreement. By dropping out of its established, centralized structure, a union of TVA employees takes a serious risk. It cannot be sure of its ability to negotiate a separate contract nearly as comprehensive as the *General Agreement* or the *Articles of Agreement.*

Moreover, the ability of TVA to use the threat of a limited bargaining scope to enforce a centralized bargaining structure has recently been heightened. In a 1976 executive order issued by President Ford, TVA was removed from the coverage of Executive Order 11491. Any union leaving the Council or the Panel may now be denied a scope of bargaining even as large as that prescribed by E.O. 11491.

The vertical centralization of power, upward to the Council or Panel level, is also reinforced by the existing labor agreements. Important types of decisions, which may primarily affect the members of a single union, cannot be made by the union itself. The decision-making power resides instead at the level of the Trades and Labor Council or the Salary Policy Employee Panel.

In both bargaining relationships, the Council or Panel, but not a member union acting alone, can take a grievance appeal to an impartial referee. Also, arbitration of future terms issues can only be requested by the Salary Policy Employee Panel or the Trades and Labor Council, which is understandable for provisions which apply uniformly to members of all the unions. Yet, in the TVA-Panel relationship, even bargaining disputes over basic salary rates that exclusively apply to a single union cannot be taken by that union to arbitration. The decision is reached by the whole Panel. This same situation applies to the trades and labor relationship since only the Council can appeal a wage impasse to the Secretary of Labor. An analysis is made of these provisions in a later chapter. Here, the point is simply being made that all of these provisions provide a continual, positive reinforcement to the high degree of structural centralization which exists on the union side.

The Management Structure

On the management side, structure is important for the bargaining process and for the administration of the results of the process. In the years immediately following TVA's creation, its activities expanded so rapidly that personnel administration by a highly centralized staff was a practical necessity. However, top management realized that TVA would engage in diverse operations over a large geographical area and would employ individuals in diverse occupations. It was felt therefore that TVA should follow a path toward the decentralization of personnel functions. Top management also favored decentralization because it believed that the functions of personnel management were inseparable from those of management in general.[21]

TVA could have committed itself to decentralization in a geographical sense only. Field personnel offices, under the central personnel staff, could have been opened in the Authority's various work locations. However, personnel decentralization at TVA would also mean the transfer of personnel responsibilities and functions to operating management. The fusion of personnel management and general management would become a reality.

The process of decentralization began early and slowly, since proceeding with the process depended upon operating or line management becoming proficient enough to effectively shoulder the additional personnel responsibilities. By 1935, the Personnel Division operated with six staff sections, and it had established six major field offices. These personnel and employment offices had little authority to operate independently of the central personnel division. Their primary responsibilities involved selection of trades and labor employees, developing training programs, and acting as intermediaries between supervisors and the Personnel Division.[22] Most matters regarding personnel administration were handled centrally by the division, and coordination among the several field offices became a major problem in these early years.

In 1936, an office was set up in the central staff to coordinate the work of the General Personnel Representatives, who served as personnel generalists in the field offices. These generalists linked the personnel staff and operating management. The chief of the Employment Division soon thereafter assumed control of all activities in the field offices. In 1940, line and staff functions within the Division of Personnel were clearly separated. The positions of Personnel officer were established. Individuals holding these positions were given the responsibility of working with operating management on personnel policies and problems. The personnel officers' activities were coordinated by a Knoxville

Personnel Office in the Employment Division. All other Division of Personnel positions, in Knoxville and in the field, carried clear staff responsibilities.[23]

The decentralization of personnel policy-making to operating management also began early in another way. In 1935, the Personnel Department was given the responsibility for representing the General Manager in negotiations with unions representing TVA's trades and labor employees. It was obvious even then that the Director of Personnel would need to work closely with representatives of the major operating divisions.

In order to facilitate a close working relationship with line management, advisory groups of line managers were formed to aid the Director of Personnel. By 1937, two advisory groups existed, for salary policy and for wage policy, under an overall Advisory Committee on Wage and Salary Policy. The advisory committee on salary policy was composed of the heads of the seven largest departments at TVA, but from 1937 to 1942, the advisory group did not meet. After the formation of the Salary Policy Employee Panel on the union side, the advisory group of line managers began to serve in a purely advisory capacity to the Director of Personnel in negotiations.[24]

In 1948, the several management advisory groups were replaced by an Advisory Committee on Personnel Administration. A Wage Panel was created the next year as an autonomous subcommittee. A Salary Panel was not created, so the entire Advisory Committee advised the Director of Personnel on policies relating to salary policy employees.[25] Actually, the thrust of management advisory efforts in these years aimed at the participation of line management with the Director of Personnel in the genuine bargaining which was being conducted with the Trades and Labor Council. Membership on the advisory committees specifically concerned with wage policy consisted of top management officials from each of the major operating divisions employing large numbers of trades and labor employees.

During the decade of the 1940s, as TVA construction work expanded to meet wartime demands, the larger organizations within TVA were unable to rely upon the central staff to effectively meet their personnel administration demands. The need for personnel administrators at the operating level became increasingly apparent even as the war years ended. The next logical step in TVA's personnel decentralization program was then to transfer the functions of the Personnel Division's own field personnel officers to the major operating organizations themselves. This was formally accomplished in 1953, as the Division Personnel Officers (DPOs) were removed from the Division of Personnel and placed under the administrative control of the heads of the operating organizations which they served. With the exception of employment and a few other functions, the Personnel Division would thereafter coordinate personnel activities of the other divisions and provide staff assistance. Day-to-day personnel matters would be left to the DPOs and to operating management, unless the aid of the central personnel staff was requested.[26]

Also in 1953, the Personnel Division reorganized its staff work, essentially dividing its work between trades and labor and salary policy personnel policies and problems. A Labor Relations Branch would handle the former group of employees, and a Personnel Services Branch would be responsible for the latter. Finally in 1953, the Advisory Committee on Personnel Administration was abolished and two separate management panels were created, primarily to advise the Director of Personnel on wage and salary negotiations. The Trades and Labor Negotiating Committee and the Salary Policy Negotiating Committee have continued to discharge this function in negotiations with the Trades and Labor Council and with the Salary Policy Employee Panel.

The next important change in management structure came in 1968. Responsibility for all relationships with unions—both trades and labor and salary policy employee unions—was centered in an Employee Relations Branch of the Division of Personnel. The Personnel Services Branch which had formerly handled relationships with the latter group of unions, became the Planning and Analysis Branch. The reconstructed branch was designed to be responsible for overall personnel planning and analysis of personnel problems, without specific reference to unions (see figure 4-1 for the present Division of Personnel organization chart).

In 1970, a final important change in management structure occurred. The position of Administrator (now Manager) of Union-Management Relations was created under the Director of Personnel. The Manager assumed the Director's role of direct responsibility for union-management programs and activities. In bargaining with the Trades and Labor Council and with the Panel, the Manager is management's chief spokesman. He utilizes the staff support of the Employee Relations Branch, and he acts as chairman of the management negotiating committees. Many of the Manager's responsibilities in both bargaining relationships are defined in the written agreements. For example, the Manager resolves unit determination and jurisdictional issues and makes the final TVA decision on grievance appeals.

The degree of management decentralization which presently exists for collective bargaining is most evident in the make-up and functioning of the two management advisory committees. The two groups are so similar that a description of the Salary Policy Negotiating Committee can be illustrative of the function of both groups in management's decentralized scheme for bargaining. The Salary Policy Negotiating Committee is appointed by the General Manager upon the recommendations of the Director of Personnel. Representation is primarily accorded to those operating offices and divisions which employ significant numbers of salary policy employees. (It is possible that the same line official may be asked to serve simultaneously on both negotiating committees.) The Manager of Union-Management Relations serves as chairman, and the other representatives are top officials in operating management. For example, the Assistant Director of the Office of Power, the Manager of Agricultural and Chemical Development,

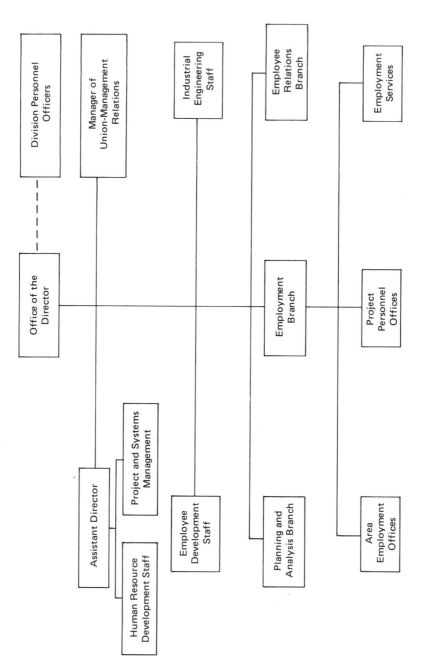

Figure 4-1. Organization of the Division of Personnel (January 4, 1976).

and the Head of Engineering Design and Construction are included (see the TVA organization chart in figure 4-2). Some of the offices and divisions are allowed additional, meaningful representation in collective bargaining, and a number of Employee Relations Branch members assist the Manager of Union-Management Relations in representing the Division of Personnel and TVA.

What is the power of the top operating managers in determining the positions of management in bargaining? The TVA Code states that the negotiating committees "assist" the Division of Personnel in bargaining.[27] This would seem to indicate that the Manager of Union-Management Relations could unilaterally make final decisions on TVA's positions during the bargaining process. In practice, decisions are normally made by consensus in the negotiating committee. The discussion of bargaining process in the next chapter more fully documents the significant power of the top operating managers to determine TVA's positions in negotiations.

Management decision-making power for bargaining is therefore centered in top management. In this sense, the bargaining structure might be considered centralized. The high-level managers are unlikely to have their bargaining positions repudiated by top management. However, the management structure is decentralized in the more important sense that decision-making power in bargaining is diffused among management in the various TVA operations.

This decentralization is a form of democracy on the management side, for operating management is a constituent of management negotiators. Practical advantages result from the decentralization. Management negotiators are assured of understanding the problems of operating management. Operating management better understands negotiated policies. This is crucial at TVA, for the administration of these policies is decentralized. Operating management is more likely to administer the policies in good faith because it played a major role in the negotiation. Finally, operating management would be unlikely to push the Board of Directors to repudiate a tentative agreement. This could be a possibility in the absence of decentralization.

TVA's decentralized structure for the administration of negotiated and other personnel policies is most evident in the activities of Division Personnel Officers (DPOs). The DPOs serve two masters. They report administratively to the directors or assistant directors of the divisions which they serve, but they have functional responsibilities to the Director of Personnel.

The DPOs are the vital link between the central personnel staff and operating management; they make decentralized personnel administration possible. On the one hand, the DPOs must communicate the problems and positions of their division upward to the Division of Personnel. For example, they are counselors to employees and are able to discern how personnel policies are performing in practice. The central staff must have this feedback. The DPOs also are instrumental in developing and communicating positions that management in their division desires to have pressed in bargaining. They may be

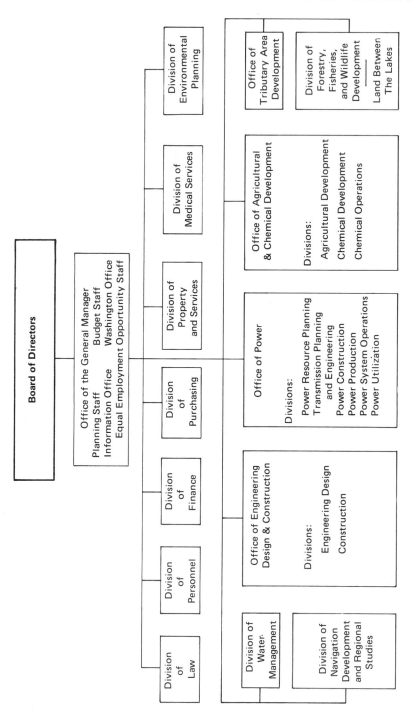

Figure 4-2. Organization of the Tennessee Valley Authority (January 4, 1976).

active both in prenegotiation and negotiation activities. They may prepare management's case in a grievance which will ultimately involve the central personnel staff.

On the other hand, DPOs are vital in the flow of policies downward from the centralized personnel staff to operating divisions. The DPOs are personnel generalists and become involved in administering most areas of personnel policy in their division: classification, pay, and staffing, for example. They must insure that operating managers and supervisors understand their own responsibilities in administering personnel policies. Policies made centrally must not be interpreted and applied differently in each division. The DPOs must not diverge significantly from the directions of the Division of Personnel, and they must not allow divergence to characterize their divisions.

Indeed, the possibility of inconsistent application of negotiated and other personnel policies is the greatest potential disadvantage of the management structure. An early commentator on TVA's personnel decentralization realized that staff influence over personnel officers in the divisions might become too weak.[28] Many union leaders and staff officials believe that the Division of Personnel did suffer a significant loss of control over DPOs in the sixties, although actions are now being taken to remedy the situation. The danger of such a development is that personnel policies will not extend uniformly into the divisions. For example, an OPEIU leader has charged in a letter to the General Manager that some operating managers, with the aid of their DPOs, subverted classification standards in the late sixties. The managers had the job titles of their secretaries changed to "clerk" or "administrative officer" to increase the secretaries in grade and salary. The changes were not supportable according to classification standards then in force.

Especially Panel unions have charged that a DPO cannot put pressure upon top managers in their division when these managers wish to interpret or apply a personnel policy in a way that would bring the disapproval of the Division of Personnel. The DPOs report administratively to the operating managers, not to the Director of Personnel. Some union leaders further believe that the DPOs must reflect, rather than mediate, the decreasing attention of many top operating managers to problems of human relations and the "hard line" of operating management in collective bargaining. The national president of the OPEIU has requested that the DPOs be placed back under the administrative control of the Director of Personnel.[29]

If significant diversity is allowed in the administration of negotiated and other personnel policies, serious problems of low morale, low productivity, and high turnover may result. The meaning of collective bargaining may be eroded. The costs of TVA's decentralized personnel administration could easily become greater than the benefits. The ability of TVA Directors of Personnel to adequately control DPOs, and to enforce the relatively uniform administration of personnel policies, has largely depended upon the abilities of the different Directors to exercise power within the management hierarchy. This should also be true in the future. Top decision-makers at TVA and in similar situations where a decentralized structure exists must make periodic appraisals of the costs and benefits of this brand of decentralization, especially with regard to the relationship between personnel officers in operating divisions and the Division of Personnel.

Notes

1. See D. Quinn Mills, *Industrial Relations and Manpower in Construction* (Cambridge, Massachusetts: The MIT Press, 1972), p. 20.

2. For an excellent analysis of crafts and crafts unions, see Margaret K. Chandler, "Craft Bargaining," *Frontiers of Collective Bargaining*, John T. Dunlop and Neil W. Chamberlain, eds. (New York: Harper and Row, 1967), pp. 51-53.

3. See Kenneth D. Alexander, "Union Structure and Bargaining Structure," *Labor Law Journal* (March 1973), pp. 164-166; and Arnold R. Weber, "Stability and Change in the Structure of Collective Bargaining," *Challenges to Collective Bargaining*, Lloyd Ulman, ed. (Englewood Cliffs, New Jersey: Prentice-Hall, Inc., 1967), pp. 14-36.

4. See Weber, "Stability and Change in the Structure of Collective Bargaining," especially pp. 15-22, for a more complete discussion of these and other reasons for union centralization.

5. See, for example, "Effects of the Structure of Collective Bargaining in Selected Industries," *Proceedings of the 1970 Annual Spring Meeting* (New York: Industrial Relations Research Association, 1970), especially pp. 502 and 514.

6. Ibid. We also know that the proliferation of bargaining units and decentralized bargaining between management and many different unions have been significant problems in the public sector. See, for example, Eli Rock, "Bargaining Units in the Public Service: The Problem of Proliferation," *Michigan Law Review* (March 1969), pp. 1001-1016.

7. Francis J. Loevi, Jr., "The Problem of Unnecessary Legislative Contract Rejections in Public Employment: An Alternative System for Ratification," *Public Personnel Review* (April 1970), pp. 118-132.

8. See Herbert J. Lahne, "Union Constitutions and Collective Bargaining Procedures," *Trade Union Government and Collective Bargaining*, Joel Seidman, ed. (New York: Praeger Publishers, 1970), p. 87. Lahne's study of the constitutions of seventy-one national unions, representing almost 90 percent of total union membership reported by the Bureau of Labor Statistics, demonstrated that over 40 percent of union members have referendum rights guaranteed in their national constitutions. Since these rights are also guaranteed in by-laws of international, intermediate, and local union bodies, or granted informally by these bodies, referendum rights should easily cover the majority of U.S. workers.

9. See William E. Simkin, "Refusals to Ratify Contracts," *Trade Union Government and Collective Bargaining*, Joel Seidman, ed. (New York: Praeger Publishers, 1970), pp. 107-145; David I. Shair, "The Mythology of Labor Contract Rejections," *Labor Law Journal* (February 1970), pp. 88-94; and Donald R. Burke and Lester Rubin, "Is Contract Rejection a Major Collective Bargaining Problem?" *Industrial and Labor Relations Review* (January 1973), pp. 820-833.

10. D. Quinn Mills, "The Construction Industry," *Proceedings of the 1970 Annual Spring Meeting* (New York: Industrial and Labor Relations Research Association, 1970), p. 501.

11. The state federations maintained an official administrative hierarchy consisting of a president and other officers who were responsible for the state-wide activities of the federation.

12. The officers of the Council generally spend much more time on TVA union-management affairs than do the other members of the Executive Board. Traditionally, the secretary of the Council has been a representative of the IBEW. In fact, the president of that international union employs two full-time labor representatives to handle employee relations with TVA. The other international representatives on the Executive Board, including the other two officers of the Council, are also appointed by their international presidents. These other representatives, however, have responsibilities for a particular region of the southeast and do not spend all of their working time on TVA matters. In fact, the international representatives who speak for only a very small percentage of TVA's trades and labor employees—asbestos workers, plasterers, and roofers, for example—are involved with TVA only during annual wage negotiations.

13. John H. G. Crispo, "Collective Bargaining in the Public Service: A Study of Union-Management Relations in Ontario Hydro and TVA," (unpublished Ph.D. dissertation, Massachusetts Institute of Technology, 1960), p. 291.

14. Matthew A. Kelley, "Adaptations in the Structure of Bargaining," *Proceedings of the Nineteenth Annual Winter Meeting* (San Francisco: Industrial Relations Research Association, December 1966), p. 24.

15. See TVA and the Tennessee Valley Trades and Labor Council, *General Agreement and Supplementary Schedules Covering Construction Employment*, revised through April 15, 1974, Supplementary schedules H-I, H-III, and H-VII.

16. Michael L. Brookshire, "Bargaining Structure in the Public Sector: the TVA 'Model'," *Journal of Collective Negotiations in the Public Sector* (Fall 1976).

17. Ibid.

18. *A Brief History of the TVAEA*, publication of the TVAEA (September 1, 1963); and personal interview with Mr. Joseph Greene, Executive Director of the TVAEA.

19. Personal interviews with the leaders of the DALU #3033, OPEIU, SEIU, TVAAPCChE, and TVAEA.

20. TVA and the Tennessee Valley Trades and Labor Council, *General Agreement*, effective August 6, 1940, Article IV.

21. Brookshire, "Bargaining Structure in the Public Sector: the TVA Model."

22. Robert S. Avery, *Experiment in Management: Personnel Decentralization in the Tennessee Valley Authority*, p. 43. See this source for a more detailed presentation of the decentralization of personnel management at TVA.

23. Ibid., pp. 42-51.

24. Ibid., pp. 65-67.

25. Ibid., pp. 67-69.

26. Harry Case, *Personnel Policy in a Public Agency* (New York: Harper and Brothers, 1955), p. 95.

27. See, for example, Tennessee Valley Authority, TVA Administrative Code III UNION RELATIONS, April 1, 1973.

28. Avery, *Experiment in Management: Personnel Decentralization in the Tennessee Valley Authority*, p. 199.

29. Howard Coughlin, International President of the OPEIU, speech to the Valley-Wide Cooperative Conference, March 14, 1974.

5

The Bargaining Process

The structure of collective bargaining, as already stated, refers to the organization of the parties for bargaining and the location(s) of decision-making power within these organizations. Bargaining process is the manner in which the parties translate their structure into action. Several topics should be covered under an analysis of bargaining process. How do the parties prepare for bargaining? What is the sequence of events in bargaining? How is decision-making power exercised in bargaining? What are the formal or informal procedures and ground rules in bargaining?

TVA and the Trades and Labor Council

The heart of contract negotiations is the wage conference, generally held in November or December of each year. Negotiations focus on basic pay revisions and on other monetary items to be incorporated into the two trades and labor contracts. Before July 15 of each year, the Council notifies TVA that it does desire to make monetary changes in the open-ended contracts. The parties then hold a preliminary conference in early September to review the need for a wage conference and to examine the process of surveying prevailing wages and fringe benefits. Both sides thereupon begin their valleywide survey of prevailing practice in wages and fringe benefits.

The annual wage conference begins with a formal meeting in mid-November. Attending are the Executive Board members of the Council, management's Trades and Labor Negotiating Committee, invited local union delegates, and other TVA and union officials who either participate or provide staff assistance for the negotiation sessions. The meeting has traditionally been held on the same day that the Council and its international union representatives start serious planning sessions with local union leaders. However, intensive bargaining does not begin until mid-December, for the Joint Wage Data Committee must first accomplish an important function.

After the opening session of the wage conference in mid-November—but before the intensive negotiations of December—the Joint Wage Data Committee meets. Composed of both TVA and Council members, this committee reviews the raw wage data and other information collected in the surveys made by TVA and the unions of the Council. Each craft comes before the committee to explain its data and to support the data which it has collected by presentation of official labor contracts from the vicinity. The committee raises or hears any questions about whether the data submitted are correct and factual. It also considers whether the data are appropriately applied to TVA jobs and whether the data submitted by the unions are supported by the proper evidence. Committee members identify discrepancies in the data submitted by both TVA and the unions and attempt to resolve disputes over conflicting data. Either TVA or the Council may present additional wage and fringe data during these sessions. After this process is concluded, the committee prepares a written report summarizing the relevant arguments made before it, records agreements reached on the accuracy and applicability of the data, and presents any additional data submitted.

Basically, the final report of the Joint Wage Data Committee represents a meeting of the minds as to what facts shall be placed before the negotiators at the wage conference. These factual data serve as the basis for wage negotiations and for the actual wage determination process. They remove from negotiations any possible debate over questions of fact. If any data become available after the committee report is issued, they can be used if verified by the Joint Committee as factual. Quite frequently, during actual negotiations, new agreements are signed by contractors and unions in the vicinity, or pending disputes are settled, and the results of such action are included in the tabulation. This process keeps the unweighted data as current as possible.

During the fall months, the international representative of each union is preparing for the December negotiations. The representative obtains raw data on prevailing wages and fringe benefits of his union's craft in the valleywide area, and he may analyze and weight the raw data. He may formulate targets for increases in wages and benefits with delegates from locals of his union which are made up of TVA workers. These same delegates will interact with the international representative as tactics and positions change during negotiations. The delegates do not, however, have the power to overrule their international representative on matters of disagreement, and no formal voting system is used during the meetings between the delegates and the international representatives. The local delegates merely make their demands known to the international representative and attempt to persuade him of the importance of the demands in the eyes of their respective memberships.

The international representatives preparing for bargaining will be speaking both for their members working for TVA and for those who might have an opportunity to work for TVA. The latter group consists of "travelers" from locals outside the area who might come to work for TVA. Wage rates to be negotiated by the international representatives would also apply to trades and labor work performed on a contract basis for TVA. Such contracts must contain a provision that not less than the prevailing rates of pay for work of a similar nature prevailing in the vicinity shall be paid to such employees of the contractor and that these rates shall not be less than the rates paid by TVA to its employees doing similar work. This is required by the written labor agreement and by the TVA Act.

Each international representative also knows that he will be negotiating on an agencywide basis and that wages, fringe benefits, and other contract terms will not vary according to local union jurisdiction. A laborer working for TVA in the Knoxville, Tennessee area and under the jurisdiction of Local Union 818 would receive the same wages and fringes and work under the same employment conditions as a laborer working for TVA in the Huntsville, Alabama area and a member of Local Union 366—both local unions being affiliates of the Laborer's International Union of North America. Contract terms negotiated by TVA and the Council will apply to all trades and labor work in the TVA area regardless of the wages and conditions of employment negotiated by various local unions with other contractors in the TVA area.

Finally, in preparing for the December negotiations, the international representatives must work together through the Executive Committee of the Trades and Labor Council. This is primarily true because many contract terms will apply uniformly to members of all unions represented through the Council. However, most of the important contract terms are now differentiated by craft and based on prevailing practice in that craft. In the contract covering construction employment, for example, contract terms on basic wage rates, overtime rates of pay, travel allowances, subsistence allowances, payments to health and welfare funds, payments to pension funds, and payments to vacation funds are differentiated by union. On such matters, coordination among the various unions in preparing for bargaining is not so important.

How does management prepare for the December negotiations? After the Wage Data Committee verifies all the data submitted by both TVA and the Council, the management members of the committee meet alone to formulate TVA's "target wage rate" and "first offer" for each classification in wage Schedule A (covering construction employment) and for each key classification in the other three wage schedules (covering operating and maintenance employment). The target rate is the wage the management members of the Wage Data Committee believe reflects the prevailing wage for that particular classification. This determination is made on the basis of all factual data reported and verified by the Joint Wage Data Committee.

The management side of the joint committee formulates what it considers to be the target hourly or annual rate, and then recommends these rates to the Trades and Labor Negotiating Committees which will either accept the proposals or alter them according to what they believe is more appropriate—given the same data as that verified by the Wage Data Committee.

To determine the "target rate" for each classification in Schedule A and for the key classifications in Schedules B, C, and D, the management negotiating team members consider a number of factors. Some of the more important evaluative standards are: consistency in maintaining desired differentials between classifications and between crafts; the average (percentage and numerical) increase of a particular classification or craft for the preceding and current years based on the number of base cities from which actual data were obtained; the rank order of the data by city for each classification and craft; the supply of available craftsmen in the area; and the projected demand for the services represented by each craft and classification.

In addition to recommending a target rate for each classification used in negotiations, the management members of the Wage Data Committee also formulate "first offers." These rates represent TVA's initial or opening wage offers for each key classification discussed in the wage conference and are calculated in order to leave plenty of room for bargaining. The Trades and Labor Negotiating Committee also has the final responsibility for deciding each first offer made in negotiations and will make its decisions on first offers just prior to the beginning of bargaining.

The management members of the Joint Wage Data Committee thus provide much of the staff work in preparing for negotiations each year and in analyzing the wage data accumulated by both TVA and the Council. Though the full Trades and Labor Negotiating Committee actually has the responsibility for negotiating with the Council and for determining TVA's position regarding any issue in negotiations, the management members of the Wage Data Committee serve an essential role in providing expertise for TVA in the wage conferences.

At the opening session of the wage conference in the middle of November, and throughout the actual negotiation sessions beginning approximately one month later, the Manager of Union-Management Relations and the president of the Tennessee Valley Trades and Labor Council serve as the official co-chairpeople of the negotiations. Thus the responsibility for the entire wage conference is equally divided between management and labor. The head of the Employee Relations Branch, Division of Personnel, and the secretary of the Tennessee Valley Trades and Labor Council serve as co-secretaries for the entire proceedings.

During the second session of the wage conference, held around the middle of December, both TVA and the Council have before them all the data on which prevailing wages and other monetary and nonmonetary items will be determined. These data have been jointly approved as factual by the Joint Wage Data Committee and have been tabulated in one complete book by the Employee Relations Branch. The data are divided into four different classifications of trades and labor positions: Schedules A, B and B-Hourly, C, and D. Anyone at the negotiation table and others in official attendance can look at the same wage and fringe data. Bargaining centers upon the wage rate to be assigned to each classification in each schedule and upon the appropriate increase, if any, in the various fringe benefit areas.

Included as part of the data-tabulation process are TVA's first offer and the union's first request for each classification of the four schedules. Each union, through its international representative, presents arguments on its own behalf if it is not willing to agree that TVA's proposal represents the prevailing wage rate for its work. Union proposals and arguments on contract terms which will apply uniformly to the Council members are presented by the president of the Council. TVA reviews the data in light of any new facts or arguments introduced by the unions and presents counter offers. As the sequence of joint meetings, caucuses of the parties, and joint meetings continues, the positions of the parties converge.

On the union side, the international representatives are receiving input from their delegates, who are present to insure that their representative well represents the interests of the membership in negotiations. Usually after each day's negotiations, or sometimes after each joint meeting, the international representatives caucus with their respective union delegates to discuss strategy and to decide on the wage or fringe increase which represents the minimum of acceptability. The international representatives also caucus in the Executive Committee to coordinate common strategy, on contract terms to be applied uniformly, for example.

During the negotiations, the Manager of Union-Management Relations serves as TVA's spokesman in the joint meetings and coordinates management's deliberations in its caucuses. The bargaining strategy used in determining how management reaches its target wage rates and other targets, or whether to go above the predetermined target, is generally decided by the members of the Trades and Labor Negotiating Committee. Traditionally, the members of the committee sit quietly during joint TVA-Council sessions, but they are quite vociferous in the management meetings held just prior to each joint session.

The joint sessions involving both the Council and TVA are primarily concerned with interpreting the factual prevailing practice data. Agreement as to what shall constitute the TVA wage rate for any particular classification has not been reduced to a set format. Generally, an agreement is hammered out in the negotiation process where TVA and the Council members take their respective management and labor positions. The prevailing wage data are primarily considered as establishing a broad band or limit within which TVA and Council have room to bargain, each recognizing the problems of the other as well as those of their own.

There is, of course, considerable variation in the wage rates being paid for any particular class of work in the seven-state vicinity from which data are collected. Thus a range of prevailing wage rates for each classification exists and varying opinions exist as to what the prevailing wage should be for each classification. There are also certain historical precedents of equity between and among classifications and crafts that must be maintained for a satisfactory wage structure to result. Certain percentage differentials are generally maintained between crafts whose work involves similar levels of skill, training, and responsibility. Also, within most crafts certain differentials must be preserved, and these are watched across the board in order to secure a consistent wage schedule.

Foremen, for example, receive a certain percentage increase above the negotiated journeymen rate and apprentices receive various percentages of the journeymen rate depending on their stage of training. Finally, the supply of workers and demand for workers in the various crafts are important in affecting the parties' movement toward a particular wage rate. Supply and demand conditions are considered directly by the parties and also affect negotiated resluts indirectly because they affect the prevailing practice data.

The wage negotiations generally last about one week and concessions are made on both sides until, as a rule, agreement is reached on all wage schedules and fringe benefits. The decisions reached in negotiations are subject to formal approval by the TVA Board of Directors, and are, by agreement, effective at the beginning of the payroll period nearest January 1. If the agreement is not reached with any particular union regarding the wage rate to be paid to (a) particular classification(s), the Council accepts TVA's last proposal but informs TVA which craft or crafts, with the approval of the Council, reserve(s) the right to appeal to the Secretary of Labor in accordance with the TVA Act. The craft (or crafts) may appeal the disputed rates to the Secretary within thirty days of the termination of the wage conference. Certainly, this right of appeal boosts the clout of the Council unions in pressuring TVA toward the union's positions.

TVA and the Council meet at times other than during the traditional fall negotiations over wages and fringes. These extra negotiation sessions are restricted to non-wage bargaining issues. Many aspects of the bargaining process in these sessions are the same as in wage bargaining, but the supplemental sessions are neither as formal nor considered as important as the negotiations in the fall.

TVA and the Salary Policy Employee Panel

The authors are able to write in detail and with significant insight about the process of bargaining for TVA and the Salary Policy Employee Panel. In the twenty-third annual salary negotiations of May 1974, one of the co-authors was given the rare opportunity to freely observe all joint meetings and all of the caucuses of both parties. The researcher had maintained close contact with the parties during their prenegotiation period, so he was able to develop a rather complete picture of the sequence of events, of the exercise of decision-making power, and of the formulation of positions and strategy in bargaining. The other co-author has observed and participated in management caucuses as well as in joint sessions.

In the annual salary negotiations of May or June, contract language changes relating to money matters are appropriate. Some topics, primarily those which are not monetary in nature, are often referred to supplementary negotiations conducted in the fall of each year.

The salary negotiations of May 1974 provided an excellent opportunity for investigation because of the difficult climate in which they were held. In the twelve months preceding the beginning of negotiations, the Consumer Price Index had risen 10 percent, and it was increasing monthly at an accelerating rate. Early in 1974, government wage controls, which had been in effect for two and one-half years, ended. Large union compensation gains and an increase in strike activity were predicted to result from the high inflation rate and the decontrol of wages.

The Panel unions were under membership pressure to produce large compensation gains. At the same time, severe inflationary pressures were pushing up TVA's nonlabor costs, especially those of fuel. The process to be described was therefore carried out under conditions of extreme stress. The durability of the process would receive an excellent test.

Although the bargaining process is most visible during the period of intense negotiations in the spring, it actually begins in the fall. Usually in November, the parties meet to set parameters for the valleywide determination of prevailing practice in money matters—the annual salary survey. The determination is bilateral; the Panel meets with representatives of the Division of Personnel and operating management who will participate in the entire process. The major parameters which must result from this meeting are the definition of the survey area, the employers to be surveyed, and the subject areas to be surveyed; that is, prevailing practice on basic salaries, shift differentials, overtime, and other indirect compensation.

This meeting with management is more important for the Panel than is the comparable meeting for the Trades and Labor Council. The Panel takes no part in the actual survey, while TVA and the Trades and Labor Council both survey prevailing blue-collar pay practice. Thus, the Panel must make its impact upon the survey before the survey begins. The Panel's nonparticipation in the survey is mainly due to practical constraints. Trades and Labor Council unions can easily survey other locals of their craft union, which bargain with those firms that TVA is surveying from the management side. But the OPEIU and SEIU, for example, probably could not find enough brother locals in the valleywide area to make an adequate survey. The TVAEA and TVAAPCChE have no brother locals, and organization among other engineers, chemists, and scientists in the vicinity is not substantial. Few of the firms surveyed would let survey teams composed of union representatives have their salary and fringe benefit data. The TVA management teams present the data received from each surveyed firm under a code number to preserve the firm's anonymity. Nevertheless, the Panel unions would probably attempt some sort of survey if they did not believe that management conducted the survey in good faith.

Management teams made the salary survey in the January-March period, and TVA tabulates the raw data. Based upon the key classes surveyed, a range of prevailing pay rates is developed to compare with the minimum and maximum rate of each TVA salary grade concerned. Prevailing practice ranges are also developed for average pay data and for fringe items.

After the raw data is compiled, a validation meeting is held between Panel representatives and, primarily, representatives of the Division of Personnel. The Panel representatives may raise questions about the correctness of data obtained by the management teams for each employer and about the appropriateness of applying certain of the data to TVA jobs. In essence, the Panel must validate the factuality of the survey data. The raw data so validated will serve as the basis for collective bargaining.

Each union then analyzes the validated salary data for the schedule(s) which it represents. The TVAEA has a special Data Analysis Committee to discharge this function. The raw data may be weighted in several alternative ways (discussed in the next chapter). However weighted, a range of prevailing data and a measure of central tendency are developed for the minimum and maximum rate of each grade represented. A range of data may also be developed for the average rate being paid in each salary grade represented.

The OPEIU follows similar procedures in analyzing the data. One or a few individuals are assigned the task in the smaller organizations. For example, the Panel representative largely assumes the task for the DALU #3033. The TVAAPCChE Executive Committee has this responsibility and then sets the first offers and targets for each grade in the upcoming bargaining. The TVAAPCChE Board of Directors has always approved the Executive Committee's decisions. Similarly, executive bodies of the other Panel organizations utilize their data analysis to set first offers and targets for each grade in the schedule(s) over which they bargain. In developing first offers, some of the unions have differed in philosophy. The OPEIU, for example, might set its first offers far above its targets to provide ample room for movement in bargaining. In contrast, the TVAEA might place its first offers closer to its targets, adding more credibility to the early offers and justifying slower movement.

The unions theoretically set their targets for the basic salary bargaining on the basis of the prevailing pay data. Yet a range of prevailing data is available. How is a position in the range determined as a target? Of course, the unions will aim for the highest positions possible in the range for each grade. Past practice in bargaining will give them an idea of feasible positions for targets in the data range. But other factors may cause a union to place importance upon obtaining a particularly high position in the data range for a certain grade. Union members at that grade may believe their salaries have slipped under prevailing practice in relation to the other grades, and they may exert political pressure on union leaders to give their grade special attention.

Almost all fringe benefits apply equally to all salary policy employees. The PSSEU bargains over allowances for the uniforms of its public safety officers, which is a small exception to the equal application of fringes. Therefore, the

Panel as a whole must analyze the survey data on fringe benefits. First offers
and targets must be set. A great deal of coordination among Panel members is
necessitated, and the Panel's Secretary is responsible for the joint-determination
process.

The Panel members culminate their joint preparation and coordination for
bargaining with a meeting just prior to the beginning of negotiations. Each union
has full responsibility over first offers, targets, and bargaining for the salary sched-
ule(s) of its members. The main coordination for basic salary bargaining must be
between the TVAEA and TVAAPCChE. Both organizations bargain over schedule SD pay rates. However, the Panel members may be inclined to decide upon
common thrusts in negotiations. They might decide to continually stress a rising
inflation rate as a compelling reason for agreement upon high positions in the
data ranges of all schedules and grades. The Panel members may also debate the
relative emphasis to be accorded basic salary increases versus fringe increases.

In this final prenegotiation meeting, the Panel members must confirm their
first offers and targets for fringe benefits. They must set priorities for compromising or dropping their proposals in the various fringe benefit areas. Interest-
ingly, the Panel decided to emphasize a proposal in 1974 designed to commit a
significant amount of TVA funds for resolving home-to-work transportation
problems of bargaining unit employees. The Panel's emphasis on this proposal
underscored a growing necessity for white-collar and professional unions, especially. The unions must not ignore the problems of their members which fall
outside of basic bread-and-butter issues.

After the validation meeting, the Division of Personnel also analyzes the data.
A range of weighted data, and a measure of central tendency, will be developed
for the minimum, maximum, and average prevailing pay rates for each TVA
grade concerned. The Division of Personnel will then begin work on formulating
targets and first offers. The operating divisions represented on the Negotiating
Committee also begin scrutinizing the validated data and considering first offers
and targets for grades and schedules of concern to their division. Division of
Personnel officials often initiate their coordination work with the "second string"
of the Negotiating Committee. Assistant Division Directors or DPOs may
substitute for their division head in these early meetings aimed at developing
management's positions. One function of the early meetings is to discover and
refine the proposals for contract changes which operating management desires
to have introduced in bargaining. Preliminary lists of proposals for nonbasic
salary contract changes may be exchanged between TVA and the Panel a month
before negotiations begin.

In formulating targets for basic salary increases, Division of Personnel and
operating management rely heavily upon data collected in the salary survey.
Other factors may be considered independently of the data. For example, management might expect significant hiring to be necessary in some grades of some

schedules. Management may have been experiencing recruitment difficulties for certain grades and schedules. Targets for these grades and schedules may be set at higher positions in the data range.

In recent years, operating management has become aggressive in developing and pressing its own proposals for contract changes. The Division of Construction urged that several contract changes be made during the 1974 salary negotiations. It desired to have more flexibility in recruitment at within-grade rates for subprofessional and professional engineering positions. It also wished to be granted additional flexibility in the announcement of vacant positions and in retaining employees at certain work locations.

The Manager of Union-Management Relations meets with the official Salary Policy Negotiating Committee in the week prior to negotiations and again a few hours before negotiations begin. The meetings may include an assessment by the Director of Personnel of the Board of Director's views and expectations concerning negotiations. Committee assignments are made in the meeting just prior to negotiations; committee members are the official Negotiating Committee and a few other operating managers, DPOs, and Personnel staff members, who are designated to become involved. Various committees are assigned to handle TVA's positions on each salary schedule and each fringe benefit area. Those operating divisions which employ large numbers of engineers, for example, would be represented on the committee determining TVA's positions on the SD and SE schedules. The committees and, therefore, the operating managers have significant discretion in developing TVA's positions during bargaining.

Finally, targets and first offers must be confirmed in management's final prenegotiation meeting. First offers are set further away from management's targets for those schedules where the union involved sets its own first offers further away from its own targets. Priorities must be set for compromising or dropping management's proposals in bargaining, and the management proposals may be ranked in importance.

In recent years, TVA and the Panel have taken an additional step in the prenegotiation period. As mentioned, TVA and the Panel exchange a preliminary list of nonbasic-salary proposals. A prenegotiating meeting may then be held between the Panel and the Negotiating Committee. Proposals may be clarified in this meeting, some may be dropped, and some may be deferred until supplemental negotiations in the fall.

The process of negotiation is, of course, carried out in both joint meetings and in the caucuses of both parties. In the first joint meeting, the Manager of Union-Management Relations might make a few introductory remarks, perhaps commenting on management's proposals for contract changes. The Panel presents its first requests on all basic salary and fringe items. A recent innovation is that in all subsequent joint meetings, each party rotates its responses to the last offers of the other party. Management may respond on basic salaries in all schedules, the unions may respond on fringe items, and responses may then be reversed in the next joint meeting.

For the Panel unions, the Secretary might begin negotiations with opening comments, perhaps emphasizing that the rate of inflation justifies liberal interpretation of the data. A representative of each Panel union would read the union's proposals for salary grades in the schedule(s) represented, and he also might preface the proposals which are made for the minimum and maximum rate of each grade with brief comments. The Secretary would speak for the Panel on all nonbasic-salary items. Early in the negotiations, the official union representatives state their proposals and counterproposals rather dispassionately. Many members of the executive bodies and other leaders of the unions are present, but they play no formal role in the joint sessions.

The Manager of Union-Management Relations is the exclusive spokesman for management on all issues. The Division of Personnel officials and operating managers participating in the negotiation process are present; however, they reserve their energies for the management caucus.

The sequence of joint meeting, caucus, joint meeting is set in motion and normally continues for five or six days. Toward the end of the period, the time between joint meetings lessens. Many proposals are dropped, and the sticking points in bargaining narrow. A striking feature of the negotiations is the constant reference to the data which is made by both parties. Proposals may be labeled "well supported by the data," "partially supported by the data," or "not supported by the data." However interpreted, the data constitute the foundation for the positions of both parties. If a Panel union stresses a high rate of inflation, for example, it is to justify settlement at a high position in the data range. Failure by the union to make reference to the data might result in an observation by management that the cost of living is not an agreed upon criterion for salary determination.

Of course, the data can be analyzed and interpreted in an almost infinite number of ways. A significant portion of the verbal exchange in the joint meetings directly relates to conflicting interpretations of the data. For example, a union proposal in the 1974 negotiations was that TVA should pay a certain number of each union's elected representatives for their time spent in negotiations. Thirteen of thirty-three employers surveyed made such payments. Management resisted the proposal because less than 50 percent of those surveyed made the payments, so the practice was not "prevailing." The unions argued that the practice was sufficiently prevailing for TVA to initiate some payments. If full pay for union representatives could not be justified, then TVA should begin paying some fraction of full pay.

After a few days of negotiations, both parties will begin dropping some of their proposals to concentrate and focus upon their priorities. Some proposals may be deferred to the fall negotiations. Toward the end of negotiations, both parties will increase their "editorial comments" as they read their counterproposals.

Typical comments are "we are well within the data range," "the data support our present position," and "you are moving your counterproposals too slowly on this item." Both parties present a united front throughout the sequence of joint meetings, and they remain remarkably cool. Some salary grades and fringe items may be settled a full day before negotiations end, while agreement on other issues will not be forthcoming until the end of the process. Mediation and arbitration procedures already described are available for impasses, but arbitration on pay matters has never been utilized.

During the 1974 negotiations, another set of joint negotiations was conducted concurrently with the regular joint meeting-caucus process. The parties made their first use of work groups. One of the groups debated the Panel's proposal for use of TVA funds to combat transportation and parking problems of employees. A compromise agreement was developed by the work group. Another joint work group was appointed after the negotiations had begun to consider the several proposals for contract changes made by the Division of Construction. This work group also reached an agreement that was made effective by a special Memorandum of Understanding. The work groups resolved rather complex problems which may have strained and lengthened the regular joint meeting process. Further use of this device in future negotiations is likely.

After every joint meeting, each party caucuses to alternatingly develop counterproposals on basic salaries and fringe items. If the Panel is responding on basic salaries, the official representatives of each union will spend considerable time on their own developing counterproposals for their schedule(s); they will periodically discuss their strategy and positions with a larger group of delegates from their union if such delegates are present.

When the Panel is responding on fringe benefits, the various union representatives must discuss counterproposals together. The Secretary has an important role in guiding the Panel to a consensus. In the 1974 negotiations, the ease with which the Panel representatives worked together was notable.

As the negotiations proceed, the union representatives frequently discuss what the data support, how an arbitrator might rule on certain issues, and what TVA's targets on various salary and fringe items might be. The experience which the parties have with each other surfaces in their use of various "keys" to the positions of the other party. For example, the Panel might recognize that TVA's last proposal on a certain grade of a certain schedule will always be divisible by twelve. The researcher noted that some of the keys which the parties used to interpret the behavior and thinking of the other party were accurate while others were inaccurate.

It also appears that, as negotiations proceed, the Panel unions compromise more readily on fringe items and focus their attention upon basic salary increases. The methods of impasse resolution may be a prime causal factor. An impasse resolution procedure which guarantees final and binding decision-making by a third party is only available for disputes over basic salaries. Therefore, in negotiations over monetary matters, the Panel unions have effective clout only in bargaining over basic salary rates and should tend to concentrate their efforts on salary bargaining. Advisory arbitration is available for disputes over fringe items, but in the end TVA may make a unilateral decision.

The Manager of Union-Management Relations presides over the management caucus, but decision-making power is diffuse. Each management committee develops counterproposals which may be discussed by the Negotiating Committee as a whole, and individuals may voice their opinions vociferously. Considerable bargaining takes place within the management group. For example, instances occur in which operating managers concerned with a particular salary schedule withhold their targets for particular grades from the rest of the group. Or they may strongly defend an upward revision of their targets. The Manager guides the formulation of management's positions. He attempts to gain a consensus of the Negotiating Committee on each salary and fringe item. Occasionally, the Manager may pressure the group into a certain stance, but he normally will not play a dominating role. It is even more rare for the Director of Personnel to enter the debate or to take a forceful position. The Director might feel compelled to intervene, however, in order to express the probable reaction of the Board of Directors to alternative management positions.

As the negotiations proceed, management will move its offers toward its targets. The rate of movement toward target will depend upon the rate of union movement toward the TVA target. If, for example, a union is further away from a basic salary target than is management, TVA's movement toward the target will be halted or slowed until the union "comes into line." The management caucus also begins to consider its positions in the data ranges and the probable decisions of arbitrators, especially on basic salary issues. Moreover, the management caucus, like the union caucus, must direct the positions of its negotiators in any ongoing work groups. Agreements in these work groups are presumably to be accepted by the full negotiating teams of both parties.

In the past few years, the give-and-take of negotiations has narrowed to a point at which TVA has stated a "last offer" on all outstanding issues. The Panel has then had the option of agreeing to TVA's final proposal or invoking impasse resolution procedures. Despite the economic environment for negotiations in 1974, all outstanding issues were resolved by the parties on the sixth day of negotiations. The ability of the parties to avoid the use of impasse resolution procedures was, in large part, a tribute to the efficacy of the bargaining structure and process, including mutually agreed-to pay determination criteria.

The bargaining process may extend to supplemental negotiations in October. Both parties will gather the issues deferred from the spring and canvass their constituencies for new proposals which are nonmonetary in nature. The full bargaining process differs somewhat from that in the spring. The negotiations will normally not exceed two days. The TVAAPCChE may not send its Panel representative, and the other unions will send considerably smaller delegations. The Negotiating Committee's "second string"—DPOs and assistant division heads—may represent management along with officials of the Division of Personnel.

The outcomes of these negotiations, however, could have important effects upon the collective bargaining relationship. For example, the Panel unions might wish to add cost-of-living changes as a criterion for salary determination. The issue might be debated in the fall negotiations, and the resolution of the issue might have a profound impact upon salary negotiations in the spring.

A Comparison

Several aspects of the bargaining process differ between the two relationships. For example, negotiations on basic salary rates and on important fringe items are primarily run by each union of the Trades and Labor Council, because the negotiated results are differentiated by craft practice. The Panel unions work together more closely formulating positions and carrying through with negotiations on fringe issues, for almost all fringe benefits apply uniformly to salary policy employees. The greater degree of differentiation for the trades and labor unions is understandable because of the traditional, overriding importance of craft practice. The international representatives of craft unions felt compelled to push for the increasing differentiation of contract terms because they believed that the relevant comparisons for determining prevailing practice on all important issues were comparisons within the craft and in the vicinity.

Craft or occupational ties were not so important for salary policy employees, so Panel unions never strongly pressed for the differentiation of fringe items by union or by occupation. Because negotiations over fringe items are not separated by union, the process of bargaining over these issues is certainly more simple than in the other relationship. Another ramification is that the Panel unions must work together more closely before and during bargaining, and their need to work together tends to increase their cohesiveness and their ability to work in common.

Another difference that surfaces in an analysis of process is the greater degree to which decision-making power is shared between union members and their negotiators in the Panel unions. This was illuminated in the prior chapter on structure, but it also becomes clear as the parties translate their structure into action. In both relationships, union negotiators discuss positions and strategy with delegates from their union locals. Yet because of the greater degree of democracy built into the structure of the Panel and its unions, the negotiators for these unions must share decision-making power with their union members through the delegates directly elected by these members. Moreover, the Panel structure is responsive downward, so decision-making power on fringe items does not solely reside with a few individuals at the top of the centralized structure.

A final notable difference in the process of bargaining is that salary bargaining is over minimum and maximum rates of each grade, and salary schedules are clearly separated along occupational lines. The process of wage bargaining is perhaps more complex because negotiations occur over wage rates for the many different classifications of work. Also, though separate wage schedules exist, management and the unions have a more difficult time insuring that negotiated outcomes do not violate traditional wage relationships between and among various classifications and crafts.

The processes of bargaining in the two relationships are also similar in important ways. The general sequence of events before and during negotiations does not vary greatly between the relationships, except that the unions also conduct prevailing practice surveys before TVA-Council negotiations. Great importance is attached to the collection, analysis, and interpretation of prevailing practice data in both processes. The exercise of decision-making power within management is very similar in both processes. Finally, the parties in both relationships are continuing to experiment with techniques designed to improve the effectiveness of their process, such as the rotation of responses to provide order in the interchange of offers and responses and the use of work groups to handle special problems.

In general, the parties in both relationships seem to have found processes with which they are comfortable and within which they can pursue their goals. The processes are carried out smoothly, even under difficult circumstances, and the central importance of prevailing practice data in the whole sequence of events seems to provide a focal point that allows the chain of events to proceed without significant interruptions or roadblocks.

6 Pay Determination

The rapid growth of public employment, the recent upsurge of government unionism, and increasing reliance on bilaterally determined employment conditions have focused considerable attention on the pay determination process in the public sector. Although some evidence exists that the actual impact of unionism on government labor costs tends to be exaggerated, union demands for pay increases continue to be of genuine concern not only to government employers and their employees, but to the taxpaying consumer of government services as well. Such concern for public wage determination appears justifiable in view of the unique role that public employees play as voters who may significantly affect their employer's tenure in office and because of the inherent, monopolistic nature of government services. A continual and inelastic demand for public services and the lack of alternative sources of supply mean that no apparent ceiling on employee wage demands exists. Highly organized public employees are theoretically in a position to extort inordinate wage or salary increases.

The monopolistic nature of government employment and the potential impact of unionism on the cost of government leads to an important question of whether specific public wage settlements are excessive, just right, or too low. Do standards or criteria exist which the parties can use to arrive at mutually agreeable compensation levels that are economically and politically justifiable? If so, how can they be used by the parties to fashion wages and salaries? What are some of the policy level as well as administrative problems in applying these criteria to particular bargaining relationships? The purpose of this chapter is to answer these questions by examining how TVA and its employee representatives utilize a specific pay criterion to determine employee compensation.

Although no scientific or purely objective bases appear to exist for concluding whether particular negotiated pay levels are equitable or economically sound, several criteria or standards exist upon which wage decisions can be founded. The more important criteria, applicable to either public or private sector wage determination, include the comparability or prevailing wage principle, cost of living, just or living wage, ability to pay, productivity, labor supply, and purchasing power. Unless legislation and/or the collective bargaining agreement requires the use of a particular criterion, the wage determination process will generally include consideration of some combination of all of these criteria. In fact, even under legal or contractual mandates requiring the use of a specific criterion, the parties may subconsciously or consciously use other wage standards. Such an occurrence is typical where the law requires the government to pay "prevailing" rates.

One of the aforementioned standards is utilized in government employment almost exclusively. Many city and state governments, as well as the federal government, are required by law to pay wages to their employees which are comparable to wages earned by employees performing similar work in private industry. This criterion is ostensibly an equitable one for determining the compensation of public workers, as most persons agree that government employees should not receive less remuneration than private sector workers performing similar tasks. Also, workers of the same "efficiency" receive the same wages regardless of their employment sector. The comparability standard is therefore considered efficient and economical because public agencies using the criterion would pay no more than necessary to attract and maintain an adequate supply of qualified workers from relevant labor markets.

The TVA case study on pay determination shows how the prevailing wage criterion functions in practice. It also identifies various factors which affect the efficacy of the criterion. These factors include the commitment by the parties to use the criterion, the classification or job evaluation system for positions remunerated on the basis of prevailing wages, the applicable labor market(s) and companies or agencies surveyed, and the data collection and analysis methods utilized to determine "prevailing wages." The TVA experience also emphasizes the problems associated with using the prevailing wage standard, and it depicts how collective bargaining influences the application of the criterion.

Trades and Labor Experience

The pay determination process for trades and labor positions in TVA evolved directly from the TVA Act. Section 3 of the Act states that all contracts requiring the employment of laborers and mechanics should mandate the payment of "not less than the prevailing rate of wages for work of a similar nature prevailing in the vicinity." When trades and labor work is performed directly on a force account basis, the Act requires that the prevailing rate of wages for work of a similar nature be paid in the same manner as though the work had been contracted out. Since most of TVA's construction, operation, and maintenance work has been performed by force account, the latter requirement has meant that wages for trades and labor employees (laborers and mechanics) have been determined by the prevailing wage criterion. Although a legal mandate, the parties have genuinely accepted the prevailing wage criterion as the most effective means of determining compensation for trades and labor positions. Their commitment to the standard is evidenced by the labor agreement incorporating the Act's requirements on wage determination and by the central role of prevailing wage data in the bargaining process as discussed in the last chapter.

Given the parties' acceptance of the prevailing wage principle, how is the criterion applied by TVA and the Council in actually establishing wages for trades and labor positions? The criterion is implemented in two distinct stages. First, TVA and the Council representatives survey a sample of the multitude of pay information existing in a predetermined labor market. Next, the parties jointly decide the prevailing basic hourly or annual wages by occupation which exist in the market, and these become TVA's negotiated wage rates. Associated fringe benefits (indirect compensation) paid by certain employers in the market are also surveyed, and prevailing benefits are determined and applied to trades and labor positions.

Representatives from both TVA and the Council make separate pay surveys, relying exclusively on primary sources of compensation data. TVA sends management representatives throughout the TVA area for purposes of securing firsthand information on wages and indirect compensation paid employees doing work comparable to the agency's trades and labor work. Actual collective bargaining contracts from hundreds of local unions are collected, local union business representatives are personally interviewed, and wage rates and other information included in the labor contracts are confirmed as accurate through interviews with representatives of contractors and contractor associations.

Council representatives survey wage rates, fringes, and other working conditions in the same labor market. They obtain copies of the same contracts secured by management representatives. Then, they submit the information to TVA for tabulation. No validation of the wage data is made by union representatives.

The TVA and union surveys generally begin in July and end by September or October. The actual interviewing and data gathering tasks involve as many as twenty different management representatives and about as many union representatives, although the union's survey is much less comprehensive than management's survey. Manpower and other costs of the surveys are relatively high. A less comprehensive survey and more reliance on secondary sources of wage information (such as the Bureau of Labor Statistics) might be just as useful and would certainly be less expensive. This seems particularly true since the Department of Labor can now furnish accurate and timely information on wages paid to construction employees.

Several important factors must be considered by agencies and firms which desire to utilize prevailing wage surveys effectively. The following sections discuss how TVA and the Council operationalize their prevailing wage criterion by addressing such factors as the classification system; the occupations, area, and firms surveyed; and the analysis and use of survey data.

Classification of Trades and Labor Positions

An important factor influencing the efficacy of the prevailing wage standard is the soundness of the job evaluation or classification system utilized by the agency conducting the survey. A system must exist for classifying similar jobs into the same wage schedules and wage grades, or at least, a system of accurately selecting key classes of positions to represent broad classes of positions for wage survey purposes must be operational. Otherwise, positions of the agency must be matched with positions of the surveyed firm in a time consuming and haphazard manner. Moreover, if certain positions of the surveying agency have been incorrectly allocated to particular wage schedules or grades, then surveys of wages for key positions of each schedule or grade will lead to wages which are "too high" or "too low" for the misallocated positions. Wage differences between and among some positions will not accurately reflect the differing skill, responsibility, and other requirements of those positions.

TVA has not given great attention to job evaluation for trades and labor construction positions since well established craft standards have been used almost exclusively. However, the increasingly complex nature of construction, operation, and maintenance work will dictate more concern for a sound job evaluation system for trades and labor positions. This is particularly true for nuclear plant construction, operation, and maintenance work. Despite the deemphasis on formal job evaluation, a rudimentary classification system does exist for all blue-collar work.

Trades and labor work at TVA is divided into five general areas according to type of work and whether the work is of a permanent or temporary nature. The broad categories of positions are designated as schedules A through D, with schedule B having two groups. All construction work is classified as schedule A; it is considered temporary and is paid on an hourly basis. This schedule represents the majority of trades and labor employees hired in TVA. Regular maintenance and miscellaneous operating work is classified as schedule B and is considered permanent or career type employment paid on an annual basis. Temporary operating and maintenance work paid on an hourly basis is labeled schedule B-Hourly. Regular operating work for chemical plant operations is classified as schedule C, and regular operating work for power plants is designated as schedule D. Each schedule is subdivided by craft or trade and further by specific job title.

A joint union-management committee (Joint Classification Committee) is assigned the responsibility for administering the trades classification scheme. Specific functions include the approval of new classes of positions, elimination of obsolete classes, modification of class titles, and approval of qualification and classification standards. All actions taken by the Committee are binding on TVA and the Council. For purposes of surveying pay rates, class or benchmark jobs are used for comparing TVA nonconstruction positions with those existing in the vicinity. The joint committee decides on these key positions.

To obtain wage comparisons for construction work, TVA uses only job titles. For some operating and maintenance work, a more comprehensive comparison is made between the duties of TVA's jobs and those of similar jobs in the survey. A real question remains as to whether TVA is comparing similar jobs.

Definition of Vicinity

Although the TVA Act requires payment of prevailing wage rates based on a comparison of pay for similar work performed in the vicinity, it specifies no definition of the term "vicinity." TVA has therefore retained flexibility in deciding on the specific geographic area for surveying wage rates and thereby determining the prevailing wages for particular types of work.

The determination of prevailing wages has been a negotiable subject since 1935, and the actual geographic area surveyed (that is, the definition of vicinity) has also been subject to collective bargaining. From 1935 to 1941 the vicinity was defined narrowly by TVA and the Council. It primarily included cities within the Tennessee River watershed area. During the 1940s, the parties agreed to expand the geographic area by including larger cities outside the watershed area and in fact, outside the Tennessee Valley area. By 1948, the parties finally reached agreement on the precise area which constituted "the vicinity" for purposes of determining prevailing wages. The official definition included three relatively high-wage cities, Atlanta, Birmingham, and Louisville, as points on the outer boundary of the vicinity. This definition of vicinity; that is, the area within the defined boundary line, remains in effect today. The actual cities surveyed within (or on) the boundary line are negotiable each year but have traditionally encompassed a set of fourteen urban centers and have included Atlanta, Birmingham, and Louisville. Wages surveyed from these cities have historically been higher than those from cities within the actual Tennessee river watershed area.

Although the three "fringe" cities have been surveyed yearly and their wage data given equal weight to that collected from the other cities, top management doubts the validity of the justification for their inclusion. The rationale for surveying these cities has always been that TVA recruits from the cities and thus that they should be included in the applicable labor market. Recent evidence indicates, however, that only about 10 percent of trades and labor positions are filled by recruits from Atlanta, Birmingham, and Louisville.

The Council fought long and hard for inclusion of Atlanta, Birmingham, and Louisville in the area from which survey data would be collected and used to determine prevailing pay. The primary reason was not only to push TVA rates higher, but also to use these higher TVA rates as leverage for driving wages up thoughout the south. This reason is still valid today. TVA, on the other hand, has benefited by its enhanced ability to recruit, but more recently is concerned about paying unnecessarily high wage rates and about its own inflationary impact on the region. A bitter struggle between TVA and the Council may result from TVA's insistence on giving less weight to data collected from the three outlying cities and from other efforts to modify the application of the prevailing wage criterion.

Unions, Contractors, and Firms Surveyed

Trades and labor employment in TVA is comprised of construction, operating, and maintenance work, and the wage determination process is subdivided along these lines. Prevailing wages are determined for construction employees by surveying the pay rates of "comparable workers" in several cities throughout the vicinity. TVA and the Council have agreed to secure wage data from only the more significant cities and industrial centers within the defined vicinity. Since 1965 the parties have finalized this understanding by agreeing to survey wage rates for each of the Council's sixteen unions from the fourteen major cities listed here:

    Asheville, North Carolina

    Atlanta, Georgia

    Birmingham, Alabama

    Gadsden, Alabama

    Huntsville, Alabama

    Jackson, Tennessee

    Knoxville, Tennessee

    Louisville, Kentucky

    Memphis, Tennessee

    Nashville, Tennessee

    Paducah, Kentucky

    Tri Cities, Tennessee

    Chattanooga, Tennessee

    Tri Cities (Florence), Alabama

For construction work and also for temporary operating and maintenance work, TVA and the unions survey local union wage rates, and indirect compensation, in each of these fourteen base cities. In addition to surveying local union rates for each of the sixteen crafts, TVA surveys certain large construction projects in the vicinity. Disagreement has resulted over the interpretation of "large construction project." However, the Wage Data Committee, comprised of union and management representatives, have officially defined a major project as being any construction activity in the vicinity which is located outside the jurisdictional boundaries of local unions other than those having their base in one of the fourteen cities. Also, the major project must be determined to have a significant influence on wage rates. This has limited surveys of major projects to the construction of dams, locks, power plants, transmission lines, or large chemical or manufacturing plants and has precluded housing projects, shopping centers, and other nonmanufacturing facilities. Obviously the sample is restricted to high wage construction projects and not necessarily to construction activities prevailing in the vicinity. In 1976, TVA and the Council agreed to survey pay and fringes of twenty-nine major projects, three of which were nonunion.

After pay data has been secured from local unions having jurisdiction in each of the fourteen cities, TVA's survey teams attempt to validate that information with local contractors who have bargaining agreements with the local unions. In cities where several contractors bargain as a group in employer associations, such as the National Electrical Contractors Association and the American General Contractors, primary emphasis is given to validating wage data through these associations.

To obtain factual data for negotiating prevailing wages for operating and maintenance work, the Wage Data Committee establishes a list of companies to be surveyed. The determination of companies to be surveyed is the heart of the entire collective bargaining relationship on pay matters.

The firms surveyed are located within ten different geographic areas within the vicinity. The areas correspond generally to the same geographic areas as the fourteen base cities. The criteria used by the parties to select the specific companies surveyed from each of its ten urban centers (usually sixty-five to seventy-five companies in total) are: (1) similarity and comparability of the type of work performed; (2) significance in terms of volume of production and number of employees; (3) willingness to disclose wage and other personnel data; and (4) existence of a professional personnel system from which reasonable job comparisons can be made. An unofficial, yet jointly recognized criterion in addition to the above, is that the companies be unionized. Only four of the surveyed companies are nonunion, and each of these companies are in a separate geographic area.

Firms in three industrial categories are included in the survey of operating and maintenance work: transportation, public utilities, and manufacturing. Power companies and public utilities are surveyed for operating and maintenance work, and firms in the other categories are surveyed for maintenance and chemical operator work. The size of the firms varies in terms of employment, but most are large, unionized firms with at least several hundred employees. Moreover, some firms, having more than one location within the vicinity, are surveyed at several locations even though the same wages are paid at each location. Such double counting gives greater weight to the pay tabulated from these multi-locational companies.

Collection and Use of Data

A wide variety of pay data is solicited from local unions and contractors in the fourteen base cities, from major construction projects, and from various companies surveyed throughout the vicinity. For construction work the surveyors obtain basic hourly wage rates for each TVA job classification except those few jobs which are unique to TVA's own work. They also solicit indirect compensation information, such as the amounts contributed to health and welfare funds, pension and vacation funds, and the amount of any transporation allowance. These types of information are usually contained in the collective bargaining agreements, and copies of each contract are obtained by the surveyors.

Descriptions of actual duties for each construction classification are not officially documented, and generally accepted craft standards are considered sufficient for basing comparisons of similar positions. In practice, few actual job comparisons are made on the construction survey. Operating and maintenance positions are described in broad terms, and the surveyors do attempt to make job comparisons and identify pay for similar positions. Only certain benchmark operating and maintenance positions are surveyed; however, indirect compensation information, similar to that surveyed for construction employment, is solicited from firms engaged in work comparable to TVA's operating and maintenance work. Other employment conditions, such as overtime, shift differentials, dues check-off, etc., are also surveyed. Thus, TVA and the Council negotiate basic pay rates as well as other monetary and nonmonetary fringe benefits on the basis of prevailing practice.

Prior to 1952, the data tabulated for each wage negotiation session depicted the number of employees receiving each wage rate surveyed. The parties concluded, however, that in most locations the rate negotiated by the local unions and the majority of local contractors was the most prevalent rate being paid in that location. Employment information was not deemed to be necessary. Thus, the number of employees in the positions surveyed is not solicited from either contractors or firms. The lack of such information casts some doubt on what rates are actually prevailing.

TVA assembles the pay data collected by its surveyors and also that data collected by Council representatives and records the data in tabular form. The format for data display varies somewhat by pay schedule. Most of the data is entered into computer storage, and the information is automatically printed in predetermined form.

Prevailing pay data for construction work are tabulated for each of the sixteen international unions. Compensation data are recorded for each craft by location (each of the fourteen cities) and by classification (job titles within each craft). Basic hourly wages, effective dates of wage increases, hourly contributions to health and welfare, pension, and vacation funds, and transporation benefits are noted for each surveyed city and job title. Also recorded on the tabulation forms is whether the pay data were submitted by management or by the union and whether the data were the same. If the TVA data differ from that submitted by the union, the printout indicates whether an employee association or contractor affirmed the paying of a particular rate or fringe. (See appendix A, for an example of the format used by the parties to record "prevailing" compensation for construction work.)

Nonconstruction prevailing pay data are tabulated for each union representing operating and maintenance work in TVA. For schedule B classifications, the metal trades group, six to ten companies are surveyed from each of the ten geographic areas within the vicinity, and wage data are tabulated for each of the metal trade unions by company and geographic area. Specific company names are coded to provide anonymity. Effective dates of the wage data are recorded as well as whether TVA or the international union reported the pay information. Generally, the unions only submit data for electricians, machinists, and operating engineers. These crafts represent the majority of work performed in schedules B, C, and D. Wage data for schedule D work are obtained primarily from power companies within the vicinity; most of this work is represented by the IBEW. Data for schedule C are obtained primarily from those companies having maintenance and chemical operator work. (See appendix B for an example of the format used by the parties to record prevailing wage data for schedule B positions.) The tabulation of all pay data collected for schedules A, B, B-Hourly, C, and D work is distributed to appropriate representatives of TVA and the Council. As the preceding chapter pointed out, this compensation information serves as a factual base, jointly agreed to by both parties, upon which collective wage determination is founded. TVA and the Council consider only these data and updated rates received after the official survey ends and approved by the parties as valid, in fulfilling the joint responsibility of determining the compensation for each trades and labor position in TVA. In the actual wage setting process, the parties typically analyze the raw pay data in certain predetermined ways. Each party emphasizes the analysis which best reflects its own bargaining position.

For schedule A work, management uses three primary types of statistical analyses of the raw pay data. The first is a simple rank ordering, by city, of the pay rates (direct and indirect compensation) for each of the sixteen unions representing TVA construction work. The TVA wage rate being paid at the time of negotiations is included in the rank ordering of the fourteen base cities. For example, the pay data collected for the Asbestos Workers Union is ranked by city, from the highest paying city to the lowest paying, and the current TVA rate for the asbestos worker classification is included in the appropriate position. The TVA rate generally falls within the lowest quartile, and often is the lowest pay rate, because the rates in the fourteen base cities were negotiated after the TVA rate was set. (See appendix C for a comparison of TVA's average hourly construction rate with the average hourly construction rates for the four major cities in Tennessee.) One objective in the pay setting process is to put the TVA rates in at least the upper half of the data. The exact ranking of the TVA rate varies by union and depends on many factors.

In addition to the rank ordering process, the basic union hourly wage rate and the total pay rates are averaged for all fourteen cities. The mean rate is compared with the previous year's mean rate and the absolute increase is calculated. Also, the percentage increase is calculated. Most trades and labor increases for construction employment approximate the average wage increase resulting from the fourteen base cities surveyed. (See Appendix D for an example of these analyses for the Asbestos Workers union.)

For operating and maintenance work in schedules B and C, the survey data collected from the various firms surveyed are compared with the previous year's data, and the increase is calculated and recorded for each firm by job classification. The dollar and cents increase for all firms reporting applicable data is then averaged. Average increases are given considerable weight by both parties in setting pay rates for these schedules.

Schedule D, operating work for power generation, is analyzed on a rank order basis, by occupation, for those power companies having work comparable to TVA. The TVA rates are included in the ordering process and generally fall near the bottom of the list. Average pay rate increases for each key occupation are also calculated from the pay data of all the power companies surveyed. Moreover, pay increases for the more significant firms (usually the top paying firms) are averaged separately.

The prevailing pay criterion as applied by TVA and the Council, along with the bargaining structure and process described in previous chapters, have resulted in peaceful wage determination and harmonious union-management relations in TVA.

Salary Policy Experience

TVA did not adopt the prevailing wage criterion as a basis for determining the pay of salary policy employees until 1951. TVA and the Salary Policy Employee Panel incorporated this criterion and two others into their collective bargaining agreement which was amended in 1952. The other criteria were later eliminated, and the prevailing rate standard is now the sole criterion used for determining the compensation of salary policy employees where prevailing data exist.

The labor contract between TVA and the Panel states that pay rates will be

determined "on the basis of prevailing rates for similar work in the vicinity."
Two important differences exist between the application of this criterion and
the one used for trades and labor pay determination. In the latter case, the prevailing wage criterion is required by law, as well as by contractual agreement,
whereas the salary policy prevailing wage criterion is required only by the contract. Thus, the Panel and TVA can change the criterion whenever they desire.
A more significant difference, however, is the fact that TVA is required to pay
its trades and labor employees "*the* prevailing rates of pay for work of a similar
nature in the vicinity," but TVA is only required to *base* salary policy pay on
prevailing rates. Thus, the salary policy parties could use criteria other than
prevailing wages to determine pay rates. This difference is a real one in language,
but it has not constituted a significant difference in application. Pay for both
trades and labor and salary policy employees is *based* on wages prevailing for
work of a similar nature in certain segments of the regional economy.

As in the case of trades and labor pay determination, TVA relies almost
exclusively on primary sources of data for determining the prevailing pay of
white-collar work in the vicinity. The agency has conducted compensation
surveys each year since 1951. It sends management representatives throughout
the TVA area for the purpose of securing direct and indirect compensation
data from selected companies and agencies employing persons who perform
work similar to that performed by TVA salary policy employees. Surveyors
personally visit management representatives of each of approximately fifty
firms or government agencies and interview them to compare jobs and to
secure pay and other information about their white-collar (exempt and non-
exempt) employees. Representatives from the Panel neither make salary surveys nor accompany TVA representatives on their survey.

TVA's pay surveys are costly in terms of manpower, time, travel, and other
resources. Less reliance on primary sources of pay data may reduce its accuracy
somewhat, particularly with regard to job comparisons, but such a contention
presupposes that the survey methods utilized do in fact yield accurate and
statistically valid pay data. Are accurate job comparisons made with each company? Would secondary sources of information be just as timely and just as
accurate as primary sources? How much money would be saved by relying more
on secondary sources? Do the benefits derived from using primary sources outweigh the costs of such a process? Is it necessary to make surveys each year?
These are questions which must be answered by any organization using primary
sources of data, and which are presently being addressed by TVA.

Classification of Salary Policy Positions

Especially for white-collar and professional workers, an effective job evaluation
and classification system is vital. Craft standards and precedent for describing

and ranking jobs in trades and labor work do not exist for salary positions. In the absence of such a system, the establishment of accurate comparability between the pay of public and private sector employees is not possible, even if the determination of prevailing practice is perfectly accomplished. Comparing actual duties, not job titles, is essential for true comparability.

TVA's present classification system for white-collar employees is comprised of six pay schedules: administration (SA), clerical and general services (SB), engineering and scientific (SD), aid and technician (SE), custodial (SF), and public safety (SG). Each schedule consists of a broad grouping of classes and class series, based on related functions and qualification requirements.[1] Schedules SA, SB, SD, and SE have several different grades of work, with each grade corresponding to a broad band or level of difficulty, importance, and responsibility. Each grade of the major schedules (SA through SE) contains eight different within-grade steps, and progression to successive within-grade steps is conditional upon satisfactory work performance and length of service.

Just as in the trades and labor experience, the job evaluation and classification system has been one of the weakest links in the prevailing pay determination process. The success of the pay system depends on accurate and current classification standards which define the kind of work and concomitant qualification requirements for each grade level. These standards are used as guides in classifying positions in the appropriate class and in establishing and maintaining sound relationships among positions. As guides to allocating positions, they must be flexible.

One fatal problem with the current classification plan has resulted in pay rates for certain positions which are completely out of line with the rates of comparable jobs in the vicinity. Schedule D, for example, includes all bargaining unit engineering positions in TVA, but it also contains nonengineering jobs such as Forester, Ecologist, Economist, Mathematician, Research Analyst, Tributary Area Representative, and Human Resource Analyst. Although one or two of these nonengineering jobs are surveyed, the engineering pay rates have predominate weight in the pay setting process and thus bias the rates for all other unrelated jobs in the engineering and scientific schedule. The parties have established a joint Panel-TVA committee to study this problem and to recommend a solution.

A special in-house task force was established in 1973 to make a comprehensive review and evaluation of TVA's job classification and pay system. As a result of its study of the classification system for salary policy employees, a joint union-management group was established to develop a new job evaluation system for schedules SD and SE. A similar system also is being established for schedules SA and SB. Basically, the system involves factor-ranking[2] and the use of benchmark job descriptions, guidecharts, and points to facilitate this allocation of positions. The new system should improve the basis upon which job comparisons are made for pay determination purposes.

Key Classes

TVA uses the "key class" or "benchmark" concept in determining what salary policy occupations are used in the comparison process to determine prevailing practice. Compensation data for jobs which are comparable to these key classes are solicited from the organizations surveyed. Four criteria are used by TVA to select which of the many hundreds of salary policy classes of positions will become key classes:

1. In terms of duties, responsibilities, and qualifications, the class represents other classes of positions at the same grade.
2. The work is clearly identifiable.
3. The class has a large number of positions.
4. The prospect of obtaining data from surveyed firms is good.

The number of actual key classes used in the survey varies each year, but averages around 150. In the administrative schedule, for example, the Accountant, Accounting Officer, Administrative Officer, Cost Accounting Officer, Data Process Analyst, Purchasing Agent, and Voucher Examiner classes at each grade level have been used as key classes for survey purposes. A brief written description of the duties and essential qualifications is developed for each key class, and these descriptions serve as the primary source of information for surveyors in making comparisons with jobs in other firms. In addition to these brief descriptions, the surveyors have access to the more detailed classification standards for most of the key classes. Pay information is not collected for all key classes from all firms in the survey. In many firms, only ten to fifteen comparisons are made. Generally, about 1,500 job comparisons are reported for each year's survey.

Surveyors are instructed to read each key class description to the company representative being interviewed and then ask if that company has a similar job. The surveyor and company representative then discuss the comparability of the jobs and match corresponding grade levels and pay ranges. TVA surveyors are asked not to compare job titles, but to compare actual duties and responsibilities. In practice, job titles are frequently considered, since previous job comparisons have often been made. In some cases, however, the original job comparisons have been made as much as five years in the past.

Vicinity and Firms Surveyed

To operationalize the prevailing wage standard incorporated in the *Articles of Agreement*, TVA and the Panel adopted the same definition of "vicinity" as that incorporated in the *General Agreement* between TVA and the Tennessee Valley

Trades and Labor Council. Specific companies and government agencies to be surveyed are selected from the following geographic areas:

Knoxville–Oak Ridge, Tennessee

Upper East Tennessee

Atlanta, Georgia

Central Alabama

Memphis, Tennessee

Northern Alabama

Central Tennessee

Louisville, Kentucky

Paducah, Kentucky

Chattanooga, Tennessee

Western North Carolina

In addition to firms selected from the above areas, federal government agencies operating within the vicinity were once surveyed as separate organizations. Now, one prevailing federal pay rate is determined for each TVA key class deemed comparable with a class of federal positions.

Several criteria are considered in deciding which organizations to survey:

1. The product or service should correspond to some major type of TVA work.
2. Positions in the firm must correspond to at least some of the TVA key classes.
3. The classification and pay plan of the organization should establish rates of pay for established classes of work and not merely for individual positions.
4. A substantial number of employees must be working in the TVA area.
5. Good personnel policies and procedures should be practiced.

The actual organizations selected each year (usually fifty to fifty-five in number) are subject to negotiations between TVA and the Panel, using the above mutually approved criteria. As a general rule, the Panel attempts to delete lower paying firms and to add higher paying ones. The survey has generally included the same organizations each year. Organizations surveyed cannot be considered representative of all employers operating within the defined vicinity. The sample of companies has traditionally been weighted toward large establishments in only major industrial categories.

Many national firms which operate in the vicinity are also included in the survey. These firms tend to provide the same pay levels at all locations, and data collected from these firms primarily reflect national, rather than regional, practice. As in the trades and labor experience, several plants of the same national organization may be surveyed, with each location counted as a separate establishment for purposes of data collection and analysis. Thus, the range of pay data collected for each grade of each schedule is biased upward because of the sample of firms included in the survey. TVA and its employee representatives tend to combine the pay-setting process with the determination of prevailing pay for comparable work in a defined geographic area. They do this by surveying large, relatively high paying firms, instead of surveying a sample of firms more representative of the universe and then setting pay rates on the basis of this sample.

The definition of vicinity appears restrictive for salary policy positions which have national recruitment markets. National rates would seem applicable for many engineering, scientific, and professional positions. One reason that TVA agrees to survey national firms operating within the region and to count some multilocational firms twice is to remedy this problem, but data are also collected from these firms for white-collar positions filled primarily by local and regional recruitment markets. The pay data for such positions are unjustifiably biased upward.[3]

Collection and Analysis of Data

The survey of prevailing practice in the vicinity is carried out by teams of management representatives a few months after the parameters for the survey have been negotiated. In addition to basic salary rate information, TVA makes a comprehensive survey to solicit data on a myriad of indirect pay practices and other conditions of employment. Pay data is collected on shift work, overtime, cleaning and laundering of uniforms, severance, and contributions made to the retirement and insurance plans. Information about the number of holidays, the vacation plans, sabbaticals, and safety equipment is also obtained. Indirect compensation, however, is not considered when negotiating a particular salary rate. Thus, total compensation comparisons are not made—salary rates are negotiated on the basis of prevailing salary rates for comparable jobs and fringe benefits are negotiated separately on the basis of prevailing nonpay benefits.

Because the survey data assume such importance in the collective bargaining process, the questionnaire method of collecting data, coupled with the interview technique, is also utilized to solicit prevailing practice information for salary policy employees. A TVA representative will typically review each of about 200 questions on the survey form with the company representative being surveyed. This allows little time for making job comparisons.

To survey and properly record basic pay-rate data, the survey teams must be well-trained in matching groups of positions in the firms surveyed with comparable positions in TVA. Even if the difficult matching process is performed properly, other problems in the survey process can thwart the accurate comparison of TVA's basic salaries with those in the vicinity. For example, the surveyors attempt to uncover the minimum, maximum, and the average rate being paid by firms surveyed for each key class. The minimum rate is supposed to represent the hiring rate used by the firm surveyed, yet the firm may have considerable discretion in hiring at rates considerably above the minimum rates of the range. If so, the minimum rate stated by the firm would be a misleading basis for establishing the minimum rate of a TVA grade.

Maximum and average rates quoted by the firms surveyed also may be misleading. TVA has a "satisfactory-service" plan for advancing to the maximum rate of each grade, but most of the firms surveyed advance individuals within each grade on the basis of merit rather than length of service. Few individuals may be expected to advance to the maximum rate. For this reason, the maximum and average rates quoted by the firm surveyed might be higher than that which it would quote under a satisfactory service plan. Thus, the surveyed rates may not be an accurate benchmark for setting TVA salaries if the prevailing data are unweighted. Hypothetical minimum and maximum rates, which are the primary bases for negotiating prevailing pay, clearly do not reflect rates that are actually being paid for certain jobs in the vicinity.

Finally, a firm surveyed might pay relatively low basic salaries, but relatively high fringe benefits. Inclusion of its minimum and maximum rates in the survey data would result in a misleading impression of prevailing practice. Adjustments need to be made in the survey data to resolve this and the other problems which distort the true picture of prevailing practice. In fact, experimentation is being conducted on means of surveying the total compensation package of firms. Surveys of this type could eliminate the distortion of prevailing practice that results because different firms pay differing percentages of total compensation in fringe benefits. TVA appears ready to seriously consider a switch to surveys of total pay packages when "total compensation cost models" are perfected by the Office of Management and Budget and the Bureau of Labor Statistics. The Employment Cost Index (ECI) appears to be a step in the right direction.

In addition to the minimum, maximum, and average salary-rate data, the surveyors record the time period for which the rates apply (hourly, weekly, biweekly, or monthly); whether the pay plan is a merit, satisfactory-service, or combination plan; the number of within-grade rates from minimum to maximum; and the total number of position steps and employees in these positions for each job which corresponds to a particular TVA key class. (See appendix E for an example of the tabulation form used by the surveyors to record pay data for a few key class positions in schedule SA.)

Raw prevailing practice data, obtained for minimum, maximum, and average rates being paid for key classes in each TVA salary grade, could be analyzed in a wide variety of ways.[4] Extremely divergent analyses by two parties in a

collective bargaining relationship would provide little common ground in negotiations. TVA and the Salary Policy Employee Panel use similar methods of
analyzing the raw survey data, and an explanation of three major methods of
weighting or analyzing follows.

In the "common entry" method of weighting the data, only a subset of the
prevailing practice observations is used. This subset consists of those observations obtained for the same key classes and from the same organizations as were
obtained the previous year. Such survey entries, in common for both years, are
assumed to provide the best indication of prevailing rate changes between the
two years. The range of common entries is prepared for the minimum and maximum rates of each grade, and a simple average may be obtained for each range.
Then, for example, the percentage increase in the average of minimum rates
paid for the same grade, from this year over last year, is determined. This percentage increase is one indication of changes in prevailing practice for minimum
and maximum rates; it is one basis of collective bargaining over pay.

Another weighting method has sometimes been labeled the "survey data"
method. Assume that for a minimum rate of some TVA grade, ten firms or
agencies were surveyed, and ten observations were obtained from each firm;
that is, each firm reported the minimum rate being paid to ten key classes comparable to the TVA key classes for the particular grade. In the survey data
method, each observation—one hundred in this example—would be reported in
the raw data range, and each observation would be given equal weight. Further
analysis of the range, determined in this way for minimum and maximum rates
of each grade, will be explained below.

An alternative method for developing a data range has been labeled the
"company practice" method. In the above example of ten observations each
of ten firms, an average of observations for each firm would be computed and
counted as one entry. Therefore, ten entries would constitute the data range,
rather than one hundred. This method means, of course, that data from a
company with one observation reported would be given the same weight as data
from a company with fifty observations reported.

The range of data compiled by one or all of these alternative methods may
be reported in several ways. As one example, the range of prevailing rates compiled for the maximum rate of some TVA grade may be placed on a graph with
salary levels on the vertical axis and percentiles from one to one hundred on the
horizontal axis. Assume that the range of prevailing practice entries was from
$8,000 to $12,000. If one entry was $10,000, then a point would be recorded
on the graph corresponding to $10,000 and the fiftieth percentile. Once the
scatter of points has been plotted, a smoothed curve is fit statistically to the
scatter diagram. Reading this curve, one can easily see what salary rate corresponds to a particular percentile in the prevailing rate range. The same information, matching prevailing salary levels with percentiles, may also be compiled
in tabular form. Obviously, the correspondence between salaries and percentiles

should differ between the "survey data" and "company practice" methods of compiling the data range.

Bilateral Wage and Salary Determination

TVA is bound to the prevailing pay principle by law and contractual agreement. Thus, for all construction, operating, and maintenance work performed by TVA on either a force-account or contract basis, the wages for work of a similar nature prevailing in the vicinity must be paid. The only statutory guidance given to TVA in applying the prevailing rate standard was that in determining prevailing wages due regard should be given to wages secured through collective bargaining. To effectuate the prevailing pay criterion, TVA and the Council and Panel have defined the geographic area (vicinity) from which prevailing pay data will be accumulated; established each year the specific firms, contractors, other employers, and unions to be surveyed; developed a method for comparing TVA jobs with those in the vicinity; and standardized methods for analyzing the pay data for purposes of negotiating the desired "prevailing" rates.

TVA's approach to setting wages and salaries combines both the pay-setting process and the process by which prevailing rates are determined. Since the law requires payment of prevailing wages, and because of the collective bargaining agreements, TVA has believed it necessary to determine prevailing pay in a manner that reflects other factors important in the setting of wages and salaries. TVA's decision to be a high-pay employer to facilitate recruitment and employment, for example, is translated into the process of determining prevailing pay. This is accomplished by giving greater, or even exclusive, weight to certain rates in the vicinity. Thus, high-pay, large, and/or unionized employers and contractors are surveyed to reflect "prevailing pay" so that the resulting TVA rates will be high enough to make the agency a high or relatively high-pay employer. This process does not mean that the negotiated "prevailing" rates are prevailing generally in the vicinity; rather, it means that the rates are prevailing within only a certain segment of the total employer population in the vicinity. In other words, the sample of pay data collected is not representative of all pay data but is a more biased sample which reflects the apparent pay-setting needs of the employer using the data. Collective bargaining has certainly contributed to this upward bias in applying the comparability criterion.

Theoretically, payment of the prevailing wage or salary is generally understood to mean the setting of a pay rate at or around the fiftieth percentile of the data range, or at or near the median or mean rate in the survey data. TVA and the Salary Policy Employee Panel have never officially agreed upon the definition of "prevailing rates." The agency has traditionally aimed at a target of the sixty-seventh percentile in the range for minimum salary rates and for a lower percentile in the range of data for maximum salary rates. This practice was based primarily on a general guideline established by the TVA Board to the effect that pay rates should be negotiated which were above average, but well below the maximum discovered in the survey. Actual rates negotiated over the years, however, have been above the original guidelines. In schedule SD, the minimum rates have ranged from the eightieth percentile to over the ninetieth percentile; and in schedule SE, from the seventieth to eightieth percentile. Maximum rates are set more conservatively but are generally well above the percentiles originally believed desirable. Among the primary reasons given for such a liberalization in pay-setting are the requirements to recruit and retain a high-quality work force and the increased bargaining power of the Salary Policy Employee Panel.

The use of such a standard in a collective bargaining environment means that the designation of firms, type of work, and the geographic locations surveyed become the very heart of the pay determination process. A rate negotiated at the fiftieth percentile of high-wage firms will naturally be higher than a rate negotiated at the same percentile of the low-wage firms. Over the years, TVA has yielded to pressure to survey union construction work, major construction projects, and large, unionized firms. Moreover, the geographic areas surveyed have included high-wage areas outside principle recruitment areas. Use of such a sample and geographic area to determine "prevailing pay" guarantees that TVA will negotiate relatively high rates. Moreover, after such a pay-setting process is started and the firms and defined vicinity are established, it is very difficult to revise the approach to include low-paying firms, to exclude higher paying firms, or to redefine the survey area. During the 1975 negotiations, for example, TVA surveyed nonunion bridge and highway construction work, intending to consider the resulting data in determining pay for trades and labor work. The Council refused to consider such data and management was forced to disregard it.

In addition to negotiating rates well above the fiftieth percentile of the data, upward biases in the application of the prevailing pay standard occur because of the unrepresentative sample of companies; the double counting of some national firm data; the lack of total compensation comparisons; the comparison of length-of-service progression plans with merit and merit/length-of-service combination plans and the consideration of hypothetical minimum and maximum pay rates; and the use of vicinity-wide data to set rates for positions filled through local labor markets.

TVA's approach to pay determination has, of course, contributed to harmonious labor relations. Employees and their representatives have generally considered wages and salaries to be equitable. TVA has been able to recruit craftsmen and professionals from all over the country and turnover has been relatively low. Voluntary terminations over the last five years have been almost nonevident. Candidates for certain jobs are in abundance. A question of paramount concern, however, is whether wages and salaries resulting from this process have been "too high" and whether they have had an inflationary impact on the economy of the region. Lower pay may have been sufficient to recruit and maintain an adequate work force. On the other hand, any upward bias to wages and salaries resulting from the survey of union rates and large firms may have been justified by increased productivity resulting either from the recruitment of better qualified candidates or by enhanced performance of those employed, or both. Savings may also have resulted from generally harmonious union-management relations and peaceful collective bargaining settlements.

It appears, however, that the application of the comparability standard has led to wages and salaries that are biased upward and do not reflect genuinely prevailing pay for comparable work in the total geographic area from which TVA recruits. One possible factor which may temper the upward bias is the centralized structure of bargaining. The Council structure tends to insulate union negotiators from rank-and-file demands. Council members are better able to consider the ramifications of inordinate wage increases on employment levels, on TVA operations in general, and on TVA consumers whose attitudes can potentially affect many aspects of TVA. Wage inflation from whipsawing demands of unions is also minimized.

Also, regional versus national surveys continue to bias downward the salaries of certain TVA professionals, despite the inclusion of establishments of national firms in the survey sample. Moreover, a "lag" problem produces a downward bias in all TVA salaries determined through the prevailing pay process. Raw prevailing pay data are collected several months prior to negotiations. After negotiations, one month elapses before new wage and salary levels become effective. An additional lag results because wage increases of the survey companies may have occurred six to nine months before the TVA survey was conducted. Especially when the rate of wage and price inflation is accelerating, the downward bias resulting from the lag problem can become serious. Although survey data may be biased above generally prevailing rates when it is collected TVA basic salary rates may not be upwardly biased, in relation to the surveyed firms, with respect to the year during which they will be in effect.

During the past several years, top management has indicated a desire to begin pushing negotiated pay rates (in percentile terms) back toward the fiftieth percentile of the data ranges and to generally improve the entire pay determination process. Given the biased sample of firms upon which prevailing pay is determined even rates of the fiftieth percentile would constitute relatively high rates for the vicinity—especially for positions filled through local recruitment. More emphasis will be placed on collecting average pay rates and on adding firms and government agencies to the sample that are more representative of employers in the vicinity. Also, total compensation package comparisons would improve the efficiency of the comparability policy as applied by the parties.

Notes

1. A class is a group of positions having similar duties and responsibilities, the same basic qualification requirements, the same salary range, and identical job titles. A series is composed of two or more classes which have similar fields of work, but differ in the relative difficulty, importance, and responsibilities of the work.

2. Factor-ranking involves comparing a particular job with all others, one factor at a time. The system is used extensively in varying forms in private industry and has been recommended for use by the classified service of the federal government.

3. To broaden the definition of "vicinity" to include the national labor market for certain positions would present certain administrative problems to TVA since its survey and pay-setting practices are presently independent of the Civil Service Commission. The regional definition of "vicinity" better assures continued independence. By including data from national firms having plants or firms in the vicinity and by tabulating pay rates for jobs other than those recruited for on a national basis, TVA gives greater weight to the higher-paying firms for nonprofessional work such as clerical, technical, janitorial, etc.

4. Bargaining actually occurs over the minimum and maximum rates of each salary grade in each salary schedule. Once these extreme rates of the grade range have been determined, a simple formula is used to determine the other within-grade rates between the extremes of the range.

7 Impasse Resolution and Work Stoppages

Impasse resolution is a broad term. It encompasses a discussion of bargaining power and of the collective bargaining process itself, for bargaining begins with impasse and the purpose of the entire process is to resolve impasse. The last three chapters have provided information on the environment and the mechanisms which serve to dissolve deadlocks in the TVA bargaining relationships and to move the parties toward final agreement. Yet, procedures must be at the end of the process to facilitate agreement on sticky issues and, more importantly, to serve as the pressure mechanism prompting both sides to make concessions. In turning to the impasse resolution procedures at the end of the bargaining tunnel, we face the most controversial area of public sector labor relations.

According to the labor contracts between TVA and the two centralized union bodies with which it bargains, five procedures are available for resolving impasses. Mediation by a neutral may be utilized in an impasse over any subject matter of the supplementary agreements. Beyond this, four forms of advisory and of binding arbitration are specified, depending upon the particular contract and upon the subject matter of the dispute.

Two analytical issues should be addressed prior to an analysis of the TVA procedures in order to put the analysis of impasse resolution at TVA in proper perspective. First, what are the major factors which should be considered in evaluating impasse resolution procedures in the public sector? Second, what are the alternative procedures and how is each evaluated according to these factors?

Five basic factors have been considered in developing and debating alternative impasse resolution procedures in the government sector:

1. Vital public services cannot be interrupted.
2. Collective bargaining cannot be meaningful unless all parties may be faced with significant pressure if an agreement is not reached in a reasonable period of time.
3. The bargaining parties themselves should ultimately decide upon all contract provisions. Neutrals may play an important role in successful public sector negotiations, but they should not have the power to make final and binding decisions over the terms of a contract, except in unusual circumstances.
4. Any dispute-settlement procedure should possess the flexibility for

differential application to the disparate types of public employees—public library workers and policemen, for example.

5. Any dispute-settlement procedure must be workable, and it must be palatable to the government employer, the government employee, and the public.[1]

Academicians and practitioners concerned with public sector bargaining have experienced great difficulty in developing procedures to adequately meet these standards. Bargainers in different settings have weighted the importance of the various factors differently and have therefore chosen different alternative procedures. The alternative procedures and their performance according to the five factors must be made clear to facilitate informed choice among the alternatives in the future.

Some public employers continue to adopt an extreme position and refuse to consider any method for impasse resolution except unilateral decision-making by management. The fact that the sovereignty doctrine can no longer be used to justify this posture by public employers was established in chapter 1. No other alternative is evaluated more poorly according to the criteria. Public services are indeed interrupted because extralegal strikes become common when peaceful and effective procedures for resolving disputes are not available. No effective pressure is placed upon the public employer in bargaining. The employer can resolve all issues unilaterally at the end of the process. The parties may not decide upon the issues; only one party may decide. Finally, this alternative is not generally palatable to public employees.

Third-party mediation is often suggested as a means for resolving impasses. The procedure is more complicated in the public sector than it is in the private sector. Public sector mediators often find that they must educate the parties about collective bargaining. Issues in bargaining are more likely to be made public during the negotiation process, points of decision-making authority in management may be difficult to locate, and budgetary problems may complicate both bargaining and mediation.[2] A staunch advocate of public sector mediation believes that use of this procedure alone would resolve most impasses, especially if mediators were introduced early into the bargaining proceedings. Even so, this advocate would prefer that factfinding and even limited strike rights be available if mediation did not work.[3]

Mediation does not entail an interruption of public services. Third parties are involved in collective bargaining, but they do not make final decisions for the parties to bargaining. Moreover, the procedure has been quite acceptable to all parties concerned with bargaining, and it has received considerable use. The drawback of this procedure is that effective pressure is not placed on the bargaining parties to reach an agreement. When the procedure is used alone, the public employer is still free to resolve impasses unilaterally. Therefore, most experts suggest that mediation may help facilitate the resolution of impasses but that it is not enough. It should be tried first for resolving deadlocks and then be followed by another procedure if the impasse is not resolved. A major reason for this viewpoint is that mediation procedures are much more effective when the parties know that another procedure, involving direct pressure and costs to both parties, will follow mediation. The parties have an incentive to use mediation fruitfully and resolve deadlocks on their own.

Factfinding by third parties, or by a panel including third parties, has also been used to resolve disputes. It has taken several forms. For example, the factfinders may simply present relevant data and analysis to the parties without recommendations for resolving deadlocks. Factfinders may also find themselves assuming the role of mediators.

Factfinding is more commonly considered as a procedure which is similar to, and is evaluated almost identically with, advisory arbitration. Third parties consider the positions of the parties to bargaining along with all relevant economic data and other information and then recommend terms for a settlement. As the procedure is normally conceived, these recommended terms will be made public so that public pressure will induce both parties toward a settlement on the basis of these supposedly equitable terms. Under this factfinding with recommendations, no work stoppage occurs. Like mediation, it can be used in situations involving all types of public employees, and it has been sufficiently acceptable to receive considerable use. The focus of an evaluation of this procedure, however, must be placed on the effectiveness of the pressure which it brings to bear on the parties and on the role of the third parties.

If both parties are committed to the acceptance of factfinding recommendations, then the procedure places pressure on the parties to reach agreement on their own and to avoid the procedure's use. However, if the procedure is used, then a third party makes decisions for the parties. In effect, the procedure becomes binding arbitration of deadlocks, and little reason exists for not substituting a formal arbitration procedure. On the other hand, one party or both parties may not be committed to accepting the factfinders' recommendations. It is then possible that the public employer might again end up making unilateral decisions on bargaining deadlocks. No effective pressure would be placed upon the employer, and the procedure would have little appeal for public employees and unions.

One variation of this procedure provides another step if either party refuses to accept the factfinders' recommendations. This party would be forced to appear before some body and "show cause" for refusing the recommendations. The entity conducting this "show cause" hearing would then either make further, nonbinding recommendations for settlement or fashion a binding settlement. In the former case, it is doubtful if an adequate amount of additional pressure would be generated to induce the balking party toward acceptance of recommended terms. The latter case is merely compulsory and binding arbitration. Public employee unions have severely criticized the use of factfinding-show cause procedures in the State of New York as largely ineffective.[4]

Another alternative procedure is final and binding arbitration. If the parties cannot resolve certain issues in bargaining, the issues are taken to an arbitrator or to an arbitration panel. The decisions reached in arbitration are final and binding on the parties. One group of critics attack the procedure because it involves third-party decision-making over contract terms. It is possible that one party to bargaining could not easily live with terms imposed by a neutral. In the public sector, perhaps a legislative body would not or could not make the terms imposed by an arbitrator effective. The parties themselves have the best knowledge of their bargaining and work environment. They are best able to fashion solutions which can be accepted by all concerned. Other critics contend that binding arbitration procedures have a "narcotic effect" upon bargaining. The parties will not really attempt to reach a solution on their own. Rather, they will leave major issues deadlocked and let the arbitrator resolve them. Bargainers might take this stance to avoid political pressure from their constituents. They can simply lay the responsibility for bargaining outcomes on the arbitrator.

Certainly, binding arbitration provides finality and a peaceful, nonstrike method of resolving impasses. The parties are pressured to reach agreement on their own unless a narcotic effect is present. The parties would face the risk that an arbitrator would cause them to "lose" more than they would have lost in the private interplay of bargaining. Indeed, the procedure would be most valuable if it effectively pressured the parties toward private settlement of all issues. In fact, most available evidence indicates that where binding arbitration is available, the parties choose not to use it in the majority of cases.

Binding arbitration is becoming an increasingly acceptable procedure for resolving deadlocks in public sector bargaining. Yet it is still true that when the procedure is used, the decision-making power of private parties is usurped. Third parties are given more latitude than in any other alternative procedure, because they have the authority to choose the terms of settlement.

In binding arbitration as it has traditionally been known, the arbitrator may accept one of the parties' positions on all disputed issues as the terms of settlement, but he is more likely to fashion a settlement which does not embrace the positions of either party in toto. Final-offer arbitration is a new variant of binding arbitration, which does not give the arbitrator such discretion. He is forced to accept the final positions of one of the two parties on *all* of the disputed issues. A complete evaluation of this procedure will be deferred until the discussion of impasse resolution in the TVA-Panel relationship, where final-offer arbitration has been specified for use in wage disputes since 1972.

Another alternative is to allow public employees to exercise the same strike rights as are available to private sector employees. The strike threat is the best known mechanism for pressuring bargainers to reach agreement on their own, and a few states allow certain public employees to use the strike alternative. Public services are interrupted under this alternative. However, it has already been argued that if there are services so vital that strikes must be prohibited or limited, they do not separate along public sector/private sector lines. For this reason, some have argued that public sector strikes should only be limited in the way that private sector strikes are limited. The president would be able to obtain an injunction to stop any strike endangering the national health or safety.

Under the alternative providing strike rights, final decisions over bargaining issues are made by the parties to bargaining, rather than by third parties. Economic pressure is placed on all concerned parties to see that impasses are resolved. The public is one of these parties, for the public may be affected both by strikes and by negotiated results. Yet it is true that full strike rights may not be feasible for some types of public employees, such as policemen, and the public's posture toward full strike rights for public employees makes widespread use of the procedure in the near future doubtful.

A number of alternative procedures are of the combination type, varying the method of impasse resolution by the kind of public employee. Under one such plan, public services would be separated into "essential" services and "nonessential" services. Bargaining impasses involving workers in essential services would be resolved by factfinding or by binding arbitration. For other services, limited strikes would be allowed. An independent commission would review each impasse situation and allow the union a certain number of hours per week to strike legally, depending upon the relative essentiality of the service involved. If a transit union was granted four strike hours per week, it might be allowed to allocate the hours to heavy commuting hours and thereby maximize the strike's impact.[5] Another plan would divide public services, and workers, into three groups. Where no strikes could be tolerated, compulsory and binding arbitration would be used to resolve impasses. Where short strikes could be tolerated, strike rights would be given to public workers subject to injunctive prevention if the public welfare was threatened. Where long strikes could be tolerated, absolutely no differences would exist in strike rights for public and private employees.[6]

Those states which now grant some strike rights for public employees do, indeed, differentiate the rights by type of public employee. The state of Alaska differentiates its public employees, and their impasse resolution procedures, into almost the same threefold classification described above. Moreover, where public sector impasse procedures exist on a de facto basis, the operation of these procedures is differentiated by the type of public employees and services involved. Strikes have been shorter and injunctions have been issued more frequently where services interrupted have been more essential.[7]

The combination plans attempt to meet the objections to the "pure" alternatives. For example, they provide strike rights and meaningful economic pressure, but only where public services are not essential. If binding arbitration is prescribed for impasses involving essential services, then the plans can provide some form of finality and pressure for impasses involving all types of public employees. Of course, third-party decision-making would occur in a significant number of public sector cases. Further acceptance may be retarded by a major deficiency of the plans: they require some entity to make more or less arbitrary distinctions of the relative essentiality of various public services.

There is a final group of alternative procedures. Several plans would artificially structure pressure on both parties to induce them to reach agreement on their own. These plans also attempt to meet objections to the "pure" procedures, and they are especially aimed at preserving decision-making power for the bargaining parties. One proposed procedure in this category is the semi-strike or nonstoppage strike. Under one possible scheme, if negotiations began and no agreement occurred after X weeks, then in each subsequent week a percentage of each worker's paycheck would be transferred into a trust fund. An equal, aggregate amount would be taken each week from the operating budget of the public employer and, perhaps, a similar percentage would be transferred to the fund from managers' salaries. If agreement occurred after a certain number of weeks, then all parties could retrieve their trust fund payments. If disagreement continued, a growing percentage of the fund would be irrevocably transferred to a predesignated charity.[8]

Therefore, economic pressure would be placed on the bargaining parties to reach an agreement. No work stoppage would occur, and the procedure could be applied to all types of public employees. On the other hand, no direct pressure would be placed on the public, which is a concerned party and one target of several of the other plans. Public pressure may be the catalyst for agreement in many instances. Another drawback is the possibility that workers would balk at participating in a procedure which dictated that they continue working full-time for a fraction of their normal earnings.

Another procedure has been labeled an income-work time gradual pressure strike. If negotiations began and no agreement occurred after X weeks, then workers would begin working fewer and fewer hours each week until they reached a predesignated minimum number of hours. Each week the workers would be paid a decreasing fraction of their regular hourly pay for the hours not worked, but normally worked.[9] Under this procedure, some interruption of services might occur, but the decreasing hours would stop before public inconvenience turned to public crisis. Crises would be much more likely under extralegal, full strikes. All three parties directly affected by bargaining would feel pressure to realize a settlement. Decision-making power would rest with the parties themselves and the basic procedure could be tailored for application to all types of public employees. Acceptability is the procedure's major drawback. A public employer may be unlikely to accept a procedure whereby he must contractually agree to make payments for time not worked. Moreover, both the semi-strike and gradual pressure strike plans have a common drawback. They are both relatively complicated and novel. Therefore, where parties wish to establish a meaningful procedure, they may hesitate to stray from more established procedures, such as binding arbitration.

The TVA-Council Approach

TVA and the Council have two different negotiated procedures for resolving interest disputes: one for wage determination and one for revisions of other substantive topics within the supplementary schedules of the *General Agreements*. The machinery for resolving impasses over wages was established by statute in 1933. The TVA Act prescribed that "laborers and mechanics" should be compensated on the basis of pay prevailing for similar work in the vicinity and with due regard being given to those rates secured through collective bargaining by representatives of employers and employees in the vicinity. The act further stipulated that "In the event any dispute arises as to what are the prevailing rates of wages, the question shall be submitted to the Secretary of Labor for determination, and his decision shall be final."[10]

TVA and the Council have incorporated the provisions of law into their labor agreements. If, upon the conclusion of any wage conference, any craft does not agree to the proposed rate of pay for any class or classes of work, the craft may appeal the dispute to the Secretary of Labor within thirty days. The wage must be based on prevailing rates for similar work in the vicinity and must take into account wage rates established through collective bargaining. Thus, the parties and the Secretary of Labor are provided two bases for reaching decisions on appropriate wage rates. The Secretary of Labor did formally exercise the authority to render final decisions on TVA wage disputes until December 1970, when he delegated this authority to the Administrator of the Work Place Standards Administration.

Since the first wage conference was held in 1935, seventeen disputes have been submitted to the office of the Secretary of Labor, sixteen from unions affiliated with the Tennessee Valley Trades and Labor Council and one from a contractor working on a TVA project. Three union appeals submitted to the Secretary were withdrawn before the Secretary rendered a decision. Of the remaining thirteen union appeals, only the first (in 1938) was decided in favor of the union. The contractor's appeal was also decided in favor of TVA's position.

The variant of final and binding arbitration utilized by TVA and the Council resembles the traditional form of binding arbitration in that no stoppage of work is involved in either proceeding, both procedures can be applied to all types of employees, and both procedures prescribe a binding decision by a third party. However, the arbitrator in the TVA proceeding is not a "true" neutral. He is directly subject to the executive and legislative will as is TVA management. Also, neither the Council nor TVA pay for the services of this arbitrator, which removes one portion of the financial barrier that parties face in invoking arbitration.

The fact that a "true" neutral is not involved in the TVA-Council procedure opens the question of whether the procedure places effective pressure on *both* parties to move toward a compromise settlement. Do the Council unions and TVA management believe that the arbitrator will be biased toward TVA's positions, especially in light of the record of decisions in management's favor? In fact, is an arbitrator in such a procedure predisposed to accept the position of his fellow public administrators? If so, TVA management would have the ability to unilaterally make the final decisions on wage issues, and bargaining over wages would be a farce. Management would not be pressured by the fear of an adverse ruling in arbitration. The Council would not be expected to utilize the procedure in such a case (unless for harassment purposes), and employee unrest aimed at the procedure would seem likely. Specifically, some incidence of strikes would be expected if trades and labor employees believed they had not other effective means of pressuring management in negotiations. Strikes outside of law and contract have become common in the public sector where effective tools of pressure are not available for use of both parties as alternatives to strikes.

Yet, the craft unions of the Trades and Labor Council do feel that the procedure places effective pressure on management to make concessions. The unions have used the threat of "going to the Secretary" in negotiations. Moreover, no impasse during negotiations has ever interfered with progress on a TVA project or resulted in a strike by any of the unions signatory to the labor agreements. The procedure has therefore proved workable and palatable to all of the concerned parties.

Another important issue arising from the use of binding arbitration in any form involves the possible effect of such a procedure in eroding the meaning of bargaining. Parties may use arbitration as a crutch to pass on hard decisions to the arbitrator and shed some of the responsibility for negotiated outcomes. Arbitration would thus have a narcotic effect on bargaining; negotiations would become a necessary charade or a tactical game to be played prior to an imposed settlement by a third party.

In the TVA-Council experience, this danger has been avoided. Seventeen appeals to an arbitrator in four decades of annual wage bargaining do not indicate the presence of a significant narcotic effect. This is especially true since the sixteen national craft unions composing the Council are not hesitant, by tradition, to use any mechanism which may significantly improve the wages and benefits of their members. Furthermore, use of the TVA procedure does not involve the financial burden of compensating the arbitrator, so Council unions should be less reluctant to use arbitration than would other unions under traditional arbitration procedures. However, the parties' application of the prevailing wage criterion may alleviate any need to be dissatisfied with TVA wage bargains.

In additon to this mechanism for resolving impasses over compensation matters, the labor contracts also contain provisions for resolving disputes over all other substantive topics contained in the supplementary schedules. Both of the *General Agreements* between TVA and its trades and labor employees state:

Rates of pay, hours of work, and other negotiated understandings established under this agreement shall be in the form of supplementary schedules attached hereto. Such schedules relating to matters other than the determination of rates of pay may be amended in joint conference called upon 30 days of notice of either party by the other after they have been in effect for one year. If, however, agreement in such joint conferences is not reached, either party may invoke the services of a mediator. The mediator shall be the joint selection of both parties from a panel of five suitable persons previously agreed to by the Council and TVA. The compensation and expenses of such mediators shall be borne jointly by TVA and the Council. A mediator so selected shall use his best efforts by mediation to bring the parties to an agreement. If such efforts to bring about an amicable settlement through mediation are unsuccessful, the said mediator shall at once endeavor to induce the Council and TVA to submit their controversy to arbitration.

If arbitration is agreed to the parties shall each appoint an arbitrator and the third arbitrator shall be designated by the mediator. The decision of the majority of said arbitrators shall be final and binding on both parties. The expenses of arbitrations shall be borne equally by TVA and the Council. If arbitration, after being proposed by the mediator or by either party, is not accepted within 10 days, the mediator shall notify both the Council and TVA to that effect and no modification or termination of any provision of any of these schedules shall be made by either party for a period of 30 days from expiration of said 10 day period.[11]

Under this procedure, mediation would be utilized as the first stage of impasse resolution. Mediation can be most effective in inducing the parties to reach agreement on their own only if they have some dread of what lies beyond mediation. Binding arbitration, and the threat of an adverse decision, lies beyond mediation in this procedure only if both parties choose to submit to arbitration. Is effective pressure placed on a party to the agreements when that party refuses to compromise on a proposed change in a supplementary schedule and that party can simply refuse to submit to arbitration? Certainly, the Panel unions, who operated for many years under a similar procedure, learned that management might stand fast by its position and refuse arbitration, and the unions would have no legal or contractual way to protest.

TVA records indicate that this procedure has never been utilized by the Council. Perhaps one reason is that the procedure may end in futility with unilateral management decision-making. Also, the subject matter covered by this procedure has not been considered as critical as the compensation subject matter covered by the other TVA-Council impasse procedure—a procedure which does provide finality other than unilateral management action. Finally, the cost of bearing one-half of the expenses of a mediator and three arbitrators does serve as a deterrent to the procedure's use.

Although disputes over any issue in the supplementary schedules are subject to either one or the other of the procedures already described, no impasse-resolution procedure is available for disputes over the content of the generalized

articles of agreement within *General Agreements.* This section of both trades
and labor contracts is limited to general principles of agreement, unlikely to be
frequently changed, and does not deal with substantive topics of wages, hours,
and working conditions. Nevertheless, the impasse resolution procedures for
the supplementary schedules are specified in the articles of agreement sections
of both contracts. Ironically, no impasse resolution procedure is available for
use in a dispute over revisions of the existing impasse resolution procedures.
No discontent has surfaced from the unions, however, because of this gap in
the coverage of procedures which provide alternatives to unilateral management
decision-making.

In the private sector and increasingly in the public sector, strikes have been
a favorite tool used by unions to gain various ends. Strikes have been used by
unions during negotiations and during the life of contracts, legally and illegally.
Although no work stoppage has occurred to date as a result of an impasse in
negotiations between TVA and the Council or Panel, work stoppages have
occurred and have exclusively involved trades and labor employees. Like most
work stoppages in the public sector, these stoppages have violated law and the
contract.

It has been pointed out that prior to 1946 neither the federal government
nor any of its agencies had statutory authority to prohibit strikes by employees.
Even without such legislative power, however, the government's implied and
indirect powers were proven effective in preventing or breaking strikes by federal employees. Major work stoppages were halted by injunctions or the threat
of injunctions. The general belief that "one cannot strike against the government" was a well-accepted dictum by most government employees, so that
strikes were not a major problem anyway.

Nevertheless, legislation directly aimed at preventing strikes by federal
employees was enacted in 1946. The Government Corporations Appropriations
Act made it illegal for appropriated funds to be used for the salaries of federal
employees who engaged in strikes or belonged to an organization which asserted
the right to strike. Federal employees engaging in strikes or belonging to organizations asserting the right to strike against the federal government would be
guilty of a felony and could be fined $1,000 and imprisoned for one year. More-
over, each government employee was required to file an affidavit with his department head declaring that he was not a member of an organization asserting
the right to strike against the government, that he would not become a member
of such an organization while in federal employment, and that he would not
engage in a strike against the United States Government.

Thus, prior to 1946, TVA employees were not specifically barred by statute
from striking. In accordance with the Government Corporations Appropriations
Act of 1946, however, TVA required each employee to sign an affidavit stipulating that he would not engage in a strike against the federal government. In
making this demand, TVA nevertheless refused to take any action against its

blue-collar employees who were members of AFL unions which asserted the right to strike. TVA did not consider these craft unions as organizations of government employees within the meaning of the Act, and therefore TVA employees could remain members of those unions.

It was not until the next year, when Congress passed the Taft-Hartley Act, that a provision concerning government employees was included in a general labor law. The provision, following the model of the Condon-Wadlin Act passed in New York in 1947, stated that:

It shall be unlawful for any individual employed by the United States or any agency thereof including wholly-owned Government corporations to participate in any strike. Any [such] individual. . . who strikes shall be discharged immediately and shall not be eligible for re-employment for three years by the United States or any agency.[12]

This provision of statutory law was superseded by the passage of Public Law 330 in 1955. This law made striking against the federal government a felony punishable by either fine or imprisonment, or both.

Long before TVA employees and other federal employees were prohibited from striking by statute, TVA had adopted a "hard line" on strikes. An important move prior to statutory prohibitions was to erect contractual barriers to work stoppages. This TVA did in its initial 1940 contract with the Trades and Labor Council. TVA and the Council agreed that neither the Council nor its member organizations would encourage or sanction employees leaving the service. In return, TVA agreed not to change any policy covered by the labor agreement except through the machinery established by the agreement. The 1951 revision of the *General Agreement* amplified and clarified this agreement with language that has been carried forward to the present labor contracts:

TVA and the Council recognize that cooperation between management and employees is necessary to accomplish the public purposes for which TVA has been established, and that such cooperation rests squarely on mutual understandings arrived at through collective bargaining. Therefore, TVA and the Council hereby agree to set up procedures to determine rates of pay in accordance with Section III of the TVA Act; hours of work and other conditions; adjustment of disputes and grievances; and to promote labor-management cooperation.

TVA on behalf of all management representatives and the Council and its member organizations, on behalf of their members, accept the responsibility to follow the procedures set forth in this agreement for the settlement of all issues and disputes. The Council and its member organizations will not permit their members to engage in work stoppages or to refuse to perform work of their craft as assigned, nor sanction their leaving the service, pending settlement of issues and disputes. TVA will not change the conditions set forth in this agreement except by methods provided herein.[13]

The quid pro quo involved in this agreement is that the Council will actually help management in preventing or halting strikes if TVA honors the agreement and if effective nonstrike alternatives are available for resolving disputes, grievances, and bargaining impasses. The Council must have felt that TVA was living up to its part of the bargain over the years, for the Council did indeed cooperate with management in ending the work stoppages which occurred.

The historical chapter on the TVA-Council experience documented the fact that infrequent work stoppages and strikes sprang up, with the most notable ones centering upon jurisdictional issues. When the federal statutory basis for dealing with strikes was laid, TVA and the Council cooperated in attempting, if possible, not to define work stoppages as "strikes." Yet, in those cases clearly definable as strikes, TVA did not hesitate to discharge strikers according to the law.

In 1952, TVA and the Council began efforts to establish a joint interview procedure by which work stoppages could be thoroughly investigated and those involved could be fairly treated. By 1962, the jointly developed policy was fully elaborated:

If on any TVA project a group of employees leaves work in violation of Article II of the General Agreement, TVA will notify the officers of the Council and the International Representative of the craft concerned. The Council and TVA each will appoint members to serve on a joint committee. This committee will go to the project and take the following action.

It will interview individually each employee who has left work. Except when requested by the committee, no business agent or steward or representative of local management shall be present while the men are interviewed.

The purpose of the interviews is to (1) determine the cause of the action, (2) determine who was primarily responsible for the action, (3) determine whether and under what condition the employees may return to work, (4) determine what statement of action shall be placed in the employees' personal history record, and (5) decide on appropriate action against individuals found to have participated in instigating the action or who failed in their responsibility to attempt to prevent the action.[14]

This procedure for dealing with work stoppages and for ruling upon disciplinary action was made a part of the written agreement in 1964. Two years later TVA and the Council agreed that no appeals procedure should be provided for the decision of the joint committee assigned to interview employees involved in work stoppages.

Although the interview procedure itself did not result in the immediate cessation of those few stoppages designated as strikes, use of the procedure led to firm handling of strikers and strike instigators. Those found guilty of violating the labor agreement were terminated and TVA did not hesitate to seek a court injunction in the one instance where such action was deemed necessary. The low incidence of strikes is certainly related to TVA's firm posture and the reinforcement elicited from the Council. Yet, the success of management's stance and

and management's ability to obtain the Council's support are attributable to the nonstrike machinery which has been jointly developed for dealing with bargaining impasses, jurisdictional disputes, and other impasses.

The TVA-Panel Approach

Like TVA and the Council, TVA and the Salary Policy Employee Panel do not specify any method for resolving a bargaining impasse over the generalized subject matter of their *Articles of Agreement.* Two methods are specified in these articles, however, for resolving disputes over the substantive subject matter of the supplementary agreements. If mediation fails, advisory arbitration is the final procedure to be used in resolving an impasse over any of the terms of supplementary agreements except basic salary rates. Thus, such important subjects as fringe benefits, classification, work scheduling, selection, and retention are subject to this procedure.

When agreement is not reached through mediation, either party may refer the matter to an arbitrator. The arbitrator is selected from a list of five neutrals composed quadrennially by the parties. The parties send written statements of their positions to the arbitrator, who may or may not hold a hearing. In a maximum of sixty days after the close of the hearing, or thirty days after the statements are received, the arbitrator renders his decision. Within thirty days after the receipt of this decision, each party informs the other of its acceptance or rejection of the arbitrator's opinion, or of its willingness to accept the opinion with certain modifications. If either party rejects the advisory award, the disputed supplementary agreement remains unchanged.

An evaluation of advisory arbitration according to our five factors is very similar to that of factfinding with recommendations. On the positive side, the procedure provides for no interruption of public services, and it can be applied to all types of employees and services. Does the procedure pressure the parties to reach an agreement on their own? If the parties consider the advisory decisions binding, then the answer is probably "yes." The parties would be pressured to reach a settlement before one was imposed from outside. But if the opinions are considered binding, then why not formalize the procedure into final and binding arbitration?

If the advisory decisions are not considered binding, then either side may simply ignore the arbitrator's opinions. Moral or public pressure may not be adequate to induce the balking party's agreement to the advised settlement. If the public employer turns down the advisory opinion, then low morale may result at least and an extralegal strike may result at most. If the union rejects the award, the government could be hindered by overproductive contractual provisions. The TVA-Panel procedure does, indeed, allow either party to ignore advisory opinions, and the potential dangers of morale and extralegal strike problems and of administrative inefficiency are not nugatory.

The procedure's specification of heavy third-party involvement, but with no guaranteed finality except management action, is a major reason that advisory arbitration has become increasingly unpalatable to public employee unions. They feel that if an advisory opinion favors management, then the recommended settlement will be adopted. Yet, if the opinion favors the union's positions, then the recommended terms may be ignored. In the latter eventuality, the union would have no further legal weapon to pressure the employer toward its own, and the arbitrator's, terms for settlement. The parties have only used the advisory arbitration procedure once since its imposition in 1972. Both parties accepted the award. Leaders of Panel unions have indicated doubt as to whether they can gain from use of such a procedure, and certainly the procedure's lack of guaranteed finality apart from unilateral management action is a significant reason for its relative nonuse by the unions.

According to the *Articles of Agreement*, if a bargaining impasse occurs over basic salary rates, and if mediation fails, then either party may invoke final-offer arbitration. If the dispute is over certain rates in a particular salary schedule, the whole schedule must nevertheless go to the arbitrator. The arbitrator decides with respect to the entire schedule whether the final position of TVA or of the Panel union shall be adopted. As has been said, this type of arbitration differs from the traditional form of binding arbitration in that it does not allow the arbitrator to fashion a compromise settlement. Each party will have its positions on all disputed issues either completely accepted or completely rejected.

To some extent, an evaluation of final-offer arbitration must be similar to the evaluation of the traditional form of final and binding arbitration. No interruption of public services is involved with the procedure, and it can be applied to all types of public employees. Unless a significant narcotic effect is operative, the procedure's existence may pressure the bargaining parties into resolving issues on their own. The procedure is realizing increased acceptability. Yet, use of the procedure means third-party decision-making over contract terms. A number of problems may result from the use of the traditional form of binding arbitration. One such problem may be labeled the "multiple issue" problem.

Suppose that a labor agreement required that all disputed issues over monetary terms of a new contract be taken to final-offer arbitration if mediation failed. Suppose that mediation did in fact fail to resolve several disputed issues. Assume that one-half of these issues were the salary rates for several salary grades, and the other issues involved fringe items, such as shift differentials and the employer's contribution to insurance premiums. All issues would be taken to the arbitrator.

The major purpose of the final-offer procedure is to pressure the parties to a compromise on all issues or, at least, very close to a compromise. Yet, in this case, what if one party took a reasonable final position on a few of the issues but an unreasonable, extreme position on the other issues? What if the other party took a reasonable final position on the latter issues but an unreasonable, extreme position on the former issues? The arbitrator would be forced to impose a much more "distorted" settlement than the parties might have developed on their own or than would have been imposed under the traditional form of binding arbitration.

A leading arbitrator did experience this problem in a final-offer case involving the City of Indianapolis and the AFSCME. He thought that a much more equitable, compromise settlement would have been reached under the traditional form of binding arbitration, because the arbitrator would not have been bound to accept one of the parties' positions on all disputed issues.[15] This is certainly a potential problem in the TVA-Panel relationship, although the scope of the danger is narrower than it might be. Since only disputes over basic salary rates can be brought to the final-offer arbitrator, multiple issues are confined to the possibility of several disputed rates within the same salary schedule.

A related danger is that, in the multi-issue case described, one of the parties would "win big" in the arbitration. Much more would be won than if the parties had reached a settlement on their own. Thus, much bitterness might be engendered to smoulder in the other party until the next bargaining period, and the future bargaining relationship might be seriously damaged.

Another serious problem has surfaced from the operation of a Michigan final-offer statute, as well as in other cases. The final-offer procedures in Michigan and in other situations provide that a hearing be held on disputed issues and that neither party be forced to state a final position until the end of the hearing. These hearings take on many of the aspects of mediation, but the danger lies in the tactical use which the parties may make of such procedures.[16] For example, the parties may negotiate, reach impasses, and go through the mediation-like hearing with a good knowledge of the other party's stated positions. If disagreement persisted, then the parties would submit their final positions to an arbitrator. However, one of the parties might submit final positons that differed drastically from the positions which it had taken throughout the negotiation process. In other words, one party might use the negotiation and mediation process simply to mislead the other party and to set the stage for a "surprise submission" designed to win the arbitrator's approval. Thus, the negotiation process would become a tactical game rather than an attempt to reach a compromise settlement on all issues.[17]

The language of the *Articles of Agreement* allows the possibility of a "surprise submission" problem. If the final-offer procedure is invoked, each party sends a brief to the arbitrator which contains a statement of the final positions of both parties. Theoretically, one party could submit a statement of its own final position which differed from the other party's understanding of the "terms" of disagreement. Presumably, if the briefs differed as to one of the party's final position, the arbitrator would be forced to accept each party's statement of its own final position. Although one of the parties could "surprise" the other in the TVA-Panel experience, both sides feel confident that neither would rely upon such a devious tactic. The relationship is too mature for either side to risk the long-run instability which might result from such a gamble for a short-run gain.

Moreover, the parties at TVA and in other bargaining settings could easily add language to their final-offer contract provisions which would eliminate the possibility of a surprise submission problem. Contracts could simply require that the mediation stage of impasse resolution would not be concluded until the mediator certified a statement of the final positions of both parties. This statement would be signed by representatives of both parties, and the arbitrator would act on the basis of this statement. All briefs would be required to be based upon this certified statement.

Finally, final-offer arbitration may exert a dangerous influence over collective bargainers. Union-management relations began in this country with small, local unions stating demands on an all-or-nothing, "meet our demands in full or we will strike" basis. Gradually, our collective bargaining process evolved whereby the parties use economic pressure, or the threat of pressure, to drive each other toward a compromise settlement. Yet, what is the orientation of negotiators facing a final-offer method of impasse resolution? Rather than striving for compromise, it may be, "How far can we stay away from a compromise solution and yet be sufficiently close to a reasonable compromise position that the arbitrator will choose our position?" If this did become the orientation of negotiators, then the institution of collective bargaining would be changed significantly and detrimentally. Also, final-offer arbitration would be exerting a powerful narcotic effect on collective bargaining, and a high incidence of usage of the procedure would surface.

With these potential drawbacks vis-à-vis the traditional form of binding arbitration, why might final-offer arbitration ever be utilized? It could be chosen because it might have one advantage over traditional binding arbitration that might outweigh its disadvantages. Final-offer arbitration might be more effective in discouraging its own use and inducing the parties to reach agreement on their own. Under the traditional form of binding arbitration, the parties realize that an arbitrator may not give them all they want on a disputed issue, but neither is the arbitrator likely to accept the other party's positions in toto. The arbitrator is likely to fashion a compromise solution on disputed issues. Seemingly, each party faces a much greater threat from a final-offer arbitrator, because he may adopt the other party's positions in toto. Each party should feel great pressure to resolve outstanding issues and avoid such a risk.

Evidence concerning the ability of final-offer arbitration to discourage its own use is still not adequate to allow a sound judgment of the procedure. The best evidence comes from the state of Michigan, which experimented with the traditional form of binding arbitration for over three years before turning to final-offer arbitration. After reviewing Michigan's final-offer experience for twenty-four months, two leading researchers in public sector arbitration reached some tentative judgments about final-offer versus traditional arbitration. James Stern and Charles Rehmus found a significant number of requests for final-offer arbitration in Michigan—around four per month. They further found that the final-offer procedure was not demonstrating any greater ability to discourage its own use than had the traditional form of binding arbitration in the three previous years.

Thus far, TVA and the Panel have had a good experience with the contract's specification of final-offer arbitration. They circumvent a serious "multiple issue" problem by utilizing the procedure only for basic salary issues and by limiting the breadth of an arbitrator's "all or nothing" ruling to a single salary schedule. Separate rulings for the union or for management must be made on each schedule. The maturity of their relationship minimizes the likelihood of a "surprise submission" problem. Most importantly, the parties have avoided use of the procedure in the annual wage negotiations which have occurred since the procedure was instituted. We can only speculate as to whether the same would have been true under traditional arbitration, but we do know that both sides have felt pressured by a procedure through which they could lose on all of their final positions in a salary schedule. The parties' experience with the procedure has been too short for solid judgments, but so far the TVA-Panel experience has shown that the advantage of final-offer arbitration can outweigh its drawbacks.

The topic of work stoppages has simply not been an important one in the bargaining relationship between TVA and the Panel. No stoppages have occurred. Federal law, of course, prohibits strikes by the employees represented by the Panel, but management has never felt the need to push for contract language which would reinforce the statutory strike ban. Probably the greatest danger of extralegal work stoppages was present in the late sixties and early seventies, until the institution of final-offer arbitration for wage disputes in 1972. The procedure provided finality other than unilateral management action for resolving disputes over the most vital subject matter of the labor contract. It bolstered the clout and self-esteem of the Panel unions, and it helped dissipate rising frustration which may eventually have boiled over into illegal strike activity.

Collective Bargaining without the Right to Strike?

Genuine collective bargaining cannot exist unless both union and management negotiate in an environment of economic or other significant pressure. If a bargaining relationship is an adversary relationship, as we assume to be true, then neither party can be expected to compromise or give up anything to the other unless it feels pressured to do so. Traditionally, the threat or existence of a strike has served to pressure the parties to compromise and reach agreement, for failure to reach agreement meant costs to both sides. Strikes have been officially forbidden and have rarely occurred at TVA; yet, genuine collective bargaining has taken place. How has this been possible?

The greatest part of the explanation is that the prevailing rate method of wage determination and machinery for the binding arbitration of wage disputes join together to replace strikes as the pressure mechanism necessary for real collective bargaining. The weight of law, contract, and tradition pressure the parties to bargain within the dictates of the prevailing rate data which they collect. Because they analyze the raw data similarly, real limits are placed upon the positions which they can take and still claim that the positions are grounded in the data. To traverse these limits and violate the spirit of the prevailing rate principle is to invite an unknown but probably aggressive response from the other side. The unions might respond with work stoppages; management might respond with various tactics aimed at destroying the unions.

Movement away from the limits provided by the data would not proceed this far in the short run, however, for the labor contracts specify use of the prevailing rate criterion, and an arbitrator called into the labor dispute would be forced to rule against the party abandoning the use of prevailing rate data in particular negotiations. In other words, the provision for binding arbitration of one form or another in all the labor contracts serves as an immediate and forceful check to the unilateral abandonment of the prevailing rate criterion. At the same time, binding arbitration provides the pressure which prompts the parties to choose a wage rate within the limits provided by the data. If the parties do not make this decision, they face the uncertainty of an umpire's interpretation of what wage rate is justified by the data for particular classes of work.

The prevailing rate principle is carried over into the determination of fringe benefits, but binding arbitration is not mandatory for a nonwage dispute in either relationship. It would seem that management is not under direct and significant pressure to compromise over nonwage issues, but in fact management does feel pressure to bargain in good faith. Nothing assures TVA that it will not be faced with strikes if it takes advantage of the lack of binding arbitration over some subject matter. Especially its craft unions know how to use the strike weapon. Blue-collar, white-collar, and professional employees have increasingly turned to the use of this weapon in the public sector. Its use by TVA employees could have a significant adverse effect upon the people and the economy of the Tennessee Valley. Thus, management cannot and does not ignore the implicit threat of strikes which it faces if it follows an unreasonable course of intransigence. Management does feel this pressure in bargaining over both wage and nonwage issues.

Another form of implicit pressure which management faces as it deals with its unions is political pressure. Organized labor has from the beginning of TVA's history (and even prior to its creation) been either an effective or a potentially effective influence over Congress on matters relating to programs and policies of TVA. Fifteen of the sixteen Council members and three of the five Panel members are affiliated with the AFL-CIO. These unions have opened the door to the use of a lobbying vehicle of considerable potency. The active support of the AFL-CIO has been particularly important to TVA's continuing efforts to remain relatively independent from rules of the Civil Service Commission (particularly with regard to hourly employees) and from other potential controls from Washington. The possible loss of such support when it is needed, or the wrong kind of support, could be of significant detriment to TVA's interests. Political pressure is therefore a tool which the unions can use in dealing with TVA over all issues. It is another element in the pressure environment which affects all sides in the TVA bargaining relationships—an environment that allows genuine collective bargaining without a statutory or contractual right to strike.

Notes

1. Michael L. Brookshire and J. Fred Holly, "Resolving Bargaining Impasses Through Gradual Pressure Strikes," *Labor Law Journal* (October 1973), p. 663.

2. Eva Robbins, "Some Comparisons of Mediation in the Public and Private Sector," *Collective Bargaining in Government* (Englewood Cliffs, New Jersey: Prentice-Hall, Inc., 1972), pp. 323-329.

3. Harold Davey, "The Use of Neutrals in the Public Sector," *Labor Law Journal* (August 1969), pp. 529-537.

4. Albert Shanker, "Why Teachers Need the Right to Strike," *Monthly Labor Review* (September 1973), pp. 48-51.

5. H. L. Fusilier and Lawrence L. Steinmetz, "Public Employee Strikes: An Operational Solution," *Collective Bargaining in Government* (Englewood Cliffs, New Jersey: Prentice-Hall, Inc., 1972), pp. 308-312.

6. Jack Stieber, "A New Approach to Strikes in Public Employment," *Collective Bargaining in Government* (Englewood Cliffs, New Jersey: Prentice-Hall, Inc., 1972), pp. 296-301.

7. John F. Burton, Jr., and Charles Krider, "The Role and Consequences of Strikes by Public Employees," *Collective Bargaining in Government* (Englewood Cliffs, New Jersey: Prentice-Hall, Inc., 1972), pp. 274-288.

8. See Fusilier and Steinmetz, "Public Employee Strikes: An Operational Solution," pp. 308-312.

9. Brookshire and Holly, "Resolving Bargaining Impasses Through Gradual Pressure Strikes," pp. 662-670.

10. 48 Stat. 58, Public Law No. 17, 73rd Congress, Section 3, p. 3.

11. *General Agreement Between the Tennessee Valley Authority and the Trades and Labor Council, Covering Annual and Hourly Operating and Maintenance Employment,* revised April 15, 1974, Article XIV, pp. 9-10; and *General Agreement Between the Tennessee Valley Authority and the Trades and Labor Council, Covering Construction Employment,* revised April 15, 1974, Article XII, pp. 8-9.

12. 61 Stat. 136, Public Law No. 201, 80th Congress, Section 305.

13. Tennessee Valley Authority and Tennessee Valley Trades and Labor Council, *General Agreement,* effective August 6, 1940, revised July 1, 1951, Article II, pp. 2-3.

14. The Tennessee Valley Authority and the Tennessee Valley Trades and Labor Council, "Understanding on Interview Procedure," approved February 27, 1962.

15. Fred Whitney, "Final-Offer Arbitration: The Indianapolis Experience," *Monthly Labor Review* (May 1973), pp. 20-25.

16. Charles M. Rehmus, "Is A 'Final Offer' Ever Final?" *Monthly Labor Review* (September 1974), pp. 43-45.

17. Ibid.

8

Other Substantive Issues

In addition to pay determination, impasse resolution, and work stoppages, several other substantive issues of collective bargaining between TVA and the Council and between TVA and the Panel are important. This chapter examines how the parties administer their collective bargaining agreements and handle employee grievances, the way in which they provide for union security, and the system they have established and maintained for distinct cooperative programs which operate alongside their formal collective bargaining relationships.

Contract Administration

Once the marriage between an employer and a union is consummated by the signing of the collective bargaining agreement, the parties begin the trials of a day-to-day working relationship. The contract provides the framework under which the parties seek to maintain a harmonious relationship, but questions of interpretation and application of the terms of the contract almost always arise.

Unions and managements provide specific machinery to adjust or attempt to resolve the inevitable complaints and problems that arise in the employment environment. This machinery is generally in the form of a grievance adjustment procedure which culminates with a final and binding decision made by an impartial third party. Both the employer and the union, as well as the employees, have much to gain by incorporating such a procedure into the collective bargaining agreement. More importantly, the public benefits by the existence of such machinery, since complaints and grievances can be resolved peacefully without undue hardship to the consumer. This consumer protection is, of course, particularly important in the public sector, where services are expected to be uninterrupted.

The TVA salary policy contract and trades and labor contracts have formalized grievance adjustment procedures which culminate in binding arbitration. The procedures are essentially the same, and neither has been changed significantly in the last twenty-five years. Both grievance adjustment procedures incorporate typical four-step appeal routes. A grievant initiates the adjustment machinery by filing his complaint with the supervisor responsible for the matter under dispute. If a solution cannot be agreed upon at this first step, an appeal can then be made to the director of the division in which the grievant works. At this level either the grievant (union representative or employee) or the division director can

195

request that a formal hearing be held to obtain the facts and circumstances of the particular grievance. A TVA management representative is then charged with conducting an in-house hearing, and a verbatim transcript of the hearing proceedings constitutes the record upon which a decision will be made to resolve the case.

If the grievance remains unsettled after the division director makes his decision, the case can be appealed to the Manager of Union-Management Relations (MUMR), who has overall TVA responsibility for union-management relations. The next and final route of appeal is to arbitration. Neither the individual grievant nor his union representative can effect an appeal to arbitration. Only the two federations of unions, the Council or the Panel, can submit a grievance to the final step. If either central body is not satisfied with the decision rendered by the MUMR, it may submit the grievance to an "impartial referee," who is selected from a panel of five persons previously designated jointly by TVA and the central organizations of unions. The arbitrator who is serving in a particular case may hold a hearing, but he generally makes the decision based on the record established during the first three steps of the procedure and primarily relies upon the record of the hearing generated at the second step. Both parties share the expenses of arbitrations.

Because TVA is a federal agency covered by the Veteran's Preference Act, employees may, under certain circumstances, appeal complaints and grievances to the Civil Service Commission (CSC), which has responsibility for administering the Act. Adverse actions, disciplinary suspensions for more than thirty days, and terminations for cause are all appealable to the CSC under Veteran's Preference if the employee has one year or more of current, continuous TVA service and if he is a veteran. When an employee makes an appeal under the commission's procedure, any further consideration of his complaint under the negotiated procedures is discontinued.

In addition to the CSC's appeals procedures, TVA employees may also file complaints of discrimination because of age, race, color, religion, sex, or national origin, under statutory procedures designed to cover such grievances. Moreover, such complaints can be processed under either the grievance procedure or the Equal Employment Opportunity procedure or under both procedures simultaneously.[1] Thus, an employee could conceivably have a grievance processed through arbitration and lose and then appeal the same issue to the courts and have his grievance sustained. Such an event could play havoc with the integrity of the negotiated grievance procedures.

Beginning in 1974, TVA management attempted to obtain agreement from both the Council and Panel to modify their respective contracts by providing that if an employee elects to pursue a statutory remedy for a discrimination claim, he may not, under the contracts, pursue a grievance based on the same discrimination claim. The Panel and Council did recently agree to a revision in their grievance procedures which discontinues the use of the negotiated procedure when a salary policy employee uses any other complaint procedure, for example, either the CSC or the Equal Employment Opportunity procedures. These contract modifications will help preserve the credibility of the grievance-arbitration machinery.

Both the salary policy and trades and labor grievance procedures are extremely broad in scope. If any employee covered by either contract believes he has been treated unfairly by his supervisor, he can file a grievance. When an employee disagrees with his supervisor as to the application of a TVA policy, he may also file a grievance under the contract applicable to him. The scope of the grievance procedures is limited only by the restrictions against employees filing grievances for the purpose of changing an established policy, procedure, or standard. Such changes are to be made through formal negotiations.

Grievances can be filed either personally by the employee or by the employee's union representative. Employees are not permitted to have attorneys represent them in a grievance under the negotiated procedures; if they use a representative, it must be a union representative. Furthermore, employees processing grievances personally have no appeal rights to arbitration. Personally filed appeals ultimately are decided by the Manager of Union-Management Relations. Under the trades and labor procedure, if an employee appeals a grievance through his local union representative, rather than through the international representative of his union, then the Manager's decision is also considered final and appeal to arbitration is disallowed.

Grievance Statistics and Analysis

The Council and TVA first negotiated their four-step grievance procedure, culminating in binding arbitration, in 1940. From this time until 1960, only eight grievances were appealed to arbitration by the Council. None were sustained by the referee. Such a small number of arbitrations is particularly significant in view of the fact that trades and labor employment for this twenty-year period averaged about 12,000 employees each year. It should be pointed out, however, that negotiated grievance procedures were not common in the construction industry during this period of time.

During the first two years of the 1960s, four trades and labor grievances were appealed to an outside third party for final resolution. Three appeals were made to arbitration from 1962 through 1971—a period of even higher levels of trades and labor employment as compared with the previous twenty-year period. Three appeals to arbitration were made in 1972, and four grievances were taken to arbitration in 1973. Not until 1972 did an impartial referee rule against TVA's decision in a trades and labor grievance. The types of issues appealed to the trades and labor grievance adjustment procedure include such management actions as suspensions, terminations for cause, warning letters, and the application of overtime provisions. Disciplinary actions have been by far the most numerous type of issues grieved, with terminations for cause ranking first.

Why is it that, during the last thirty years, only nineteen trades and labor grievances have been appealed to arbitration? One obvious reason is that no single employee or no single union bargaining representative can effect an appeal to arbitration; only the Council itself can appeal grievances to the fourth step. The Council has the opportunity to screen out frivolous or unmeritorious grievances and to appeal only those considered to have sound bases. The mere mechanics of getting the Council members together and obtaining agreement to appeal to arbitration also reduces the number of arbitrations.

Another reason that so few cases have been appealed to arbitration is the underlying management philosophy regarding employee complaints and grievances. TVA management has traditionally believed that opening the grievance procedure to practically any complaint concerning the employment relationship permits the use of the grievance procedure as both a means of communication and a method of resolving employee dissatisfactions. TVA management has adopted a "clinical" approach to handling grievances.[2] The negotiated procedure emphasizes thorough investigation and treatment of the root causes of employee complaints by encouraging the parties to discover the underlying causes of grievances and then to resolve these grievances peacefully without resorting to arbitration.

A former General Manager of TVA explained what he considered to be the primary purpose of a grievance adjustment procedure:

(1) To assure employees a way in which they can get their complaints considered rapidly, fairly, and without reprisal; (2) to encourage the employee to express himself about how the conditions of work affect him as an employee; (3) to get better understanding of policies, practices, and procedures which affect employees; (4) to instill a measure of confidence in employees that actions are taken in accord with policies; (5) to provide a check on how policies are carried out by management; and (6) to give supervisors a greater sense of responsibility in their dealings with employees.[3]

The adoption by top management of such a philosophy has encouraged the settlement of grievances prior to arbitration. Although no data are available on the number of grievance cases settled at the first step, information on those settled at the second and third stages makes it clear that the majority of trades and labor grievances are settled at the lower levels of the procedure. Some TVA managers will sustain a grievance before it is appealed to the second step unless the supervisor's action is clearly supportable and in accordance with negotiated policy and procedures.

The machinery for holding hearings and gathering the facts of a particular case at the second step of the procedure is indicative of the attempts to settle grievances within TVA. At this level a verbatim transcript of a formal hearing on the appeal is made to assure a complete record of the grievance. Both the division director and the Manager of Union-Management Relations base their decisions upon that record. Such a situation encourages both parties to concentrate on making a complete and factual record early in the grievance adjustment process.

A final, possible reason that so few cases have been appealed to arbitration is that the Council may have screened out grievances which were *not* frivolous. The Council wields considerable power over rank and file members, as well as over local business representatives, who generally handle employee grievances at the early stages of the procedure. International representatives on the Council are insulated to some degree from rank and file pressures and may be less likely to be in political danger if they refuse to appeal a grievance with some merit to arbitration. Also, the employment relationship in the construction industry within TVA, where most of the trades and labor employees work, is temporary in nature, and rank and file members traditionally have been more reluctant to file grievances.

On the salary policy level, a four-step grievance procedure was included in the 1950 *Articles of Agreement* between TVA and the Salary Policy Employee Panel. In no single year between 1950 and 1965 did the number of salary policy grievances settled at the second step or above exceed ten. Since the mid-sixties, a definite upward trend has occurred in the number of white-collar grievances settled at the division-director level and above. The figures on grievance appeals which appear in table 8-1 include the few appeals made to the CSC under the Veteran's Preference Act.

Since the mid-fifties, an increasing percentage of all grievance appeals to the division-director level have been taken beyond this second step of the procedure. Moreover, an upward trend is evident in the percentage of total grievance appeals taken to an impartial referee. This increase has been especially notable since the mid-sixties, with the percentage climbing from under 10 percent in 1966 to around 30 percent in 1972 and 1973.

A major reason for these trends in grievance appeals was the change in attitude by union members and union leaders, which was discussed in chapter 3. During the sixties, both white-collar and professional employees became less reluctant to grieve. At the same time, the leadership of Panel unions became more inclined and better prepared to press grievances toward a satisfactory solution.

Moreover, in the years after 1960, the Panel unions developed a good record of pursuing grievances successfully, and this development certainly bolstered their inclination to appeal more grievances. During most of the years after 1960, Panel unions gained a reversal or, in the least, some modification of management actions in the majority of grievance appeals. Their record in pursuing grievances is adequate to support the thesis that when a Panel union decides to challenge and appeal an action by management, there is likely to be some substance to the

Table 8-1
Number of Grievances by Salary Policy
Employees Settled at the Division-Director
Level or Above, 1950-1975

Year	Number of Grievances
1950	5
1951	5
1952	5
1953	2
1954	7
1955	7
1956	9
1957	7
1958	5
1959	10
1960	6
1961	7
1962	6
1963	8
1964	7
1965	7
1966	11
1967	11
1968	7
1969	19
1970	19
1971	26
1972	34
1973	28
1974	38
1975	22

Source: TVA Memoranda, "Grievances of Salary
Policy Employees under Supplementary Agreement
S-11," Chief, Employee Relations Branch to Heads of
Offices and Divisions.

union's complaint. Thus, the union is likely to pursue the grievance all the way
through the appeals process, and the union has a reasonable probability of win-
ning some reversal or modification of management action. Of course, the unions'
relative success has also been attributable to the increasing experience and expertise of union leaders in handling grievances.

The majority of salary policy grievances filed since 1960 have primarily
involved four different issues: job classification, selections for higher level positions, terminations, and performance evaluations. By far the largest percentage
of total grievances has occurred over questions of classifications and selections.
In all but two years since 1965, the majority of grievances appealed above the
first step have involved either a classification or selection complaint.

Why the relatively large number of grievances over classification matters?

One part of the explanation is that classification decisions have a major impact upon the employee's status and pay. Therefore, employees have much to gain if they can improve their classification status through the grievance procedure.

Moreover, the classification system is quite "open" at TVA to both employees and their unions. It is open in the sense that job descriptions are explicit and available for inspection, as are the standards for allocating positions to grades. Thus employees and their representatives can easily compare jobs in different grades and analyze the allocation of jobs to particular grades. The access of employees to this information may lead them to push their union into a greater number of grievances than the union might have pursued otherwise. To the extent that a relatively large number of grievances are filed because of the availability of information, the grievances strengthen the health of management-employee relations. The classification grievances serve as a check on shortcomings and inequities in the classification system, and they lead to management action on the legitimate complaints of employees.

Finally, many classification grievances may have occurred since the late sixties because serious flaws existed in the classification system. A management study group underscored many weaknesses in the system which was used through the early seventies. For example, the use of broad, narrative standards instead of more quantifiable criteria for allocating positions to grades was not considered to be effective. The group also found that no systematic means was operative for checking and rechecking the validity of the system. The recommendations of this group may lead to the use of a more objective, quantitative factor-ranking system for classification; the use of such a system may, in turn, reduce the number of classification grievances.

Why the relatively large number of grievances in the area of selection? Probably the main reason is the nature of the contract language which governs the selection of salary policy employees for promotion and transfer:

Selection for promotion or transfer . . . is made on the basis of merit and efficiency; among employees who are relatively equal in merit and efficiency, the employee with the most TVA service is selected.[4]

The selection of employees on the basis of what is, in effect, a "relative ability" seniority clause obviously involves subjectivity. It is, therefore, vulnerable to second-guessing and to challenge via the grievance procedure. The probability is high, for example, that a senior employee will grieve if a promotion is given to a junior employee working in a similar position in his department. The senior employee will tend to question management's judgment that the junior employee rates higher in merit and efficiency. Why is the agreement not amended to make criteria for selection more objective and specific? Normally, the answer in both the public and private sectors is that the parties simply cannot agree on more specific contract language or more objective and specific criteria. They are willing to let arbitrators resolve selection issues in the light of past practice and the circumstances of particular cases.

Other possible reasons for the relatively high number of selection grievances are similar to the reasons for classification grievances. Selection decisions are certainly important to employees, as they may affect both status and pay. Furthermore, the selection process is also very open at TVA, and the availability of information may contribute to the number of grievances. Most vacant positions in bargaining units represented by Panel unions must be announced to employees, and these announcements are given adequate publicity and are circulated to reasonably broad groupings of employees. Therefore, many employees are likely to apply for positions, and many must be rejected. Yet, grievances that result from the adequacy of information need not be considered as indicators of problems in management-employee relations. Indeed, the grievances may result even though selection procedures are generally sound.

Problem Areas

One of the most unique features of both the trades and labor and salary policy grievance procedures involves the in-house hearings conducted at the second step. Such an arrangement has served the parties well for many years, as a majority of grievances have been settled within TVA. Management, however, had taken a rather paternalistic approach in handling grievances, and the Director of Personnel traditionally has been considered as something of an impartial neutral in his role as TVA's final decision-maker in grievances. More recently, TVA unions, particularly the Panel unions, have matured, grown more independent, and become better able to aggressively represent employees. Thus, the Director of Personnel and the Manager of Union-Management Relations now consider themselves more as arms of management than as protectors of the employees.[5] The MUMR still overturns second-level management decisions on grievances, but these reversals involve only the more obvious management violations of policy. With this kind of changing philosophy, the parties are reexamining the second-step hearing procedure and considering other alternatives, such as the more generally accepted practice of holding the hearing at the arbitrator's level rather than at the second level. Panel unions have made such a proposal in formal negotiations.

A primary weakness of holding grievance hearings in-house is that, when the case is appealed to arbitration, the arbitrator neither has the opportunity to observe firsthand the witnesses nor to ask questions which he considers appropriate. Such an opportunity is especially important in cases involving disciplinary action or termination and in cases involving complex issues or conflicting testimony. Moreover, the grievance hearings in TVA are conducted by management representatives who are typically untrained in the art of holding grievance hearings, who are unfamiliar with labor arbitration in general, and who either fail to ask important questions or ask wrong questions that are inappropriate or tend to strengthen one side's position. The process is also costly to management in terms of time and record documentation. Generation of a factual record at an early stage of the grievance procedure is, of course, desirable, but it could be gathered in a manner other than through a formal hearing. Also, a hearing record is not particularly necessary for every grievance appealed to the second step. But even more importantly, a second step hearing tends to formalize and finalize the parties' position at a early stage and thus make compromises more difficult.

Another possible weakness of the TVA grievance procedures is the requirement that only the Panel or Council can appeal grievances to arbitration. Historically, this arrangement was established as one means of binding several unions together to make a more effective and responsible structure for collective bargaining. Today, this aspect of the grievance procedure has the potential of creating exactly the opposite result. This possibility has already surfaced on the salary policy level because both the TVAEA and the OPEIU have used the procedure as a club to prevent the other from taking an important grievance to arbitration. Each has done so in order to seek concessions or cooperation on various issues from the other. If the grievance procedure is to be truly clinical in pinpointing trouble spots and if it is to act as an effective check upon unfair management action, each duly recognized bargaining representative should have the autonomy of carrying the grievances of those whom he represents to arbitration.

A third problem area in the grievance procedures is the length of time consumed by the grievance process. The negotiated procedures place maximum time limits on the completion of each stage of the grievance procedure. However, the length of time from the beginning of the first step to the appeal to an impartial referee may be as long as 155 days—or even longer if the parties agree to waive certain time limits. Then, of course, six months or more may elapse before the referee is selected and renders a decision.

The trades and labor agreements have been revised to provide a special expedited procedure for handling grievances arising from letters of warning or reprimand which are effective for six months or less. No hearings are permitted in such appeals, and the employee (or his representative) must present his case in writing to the division director. This procedure has saved a considerable amount of time in processing grievances over these matters.

Another problem has arisen over the submission of grievances to arbitration. The issue to be decided by the arbitrator is generally stated as "whether the decision of the MUMR was proper." Yet, the specific issue decided by the Manager is usually not spelled out for the arbitrator, and often neither party has clearly and concisely stated the particular grievance issue to be decided. A jointly agreed to submission, stating the precise issue to be decided by the arbitrator, would benefit both parties in better insuring that the arbitrator's decision does not exceed mutually agreed upon parameters. If the parties failed to agree on the exact issue or question to be decided through arbitration, the parties could each frame the issue in their own terms and let the arbitrator formulate the issue.

The lack of established procedures for trades and labor employees to grieve decisions applicable to the salary policy agreement also causes problems. If, for example, a trades and labor employee applies for an announced salary policy vacancy and is not selected, he has no route of appeal. He cannot appeal under the blue-collar contract because the action complained about resulted from an application of the salary policy agreement, and he cannot appeal under the white-collar contract because he is not covered by the terms of that agreement. The same problem occurs when a salary policy employee who is represented by a Panel union is turned down for a trades and labor position or for a management position outside of the bargaining units. No channel is provided for such appeals, and this fact constitutes a gap in the capability of grievance adjustment to air employee dissatisfaction and to give these complaints meaningful consideration.

Union Security

Union security contract provisions are those which enhance the prestige or status of a union and make it easier for a union to gain members or collect dues. The primary objectives of such provisions include worker encouragement to join a union, protection of union members and leaders against employer discrimination, and prevention of the defection of employees from a union. Traditional union security devices have ranged from the closed shop, which prevents the hire of nonunion members, to the agency shop, which forces employees to at least pay some fee to a union after some employment period. Union shop and dues checkoff provisions are quite common and maintenance of membership provisions, which prevent union members from terminating their membership during some stated time period, have recently been utilized in some public sector settings.

Next to the strike issue, union security is probably the most controversial subject in public sector labor relations. Many claim that the traditional public sector rule basing appointments and promotions on the relative merit and efficiency of individuals is incompatible with the operation of union security devices. The TVA Act required TVA to make appointments and promotions on the basis of merit and efficiency. The Act forbade political considerations in such decisions but it did not elaborate further. With this statutory direction, TVA has taken the stance that it cannot officially agree with a labor organization to adopt any of the traditional union security devices, except the dues checkoff. However, management has worked with its labor organizations in formulating a unique approach to the union security issue.

Union security measures for trades and labor employees in TVA evolved over a period of twenty years from that of a position of management neutrality regarding union membership to a more prolabor position of including unionism as one factor to be considered in appraising the relative fitness of employees in selections and promotions and, finally, to a policy of actually encouraging employees to become and to remain union members. The latter position was based on the supposition that union membership per se is a positive factor of merit and efficiency and that it should be so considered in appraising the relative fitness of candidates for TVA appointments and for promotions. Such a philosophy was, and is, in keeping with TVA's general position to adopt as prounion a policy as possible without violating applicable laws.

The present union security device incorporated in the TVA-Council agreements mandates that union membership be a positive factor in appraising relative merit and efficiency and that employees be encouraged to become and to remain members of the appropriate union. Moreover, the contracts stipulate that union members are selected and retained in preference to qualified nonunion applicants for TVA employment. Thus, if two qualified trades and labor candidates apply for a TVA vacancy and only one of them is a member of a union affiliated with the Council, the union member receives employment preference over the nonunion member. The rationale upon which this policy is based appears in the official TVA policy statement on union relations:

The success of TVA's program depends to a large degree on mutual understanding and unity of purpose among employees and between employees and management. Responsible unions, recognized by TVA as exclusive representatives of employees in defined bargaining units and working together through the Salary Policy Employee Panel and the Tennessee Valley Trades and Labor Council, provide an orderly and effective means through which mutual understanding and unity of purpose can be achieved. Through them, employees participate in forming administrative and personnel policies and rules under which they work and in increasing interest, initiative, and cooperative effort on behalf of the TVA program. For these reasons, TVA encourages employees represented by these unions to become and remain members of such unions; and TVA negotiates agreements with the Salary Policy Employee Panel and the Tennessee Valley Trades and Labor Council and otherwise deals with them and their constituent unions in a manner which recognizes their contribution, and the contribution of the employees they represent, to the TVA program.[6]

The language of the labor agreement is clear in that the employment of nonunion applicants is not prohibited. No specific provision requires that employees who do not become or remain members of the appropriate unions must be terminated. In actual practice, however, TVA gives the appearance of operating a closed shop in recruiting and employing persons for certain crafts in construction work and, to a lesser extent, for temporary operating and maintenance work. Local building and construction unions are the primary, and in some cases the exclusive, recruitment source for TVA trades and labor construction employment. In view of the lack of qualified skilled craftsmen in the Tennessee Valley area and the increasingly high demand for such services, however, TVA is beginning to rely more on other recruitment sources.

The importance to the unions of hiring only union members and the importance to TVA of being able to employ the required manpower regardless of the recruitment source can be highlighted by examining a work stoppage which occurred at TVA's Browns Ferry Nuclear Plant construction project in September 1973. The local union of the United Association of Journeymen and Apprentices of the Plumbing and Pipe Fitting Industry (UA), having jurisdiction over the project, could not furnish sufficient qualified steamfitters to TVA, so TVA decided to employ two "nonunion" candidates.[7] When TVA employed these individuals, the UA local called its members off the job. The project closed operations for several days before the international representative of the UA took jurisdiction from the local union. TVA ultimately terminated most local union members for engaging in a work stoppage—it was not designated a strike. Construction activities resumed shortly thereafter, but several hundred local UA members filed unfair labor practice charges against TVA under Executive Order 11491, as amended. The complaint alleged that TVA discriminated against employees on the basis of union membership because nonlocal members were not terminated. TVA maintained that, since local union members were responsible for the work stoppage, the nonlocals—transfers working out of the UA local— need not be terminated. The case was settled between TVA and the attorney representing the UA local members without a final decision from the Department of Labor.[8]

There are, of course, several advantages to relying on unions as a primary, or even exclusive, recruitment source. The union is a ready and easily accessible source of skilled manpower, and by hiring only union members, a contractor or firm helps assure peaceful union relations. Such a practice is prevalent in unionized construction, in spite of the illegality of the closed shop arrangement, and conformance with the practice has contributed to labor peace. The major disadvantages of relying exclusively on unions as recruitment sources are the inability to recruit from other sources when the union is unable or unwilling to furnish qualified manpower, the possible interference with rights of nonunion candidates who are equally or better qualified than union members, and the retardation of progress in employing minorities who have historically been excluded from construction craft unions.

The union security device which is legally available in the construction industry under the terms of the Landrum-Griffen Act of 1959—requiring union membership after seven days of employment—appears to be a realistic alternative to the union security arrangement professed, and to the one practiced, by TVA and the Council. If such an arrangement is considered in violation of the TVA Act's requirement to make appointments on the basis of merit and efficiency, then so should the application of the existing TVA-Council agreement, which gives preference to union members in appointments. The Landrum-Griffin arrangement would still preclude the possibility of some workers receiving the benefits of unionism without bearing the risks and obligations of union activities, it would provide stability and security to the unions, it would reduce the problems of low worker morale and dissatisfaction between union and nonunion workers, and it would provide the employer with more flexibility in recruiting needed manpower. Moreover, the merit-and-efficiency principle can more easily be maintained under this arrangement and potential for unfair, discriminatory hiring can be reduced. Such an arrangement could, however, lessen the dependency of rank and file members on their union in locating employment opportunities, and it would not be readily embraced by members of the Council.

Unlike the blue-collar agreement, the provisions of union security applicable to the salary policy employees do not pertain to giving preference to union members in appointments. Salary policy employees are not members of the bargaining units prior to employment, and they do not rely on unions to seek employment for them. Preference to white-collar union members is applicable with regard to selections for promotions, transfer, and retention in TVA. Since 1954, salary policy employees who have joined and participated in the appropriate union have been given preference in selections over other employees who are not members of or participants in a union. Specifically, the TVA-Panel contract states that union membership and participation "are among the positive factors of merit and efficiency to be considered in selecting employees for promotion, transfer, and retention."[9]

The practical effect of such a provision is that nearly 90 percent of all non-management, salary policy employees are members of unions affiliated with the Salary Policy Employee Panel. Obviously, such a policy interferes with the right of employees to refrain from joining a labor organization, and this fact could be a genuine concern among white-collar employees—perhaps more so than among the trades and labor employees. Moreover, it would be exceedingly difficult to demonstrate conclusively that union membership and/or union participation is related to job performance or to valid qualification requirements.

An arrangement where no employee has to join or remain a member of the union as a condition of employment, but rather pays a service fee to the certified majority representative, may be a more viable form of union security for salary policy employees. This device, the agency shop, would compensate the union for acting as the employee's agent in collective bargaining and in the administration of the contract. The agency shop should also be compatible with the merit-and-efficiency principle, since the employer retains the right to appoint or to make selections for promotion without regard to union membership.

Union and Management Cooperative Programs

Formalized programs designed to promote cooperation between management, supervisors, and employees, through unions representing TVA employees, were envisioned early in TVA's history. The Board of Directors stated in the 1935 *Employee Relationship Policy* that they looked forward to the establishment of joint conferences between management and union representatives for the purpose of promoting employee-management cooperation. Such a cooperative program was, and continues to be, viewed as a mechanism to supplement and to facilitate a formal collective bargaining relationship. It has not been considered a mechanism to compete with unions or to replace collective bargaining.

Since the early 1940s, joint groups of union and management representatives have met outside the formal collective bargaining arena for the purposes of establishing cooperation and maintaining harmonious employee-employer relations. These groups are comprised of supervisors, other management representatives, bargaining unit employees, and employee representatives. Trades and labor employees and salary policy employees have separate, formalized cooperative programs with TVA management. The groups of management and non-management employees and division representatives function primarily at the plant, local project, and division levels. Recently, several trades and labor and salary policy groups have joined to form cooperative groups.

Two TVA-union organizations give overall direction to the cooperative programs. The trades and labor program is spearheaded by the Central Joint Cooperative Committee (CJCC), and the salary policy program is directed by the Central Joint Cooperative Conference (CJCCF). Both central organizations coordinate and provide guidance to the activities of a number of different local committees (trades and labor) and local conferences (salary policy) established at the various plants and divisions. The central bodies also act upon matters of TVA-wide interest with respect to their various constituencies.

The Central Joint Cooperative Committee is made up of the Executive Board of the Tennessee Valley Trades and Labor Council and representatives of top management of TVA. Management representatives include several top officials of the major TVA organizations. The manager of Union-Management Relations serves as the management cochairman, and the president of the Council serves in a similar capacity for employees. Although this committee of top union and management officials meets only periodically throughout the year, it serves as a continuing source of leadership for the entire trades and labor cooperative relationship. The specific responsibilities of the committee are defined in the labor agreements and include developing basic guidelines for the employee-management program, promoting the formation of local committees throughout the Valley, reviewing the progress of the local committees, acting on any suggestions from local groups, and sponsoring programs to provide information of general interest to employees.

The Central Joint Cooperative Conference has seven employee representatives designated by the Panel—two each from the TVAEA and OPEIU and one each from the three smaller unions. An equal number of management officials represents TVA. One employee representative, usually not the Secretary of the Panel, is designated as one co-chairman, and the Manager of Union-Management Relations is the other co-chairman. The major responsibilities of the CJCCF are similar to those of the Committee.

A representative from the Division of Personnel provides continuing assistance in the administration of the overall cooperative programs for salary policy and for trades and labor employees and serves as secretary of both the CJCCF and CJCC. All decisions made by either a committee or a conference must be reached by consensus. No procedures exist for resolving disputes or disagreements.

Trades and labor and salary policy employees actively participate in the cooperative programs through local organizations, not through the central joint committee or conference. Local cooperative committees of management and of trades and labor employees form the heart of the cooperative program for blue-collar workers, while local cooperative conferences of management and of salary policy employees constitute the fountainhead of the white-collar cooperative program.

Local joint cooperative committees at various construction projects and plant locations are established only when those local union and management officials agree that such an endeavor might serve a useful purpose. This policy is based on the belief that the committees will prove effective only if they are created at the instigation of the local parties themselves. The size of these committees varies, according to whether they are organized on a plant, project, or division-wide basis. Each local committee designates the scope of membership coverage (plant, project, or division), but each must provide for the inclusion of all employee units represented by the Council within the defined area. The following guidelines for local joint cooperative committees are established by the *General Agreement:*

Management and employees each designate members to serve on the local committee; the numbers need not be equal. All members shall be TVA employees. The employee representatives are designated by the labor organizations participating in the local committee and must be approved by the Council. The management members are designated by the top supervisor of the administrative unit served by the committee. The top supervisor serves as a member.

The local committee elects a chairman and a co-chairman, one each for management and labor. The committee also elects a secretary.

The co-chairmen and the secretary act as a steering committee which provides the leadership for planning and carrying on committee business and which handles matters between meetings.

The local committee schedules regular meetings. Special meetings are called by the steering committee. Committee members attend without loss of time. The committee receives suggestions made by either employees or supervisors.

The committee evaluates each suggestion. Action is taken by unanimous concurrence. Suggestions relating to activities which extend in scope beyond the
unit in which the committee operates may be referred to another committee
or to the central committee.[10]

The designation of members to the local committees is not made, however,
by management and employees. Management representatives serve by virtue of the
positions which they occupy, and employee representatives are generally elected
by small groups of their fellow union members. In the Division of Construction,
where most trades and labor employees are engaged in construction work at various
projects around the valley, the employee representatives of local committees hold
the position of job steward in their union.

Cooperative Committees in Action

A primary function of the various local committees (twenty at the present time)
has been the consideration of suggestions from rank and file employees,
supervisors, or management employees. The committees are charged with
addressing such matters as the elimination of waste; the conservation of materials,
supplies, and energy; the improvement of quality, workmanship, and services;
the promotion of education and training; the correction of conditions creating
misunderstandings; the encouragement of courtesy in the relations of employees
with the public; the safeguarding of health; the prevention of hazards to life and
property; and the strengthening of the morale of the service. By focusing a
formal suggestion system upon these needs, the local committees can provide a
mechanism whereby employees can participate in improving their own work
methods and conditions.
    Cooperative committees are designed to meet other goals. They serve as a
means of communication by which management can disseminate information
to employees and, in turn, receive information from employees, and they serve
as a vehicle by which employees can participate in the affairs which affect their
immediate work environment. Of course, the underlying purpose of the program
is to improve efficiency and build employee morale by promoting harmony and
rapport between TVA employees and management.
    Although the committees have no authority to deal with collective bar-
gaining problems for which machinery has been established under the *General
Agreement*, discussions are often held which pertain to problems relating to
various issues which could probably come under the scope of the agreement.
The chief business activity of the committee, however, is that of handling
employee suggestions and also providing a forum for communication. The suggestions are generally handled in much the same way as in other industries, but
with the important difference that no cash awards are given for suggestions.

This policy has been established by the joint committees themselves and has continued in effect to the present time. The primary reason for such a policy is the view that cash awards tend to glorify and reward individual achievement, rather than the group contribution. Many suggestions are derived from groups of employees where no one individual is directly responsible for the suggestions. The cost of administering a cash awards program in this type of suggestion system would be inordinate.

The general feeling is that employees (management and nonmanagement) should make suggestions because of a desire to increase the efficiency of TVA operations, rather than for the purpose of increasing their income. Suggestions from operating and maintenance employees average about ten to twenty suggestions per one hundred employees. The number of suggestions submitted by hourly construction workers is much smaller in comparison with the number submitted by annual trades and labor employees in maintenance and operating work. This difference generally has prevailed throughout the history of the program because of the temporary nature of hourly construction work.

Conferences and Groups

For salary policy employees, the 1950 *Articles of Agreement* gave formal status to joint union-management cooperative activities. Today, the parameters within which the program operates are set out in Supplementary Agreement 13 of the contract. This section encourages the establishment of joint conferences for the purpose of promoting cooperation between management and labor. Like joint committees, local joint cooperative conferences have always been the heart of the program. In any administrative unit, representatives of employee organizations can join with management to inaugurate a local conference. Normally, local conferences have originated at branch levels. At present, more than fifty local conferences are in operation, and these conferences cover over 9,000 employees in Panel bargaining units.

The employees in any administrative unit determine the number of their representatives for the local conference in conjunction with management. This decision is a joint one because the employee representatives are to be excused from work for a few hours each month with no loss of pay. Then, the employees in the particular unit elect their representatives for the conference. These representatives often are not the elected officers of the local union, although union business representatives may also sit in on the conferences. Management representatives are designated by the top supervisor of the administrative unit. The number of employees and management representatives need not be equal.

The top management supervisor, or his agent, and a chairman designated by the employee representatives serve as the conference's co-chairmen. A secretary is also elected by the conference. The three officers act as an agenda committee, they are responsible for the maintenance of adequate records, they see that minutes of meetings are distributed, and they perform other administrative duties.

Local conferences are encouraged to meet regularly. A two hour meeting is usually held each month during working hours, and it involves from ten to twenty individuals. Three subjects are held to be beyond the scope of these conferences: jurisdictional issues arising among unions, grievances, and items subject to negotiation. Given these limits, a significant range of important subjects is considered or acted upon:

Cooperative conferences consider such matters as strengthening the morale of the service; improving communications between employees and management; conserving manpower, materials, and supplies; improving quality of workmanship and services; eliminating waste; promoting education and training; correcting conditions making for grievances and misunderstandings; safeguarding health; preventing hazards to life and property; improving working conditions; and encouraging good public relations.[11]

Decisions on matters being discussed are never reached by vote. Rather, discussion continues until a consensus is reached and until the presiding chairman can induce agreement to a conclusion of the conference. Management may not take any action, but it at least must explain to the conference its reasons for inaction. If a consensus cannot be reached on an issue, perhaps because it is too controversial, then either a decision will be postponed until later, or the issue may become a topic for collective bargaining.

Local conferences also promote a suggestion system so that individual suggestions for policy changes can be made. In 1975, these conferences considered 2,000 employee suggestions. Most of the many hundreds of suggestions made annually concern job improvement and efficiency, although others relate to training, health, safety, and other subjects. Certainly, this mechanism for direct input by employees into the joint decision-making process is an important dimension of the cooperative program. Finally, local conferences are used as a sponsoring vehicle for bond drives and charitable-giving campaigns. They may sometimes sponsor speaker programs or other programs of special interest to those in the administrative unit concerned.

An innovation in cooperation at the local level began in the mid-sixties. Many problems affected management, salary policy employees, and trades and labor employees. The problems could be most fruitfully discussed by representatives of all three parties. Therefore, cooperative groups were formed, to be composed of representatives of these three parties and to discuss problems of common interest. Between 1967 and mid-1974, the number of local cooperative groups increased from four to twenty-three. The groups are intended to supplement, rather than to replace, the use of cooperative conferences in the TVA-Panel relationship and the use of cooperative committees by TVA and the Trades and Labor Council.

Perhaps the major function of the Central Committee and the Central Conference is to plan and administer annual, valley-wide cooperative conferences. The Committee and the Conference each have annual valley-wide meetings, which climax the year's local committee and local conference activities. On these occasions, representatives from the local conferences (committees) gather to discuss matters of general concern; from 300 to 400 union and management representatives may be involved at the respective conferences. Both annual conferences are formal programs, in contrast to the very informal local conferences and committees. Normally, the programs span two days and include speeches, panel discussions, and workshop sessions.

An extremely useful aspect of the valley-wide conference is the fact that top TVA decision-makers speak directly to a large number of employee representatives. Top managers explain the rationale for management decisions affecting employees, and they discuss problems affecting the organization as a whole. For example, at the 1974 conference, the General Manager explained the reasons for constructing a major TVA office building in downtown Knoxville, rather than in the suburbs. He also discussed the ways in which environmental lawsuits against TVA were affecting the Authority's dam-building program. Such appearances by top managers may tend to make those present feel a more integral part of the organization.

Notes

1. In Alexander V. Gardner-Denver Co. 415 U.S. 3c (1974), dealing with a nonfederal employee, the Supreme Court held that both statutory and contract grievance rights could be asserted by the employee claiming discrimination on protected grounds.

2. See Benjamin M. Selekman, *Labor Relations and Union Relations* (New York: McGraw-Hill Book Co., Inc., 194), pp. 75-110.

3. Louis V. Van Mol, "Effective Procedures for the Handling of Employee Grievances," Personnel Report Services, No. 531 (Chicago: Civil Service Assembly, 1953), p. 1.

4. *Articles of Agreement and Supplementary Agreements*, Supplementary Agreement 5, p. 64. Prior to 1973, the provision contained no reference to length of service.

5. Line management has yet to be completely convinced that Personnel is an "arm of management." This is primarily because the Division of Personnel is responsible for assuring that various nonproductivity oriented laws and regulations are enforced throughout TVA.

6. Tennessee Valley Authority, *TVA Code III Union Relations*, April 1, 1970.

7. These candidates were union members but not members of the UA. They were employed as "assignees;" that is, not fully qualified journeymen.

8. TVA contended that Executive Order 11491 did not apply because the savings clause of that order excluded TVA and its trades and labor contracts from coverage. In January 1976, President Ford amended Executive Order 11491 to specifically exclude TVA from coverage.

9. Under such a provision a qualified union member will generally be selected for a promotion to a higher-level position over a qualified nonunion employee.

10. *General Agreement Between TVA and the Tennessee Valley Trades and Labor Council*, Supplementary Schedule X.

11. See *Articles of Agreement and Supplementary Agreement and Supplementary Agreements*, Supplementary Agreement 13, pp. 105-110 for the details of the organization of the cooperative conference program.

9   Conclusion

The TVA experience in union-management relations encompasses a broad range of substantive collective bargaining issues. This study focused specifically on five of these issues: structure and process, pay determination, impasse resolution, contract administration, and union security. The study also reviewed briefly the TVA experience with joint-union-management cooperative programs. In addition to these more substantive issues of bargaining, an historical review of the evolution of collective bargaining for both trades and labor and salary policy employees was presented in considerable detail.

The substantive collective bargaining issues discussed in this study were presented with two primary purposes in mind. The first was to determine the efficacy of how TVA and unions of its employees approached particular aspects of collective bargaining. The second purpose was to facilitate an evaluation of how the more successful TVA approaches might be transferred to other union-management situations. The historical review of the bargaining relationships and discussions of the environment and times within which the parties developed their approach to labor relations were presented to better accomplish these two purposes.

In this final chapter we will discuss in general terms the efficacy of some of the major features of collective bargaining at TVA. Two standards are used in making such an evaluation. First, has the TVA-Council or TVA-Panel approach to a particular collective bargaining problem served the needs and purposes of the parties directly involved? Second, do these particular approaches or mechanisms contribute to, or are they at least in keeping with, the interests of the public? The public interest would include the primary goal of TVA which is to provide electricity throughout the Tennessee Valley region at the lowest possible cost. Another related interest of the public involves TVA's charge to improve the economic and human resources of the Tennessee River Valley area. In addition to evaluating the effectiveness of the various TVA approaches to the major problem areas of collective bargaining, we will also point out the more successful aspects of the overall collective bargaining relationship which might be transferrable to other settings.

Efficacy and transferrability will first be discussed with regard to certain nonsubstantive, environmental, or procedural matters of collective bargaining which have had, and continue to have, an extremely important influence on TVA labor-management relations. These matters include the philosophy and attitudes adopted by the officials directly involved in the collective bargaining institution, the legal environment for bargaining, the unique political nature of TVA employment, and the funding and budgeting process at TVA. These aspects are particularly important in considering the transferrability question.

Nonsubstantive Matters

Philosophy and Attitude

The TVA Act of 1933 did not mandate collective bargaining. In fact, the authors of the law seemed to envision that most of TVA's construction and even its maintenance work would be done on a low-bid type contractual basis. The first TVA Board of Directors, however, decided "neither to evade nor to shift the responsibility for democratic relations between management and the employees of TVA."[1] The Board stated:

The TVA is a democratic institution. Its purpose is to further ends of democracy by democratic methods, and our feeling from the very outset has been, and today is perhaps even stronger than before, that you cannot further democratic objectives without applying the democratic approach within your own organization. You cannot ask the country or region to follow democratic methods of organization unless within your own organization you are organized to operate democratically. TVA's relations with its workers are the very essence of the Board's belief in democratic methods.
    By contracting our work we could evade or at least avoid that (democratic) responsibility. We chose not to avoid it, but to accept it as part of our job and to seek to bring to this region a modern and, we hope, thoroughly efficient conception of labor relations on a big operating job.[2]

With regard to unionization and collective bargaining, such pronouncements implied that to insure meaningful participatory democracy, employees must be permitted to organize and bargain collectively. Collective bargaining was therefore sanctioned by top TVA management as a viable institution which brought employee representatives and management together for the purpose of reaching agreement on the rules governing the conduct of work and the employment relationship. In this sense, collective bargaining itself was considered a system of government for the employer-employee relationship.

    Such a philosophy on the part of certain influential TVA management officials was particularly prevalent during the formative years of the agency's labor policy. The philosophy was in harmony with that of the New Deal and in conformance with prevailing legislative and judicial measures designed to make labor stronger and on parity with the economic strength of corporations. Such legislation included the National Industrial Recovery Act (NIRA) of 1933, which was intended to promote economic recovery by making it possible for employees to organize and bargain collectively without employer interference, and the National

Labor Relations (Wagner) Act, which strengthened and extended workers' rights provided by the NIRA. In addition to such pro-labor legislation, the Railway Labor Act had also been amended in the 1930s with substantial improvements. Judicial opposition to unions was also reversed during the New Deal period. Thus, the labor movement in this country was becoming an integral part of the economic picture.

The procollective bargaining philosophy adopted by top management was not only in consonance with the federal government's pronouncements but was also in line with the underlying objective of TVA as stated in the 1933 New Deal legislation creating the agency. The unilateral acceptance of unionism and collective bargaining by TVA gave management the upper hand in designing bargaining structure. The partnership arrangement that evolved from centralized bargaining and from the unique management philosophy regarding collective bargaining benefited the parties involved as well as the public. Public interests were served primarily by the absence of labor strife, by the increase in regional aggregate demand, output, and income generated in part by TVA employment, and through relatively efficient construction of dams and steam plants which enhanced both natural and human resources. Society benefited also from the increased supply of skilled workers.

TVA's goals and objectives have changed over the last twenty years. Although still considered a resource development agency, TVA priorities have shifted to the production and distribution of electricity at the lowest cost feasible. The partnership or team approach to collective bargaining may not be particularly applicable or beneficial in such an environment if it leads to collective dealing or to collusion. Overemphasis on cooperation may cause the parties to lose appreciation for the fact that collective bargaining is inherently an adversary relationship and must continue to be so if the institution is to serve the public interest. Top managers at TVA do seem to be realizing that cooperation should not be carried too far, and should serve limited objectives in an otherwise adversary relationship. This seems particularly true as key members of the Division of Personnel are taking a hard look at any upward biases in the compensation-determination process, at the structure and process of bargaining, and at union security arrangements. But the unions at TVA, notably the Panel unions, have also rejected an extreme in cooperation which took the form of management paternalism. On both sides, the adversary nature of union-management relations is emerging. The critical question to be answered is whether the spirit of cooperation, and its morale, productivity, and other advantages, can nevertheless be maintained.

Legal Environment

TVA union-management relations function with relatively little interference from outside legislative mandates. The government corporation is not covered by national or state labor legislation applicable to private sector employers. Moreover, TVA is not covered by Executive Order 11491, as amended, which applies to most all other federal agencies. With a few exceptions, it also operates independently of the U.S. Civil Service Commission (CSC) which controls personnel policies and procedures of most other federal employers. The only legislation having direct impact on TVA's collective bargaining and its union-management relationship, other than Public Law 330 prohibiting federal employee strikes, is the TVA Act. How has this independence from labor legislation affected TVA's collective bargaining program? What are the possible advantages and disadvantages of such freedom?

The unique New Deal role of TVA, coupled with early top management support of unionism and collective bargaining, resulted in TVA's voluntary adoption of certain collective bargaining principles established under the National Industrial Recovery Act and under the Wagner Act of 1935. TVA also adopted many of the labor policies established under the Railway Labor Act in 1923, as amended in 1933. The absence of direct coverage by federal or state labor legislation, however, meant that TVA could apply those principles it deemed appropriate or desirable. Morover, after agreeing to abide by specific provisions or policies, the principal parties could modify or rescind them as their needs changed. Also, the parties could negotiate provisions which were in fact contrary to labor legislation applicable to other employers and employees.[3] This relative freedom from outside legislative mandates has avoided many of the problems inherent in the regulating and judicial processes applicable to collective bargaining.

Although relatively free from the constraints of labor legislation, the negotiated terms and conditions of employment stipulated in TVA's labor contracts are enforceable through the procedures agreed upon by the parties. The contractual rights of TVA employees in positions represented by both the Council and the Panel are enforceable through the negotiated grievance procedures, which include final and binding arbitration. The broad scope of TVA's negotiated grievance procedures makes such appeal routes more comprehensive than the appeal routes available to most other federal, state, and local government employees. Moreover, the appeal procedure for TVA's white-collar employees represented by the Panel is much broader than comparable procedures in the private sector. In addition, rights under the negotiated agreements are enforceable in many instances through the federal judicial system—provided, of course, that proper administrative and contractual relief measures have been exhausted.

The fact that grievances can only be appealed to arbitration on behalf of an aggrieved employee by the Panel or the Council makes the grievance machinery somewhat less effective as a means of disposing of employee disquietude than if the employee could appeal to arbitration without Panel or Council support. However, both salary policy and trades and labor employees can exhaust their administrative remedies under the TVA labor agreements and seek judicial review of agency action without the assistance of the Panel or the Council.

Although the CSC does not regulate TVA personnel policies and procedures, it does become involved in administration of the Veteran's Preference Act which gives TVA employees with veteran's preference status certain appeal rights. This channel of recourse, plus the equal employment opportunity complaint procedure, the Freedom of Information Act, and the Privacy Act, have introduced outside interference into employee relations matters which had previously been subject to internal control.

The absence oi directly applicable labor legislation has benefited TVA and its unions and has actually strengthened the overall collective bargaining relationship in TVA. Freedom from legislative restrictions has allowed TVA to establish and maintain a collective bargaining relationship tailored to meet its own unique circumstances when coverage by federal legislation could have hampered such efforts. Over the years, the legislative independence inherent in the collective bargaining process in TVA appears to have resulted in an efficacious relationship.

A potential weakness of such independence from labor legislation involves the possible abuse of individual applicant and employee rights. This can be a particularly important problem in cases of alleged unfair union representation and is even more critical where such issues involve an employee claim of improper termination. In the TVA setting of official encouragement of unionism and collective bargaining, management abuse of employee rights to fair and nondiscriminatory treatment seems less of a threat. Yet, at the other extreme, employee rights to *refrain* from union activity may be abused in the absence of NLRB-type controls. More importantly, TVA employees (bargaining unit and management) have little knowledge of specific employee and/or union rights under national labor legislation or even under Executive Order 11491. They have become unaware of the benchmarks which can be used for a comparison with their own rights existing in the absence of a legal framework.

Another weakness, applicable primarily in blue-collar employment and especially for operating and maintenance employees, involves the bargaining structure. Can fair and complete representation of employees result from a highly centralized union organization composed of union representatives not elected by the rank-and-file union members? The major disadvantage of noncoverage has indeed been the tendency for TVA and the Council to engage in "deal bargaining" as opposed to collective bargaining.

Although the advantages to TVA of legislative independence appear to have far outweighed possible disadvantages, we are by no means suggesting that collective bargaining in general would be enhanced by repealing the NLRA and labor legislation applicable to other employers and unions. Nor are we suggesting that parties at the federal, state, and local levels of government be denied necessary legislative guidance. TVA labor relations prospered in the early decades because of an enlightened and farsighted management and by the adoption of personnel policies which reinforced and strengthened collective bargaining. In fact, we would contend that if other employers had adopted some of TVA's approaches to collective bargaining, less need would have existed for some of the legislation and outside interference in labor relations that we see today.

Unique Political Nature of TVA Employment

Workers employed in state and municipal governments, and their friends and relatives, constitute a large pool of potential votes which no governor or mayor can completely ignore. Although these individuals may not actually vote in bloc, elected officials may not want to take that risk. Therefore, unionized employees at the state and local levels, and to a lesser extent at the federal level, have a potential source of bargaining strength which is not available to private sector employees. Those in private employment do, however, have the strike weapon as part of their arsenal of weapons, but public sector unions can always strike in spite of legal prohibitions.

TVA employees do represent a large potential voting bloc; yet, TVA officials are not elected by popular vote and this type of political influence is absent during contract negotiations. In this sense, TVA is very similar to private sector organizations except for the fact that TVA craft unions do have considerable political influence through the AFL-CIO, and particularly through the Building Trades Department. TVA respects this potential political clout and benefits from it. Whenever legislation is proposed which would erode TVA's relatively independent personnel system, TVA looks to national leaders of the craft unions to lobby against it.

The political influences of the Council also affect TVA labor-management relations in another way since the Council can use its clout to make its demands known to the TVA Board of Directors. The Council can do this either directly, which they have done, or they can influence congressmen and senators to put pressure on TVA. Because of organized labor's influence in Washington, the TVA Board gives careful consideration to the Council's demands. Nevertheless, lobbying and related activities by unions at TVA have not been as prevalent as in many other government settings and have not had the effect of undermining the credibility of the collective bargaining process.

Financing and Budgetary Process

Government services are typically financed by revenues generated through taxes. Public sector employees are thus ultimately dependent upon the taxpayer for their livelihood. This factor injects a third party (the taxpaying public as represented by legislatures or councils) directly into the employee-management relationship. Local school teachers, for example, must negotiate increased salaries not only with the mayor or school board, but also with the city council which controls the purse strings of the budget by its authority to request increases in property taxes. Since membership in that governing body is based on city-wide elections, its officials are reluctant to alienate the voter by increasing taxes. Politics once again enters the public sector bargaining arena.

TVA, like other governmental businesses and private employers who make money by selling a product or service directly to the consumer, is a financially self-supporting entity. Only its nonpower related activities depend on congressionally appropriated funds, and employment in these activities is minor compared with that supported by funds generated through the production and sale of electricity.[4] Since 1959, the power program has financed all operating and maintenance expenses and most of the construction costs from power revenues and power revenue bond sales.

Being the sole producer of electricity for the Tennessee Valley region and facing no regulatory control over its rate-setting process, TVA adjusts its power rates to cover the total costs involved in producing and selling electricity. In fact, it would be illegal for TVA to do otherwise. Also, since the demand for electricity tends, over the short run at least, to be relatively price inelastic, the agency has some latitude in adjusting the price of its product to cover costs without fear of losing revenue.

TVA presently has no formal budgeting process for anticipating and incorporating increased wages and salaries. These costs, whatever they happen to be, are included in the total cost figures and, if revenues are insufficient, the price of the product is adjusted to cover them (see the TVA cost figures in table 9-1 which indicate the declining proportion of payroll costs to total costs). The TVA Board of Directors has final TVA authority over the amount by which wages, salaries, and other labor costs are increased each year. However, the Board must be guided by the fact that trades and labor pay rates must be those prevailing in the vicinity and that the salary policy rates are to be based on prevailing pay. In the event of pay disputes, the Secretary of Labor has final authority over trades and labor wages, and an outside neutral has final authority over salary rate increases in the event of an impasse.

Although the Division of Personnel is responsible for actually negotiating pay changes with the Council and Panel, the Board and the General Manager are actively involved in management preparations for negotiations and are also consulted during and after the bargaining sessions. Such complete involvement in the pay determination process helps assure that what the Division of Personnel negotiates with the unions will be ratified by the TVA Board. In reality, the General Manager and the Board know (or dictate) the approximate pay increases to be negotiated since the prevailing pay determination process allows the Division of Personnel to rather accurately estimate the increases to

Table 9-1
Personnel Compensation and Other Major Costs, 1964–1975
(in millions of dollars)

Cost Categories	FY64	FY65	FY66	FY67	FY68	FY69	FY70	FY71	FY72	FY73	FY74	FY75
Personnel compensation	130	134	142	149	177	189	214	278	319	312	328	384
Personnel benefits	13	14	16	18	21	25	29	39	46	51	55	67
Total pay	143	148	158	167	198	214	243	317	365	363	383	451
% of total costs	39.2%	41.1%	37.8%	34.6%	36.7%	34.7%	31.9%	32.8%	32.4%	31.6%	29.8%	22.2%
General services	37	44	47	61	62	65	79	107	98	122	142	306
Supplies and materials	112	108	134	144	150	169	214	233	257	313	381	531
Equipment	43	28	41	53	61	99	136	190	260	156	168	383
Interest and dividends	9	11	14	20	27	39	62	78	100	139	183	229
Other	20	21	23	37	41	30	30	40	44	55	60	130
Total costs	364	360	417	482	539	616	764	965	1124	1148	1317	2024

Source: U.S. Bureau of the Budget, *The Budget of the U.S. Government* (Washington, D.C.: U.S. Government Printing Office, 1964–1976).

be negotiated. The Board may either approve Personnel's estimated pay increases or ask management to attempt to negotiate a lower rate. This is true regardless of what rates may be considered to be "prevailing."

Substantive Issues

Bargaining Structure and Process

The highly centralized bargaining structure on the union side, although reluctantly accepted by the unions of salary policy employees, is now an established TVA institution. Both parties reap advantages from centralized bargaining. One major benefit to management has been efficiency. TVA has bargained with as many as 30,000 construction and operating and maintenance employees using only two labor contracts. One alternative would be separate bargaining with each of the sixteen building, construction, and metal trade unions, some having few or no members employed by TVA. Another alternative might be separate contracts with each local union. For salary policy employees, TVA is concerned with only one contract covering about 10,000 employees who are represented by five unions. Instead of a total of twenty-one separate bargaining sessions, management representatives are therefore involved in only two periods of wage negotiations annually for all of its represented employees.

Management also finds it easier to train supervisors in contract interpretation and administration and to transfer supervisors when only three contracts cover all employees. Uniform, negotiated results from centralized bargaining have been found to obviate morale problems which may result when workers compare disparate results achieved by their respective unions. Furthermore, management has realized what it desired the most from the centralized union structures—responsibility. The union negotiators, particularly on the trades and labor side, are somewhat removed from direct pressure and observation by the rank and file. They can move responsibly toward an agreement which is not accomplished through strike threats or illegal slowdowns or work stoppages.

Advantages from centralization have also accrued to the unions. They combine their strength and their staff support for bargaining. Uniform results on most of the subject matter of bargaining do not make some negotiators appear inept relative to others. At the same time, wage increases need not be uniform, and each union has the ability to represent itself through the Council or Panel in bargaining over wages or salaries for its members.

What about the impact of centralized bargaining on the public? If uninterrupted services are considered end products, then we must conclude that at TVA the results of bargaining with centralized union structures are not unreasonable. The complete absence of work stoppages in the production and transmission of power is clearly in the public interest. The centralized structure has also moderated the leapfrogging pressures which have otherwise contributed to further upward bias in the application of the prevailing pay criteria.

A centralized union structure is efficient for both management and labor and tends to yield increased responsibility on the union side because negotiators are given some isolation from direct rank-and-file pressures. Centralization can, however, be carried too far. Coupled with a lack of referendum rights and with ineffective election controls, it can mean employee inability to influence the structure which purports to represent them. The lack of representation is particularly acute for operating and maintenance employees who represent nearly 30 percent of the total trades and labor work force. These employees have more need for representation than construction workers but are unable to achieve it through the present Council arrangement. Thus, the trade-off between the advantages of centralization and the potential dangers of inadequate democracy cannot be ignored by parties to collective bargaining.

While the union structure for bargaining and for contract administration is highly centralized, both horizontally and vertically, the management structure is decentralized so that administrative responsibilities for personnel decisions and union-management relations are shifted from the Personnel Division to line management in various operating divisions. Management organization for bargaining is also decentralized in that top line managers comprise the negotiating teams and in fact can wield considerable authority in the bargaining sessions. Although decentralization has produced positive results in establishing two-way communication between line and staff management, such a structure for bargaining can play havoc with consistent application of personnel policy and with sound personnel policies which are in the best interests of the entire organization. A Director of Personnel must have considerable authority from top management if he is to effectively establish and maintain a viable personnel program. This is more difficult in TVA since the Director's position is subservient to that of the heads of the two major line organizations. The problem is even greater during negotiations, since the position of Manager of Union-Management Relations is below that of the Director of Personnel and of members of the negotiating committees.

Although decentralized in the sense that line managers play a major role in contract negotiations, the management negotiating committees do have sufficient authority to commit TVA to binding settlements. The TVA Board of Directors has final authority to approve negotiated settlements, but it has never refused to accept an agreement negotiated between management committees and either the Panel or Council. One Board member did, however, indicate reluctance to accept the 1976 salary pay increase of 8.4 percent on the grounds that it was highly inflationary. He also criticized the interest arbitration procedure as unduly restrictive of the Board's flexibility in dealing with potentially inflationary pay settlements. The procedure has since been modified to provide the Board a direct voice in the arbitration proceedings.

The Director of Personnel and Manager of Union-Management Relations confer with the General Manager and the Board prior to and during negotiations, and these top decision-makers give the management negotiators guidance as to the kinds of agreements they will approve. Only major personnel policy issues, such as pay, need Board approval prior to the culmination of negotiations. Other matters are handled solely by the negotiating committees.

Pay Determination

Both TVA and the Council and TVA and the Panel have established a significant amount of common ground for bargaining through their use of the prevailing pay standard. The parties have traditionally followed well established processes for the collection, analysis, and use of prevailing practice information. One important result has been a stable collective bargaining relationship, with a low incidence of strikes and little use of outsiders to aid in resolving bargaining disputes. TVA has also found that the results of its wage and salary determination process have generally allowed the recruitment and retention of a top quality work force for most of its positions. It has also minimized recruitment costs. Finally, employees have seemed reasonably satisfied with the compensation-determination process and with the results of the process, and positive benefits have accrued in the form of reduced turnover and enhanced productivity.

What is the price of labor peace and employee satisfaction to TVA, its customers, and society in general? Have negotiated compensation increases, based upon the prevailing rate standard, been so high that the costs of using the standard have exceeded the benefits? Certainly, the bias in survey samples toward high-wage areas and high-wage, unionized firms, along with pay settlements above the fiftieth percentile in data ranges, indicate that compensation levels at TVA exceed those generally prevailing in the region and that percentage increases at TVA have been somewhat higher than the mean of percentage increases for similar jobs in the southeast. In fact, the increases are comparable to national trends. Table 9-2 presents the record of annual, percentage increases in wages and salaries negotiated by the Panel and Council on the basis of survey data. From 1960 to 1973, when wage inflation was a severe problem in the building trades, the average annual increase in hourly wages for a composite of U.S. building trades was 6.05 percent.[5] The annual average negotiated by the Trades and Labor Council for comparable positions was 5.58 percent. The Bureau of Labor Statistics also publishes average annual increases in salaries for professional, administrative, technical, and clerical positions across the nation. From 1961 to 1975, the annual average increase for this group was 5.03 percent.[6] Annual increases negotiated by the Salary Policy Employee Panel averaged 5.40 percent.[7]

Also, if one compares TVA's average hourly or weekly earnings for its construction (schedule A) employees with the earnings of nationwide employees

Table 9-2

Average Wage and Salary Increases Negotiated Annually for Employees
Represented by the Trades and Labor Council and by the Salary Policy
Employee Panel

Year	Average Wage Increase Negotiated by Trades and Labor Council (percent)	Average Salary Increase Negotiated by Salary Policy Employee Panel (percent)
1940	0.4	Not Available
1941	4.6	Not Available
1942	2.9	Not Available
1943	3.0	Not Available
1944	3.8	Not Available
1945	2.5	14.7
1946	5.3	14.5
1947	14.8	No Increase
1948	10.5	Flat $330
1949	12.2	Average $140
1950	3.0	No Increase
1951	10.5	11.6
1952	5.7	2.6
1953	5.3	2.9
1954	4.7	3.1
1955	3.3	2.6
1956	4.6	4.8
1957	5.4	5.2
1958	4.9	5.1
1959	4.7	4.5
1960	4.4	4.5
1961	4.3	3.5
1962	3.8	3.0
1963	3.6	4.2
1964	3.1	2.9
1965	3.0	2.9
1966	3.7	3.8
1967	3.9	6.7
1968	5.2	5.2
1969	6.5	5.7
1970	8.0	7.2
1971	10.1	6.2
1972	7.9	6.2
1973	5.1	5.3
1974	5.7	7.0
1975	8.9	9.3

Source: Adopted from material in personnel correspondence files of the Tennessee Valley
Authority.

in contract, general building, heavy or special trade construction, he would find
that TVA pay is at least equal to, if not greater than the pay of employees in the
latter group. A primary reason for the relatively high TVA earnings is that the
average weekly hours worked by TVA construction employees is consistently

higher than national averages for construction employment (including special trade contractors).

In applying the comparability or prevailing pay standard government employers must consider at least three conceptual problems that, based on the TVA experience, make the criterion insufficient for pay setting purposes when used alone.[8] First, the prevailing pay standard does not consider the supply of or demand for manpower. It assumes that the only information necessary for determining government pay is the rate(s) for that job level prevailing in the applicable labor market. An overabundance of qualified applicants for certain types of positions, however, would make substantial wage increases appear economically unnecessary. Such labor queues may either reflect higher wage and/or higher nonwage advantages in the agency using the comparability standard.

A second conceptual difficulty is that the theory behind the comparability pay policy assumes that the prevailing pay rates are set on the basis of competitive market forces. This does not always reflect reality. Prevailing wages may be higher or lower than those that would prevail under competitive conditions. Application of the policy should therefore include consideration of such factors as the representativeness of the sample of firms used to determine what rates are prevailing, unionization, unfair discrimination, and extent of monopsony prevailing in applicable recruitment areas.

An additional reason for the insufficiency of the prevailing pay policy is that government employment generally operates in a political environment.[9] Public employers must consider the reactions of both government workers and other voters to any wage decision—and government workers constitute a large bloc of potential voters. Public managers may therefore be overly concerned with the economic welfare of their voter-workers. If collective bargaining over pay matters is to succeed, however, "the chief executive officer must act first as a manager, although he understands that hard choices, if they are politically unpalatable, may ultimately drive him from office."[10] Also, employee representatives must accept the legitimacy of management acting like management.[11]

The TVA experience illuminates two other types of political influences on public management. One involves the political clout of organized labor through the AFL-CIO which has and may continue to influence management behavior in negotiations. The other involves the influence of "consumer power." The general population of the region has experienced unusually high increases in their electricity rates and despite valid cost justifications (primarily nonlabor) the public is demanding agency fiscal responsibility. Such pressures are being transmitted to TVA's bargaining parties via the Board of Directors which feels the brunt of these political forces. Specifically, the Board wants to minimize public criticism by making wage and salary increases at least appear reasonable and in line with regional and even local increases.

The TVA experience not only reinforces the need for a more sufficient prevailing wage standard, but it also reveals the need for an unbiased application of that criterion. Government employers characterized by monopoly in product/ service markets, by monopsony in labor markets, and/or by relatively inelastic demands for labor, should be required to set compensation levels that are in conformance with an unbiased application of the prevailing pay criterion. Compensation levels should also be fair to other employers competing for the same labor and to the public in general who must pay for increasing costs of services and who suffer the consequences of possible misallocations of human resources.[12] The inherent economic objective of an unbiased application of the prevailing wage criterion is to promote such public purpose interests as well as to meet recruitment, employment, and productivity goals of the employer utilizing such a policy.

In situations where collective bargaining determines pay rates based on the comparability policy, government employers and others must particularly assure that its application includes consideration of the insufficient nature of the policy. Also, the employer must carefully evaluate the impact of yielding to union pressures to upwardly bias the application of the criterion. The problems of implementation, as reflected by the TVA experience, involve determining the appropriate geographic area from which rates are gathered; the particular employers chosen within that area; the jobs used for survey purposes and how they are compared; the lack of use of total compensation comparisons; whether the survey should produce regional or local rates; and the analyses of pay data and of what rate constitutes "the prevailing" rate.

In combining the pay setting process with the process of determining what rates are prevailing in the vicinity, the TVA bargainers have included upward biases in the application of the prevailing wage criterion. Prevailing pay rates are "negotiated" in such a manner as to include the parties' needs and desires in establishing pay rates for TVA employees. Such requirements may include considerations of fairness, ease of recruitment, turnover, labor peace, costs, and projected inflation. The economic consequences of such a biased application of the prevailing wage standard involve possible redistribution of income to TVA employees at the expense of those paying taxes and electricity bills, misallocation of human resources, and unfair competition with other employers demanding similarly qualified manpower as TVA.

Impasse Resolution

The legal requirement to use the Secretary of Labor as the final arbiter of trades and labor wage disputes has effectively served the interests of the parties as well as the public. Relatively few wage impasses have occurred over the last forty years. Decisions resolved by the Secretary of Labor have been accepted by both parties and no wage dispute has ever resulted in a work stoppage. This "arbitration" procedure, coupled with the parties' application of the prevailing pay mandate, seems to provide sufficient pressure on the parties to engage in good faith bargaining and to reach mutually agreeable pay decisions.

On nonwage issues, the Council and TVA have negotiated a combination mediation and arbitration procedure for resolving impasses. This machinery should be considered effective since the parties have mutually resolved such issues without third-party involvement and without resort to strikes or lockouts. The difficult question to answer precisely is whether the negotiated settlements have resulted in unjustifiable cost increases or inefficiencies which outweigh the benefits of labor peace.

A unique feature of the trades and labor agreements involves the joint union-management approach to handling work stoppages. This procedure has served the parties, and the public, extremely well in the past and deserves careful consideration by parties who are faced by extralegal or wildcat strikes.

The present TVA-Panel machinery for impasse resolution has been of very recent origin and is thus more difficult to evaluate. To date the procedures appear successful primarily because the final-offer arbitration stage has not been utilized by the parties. The arbitration procedures have effectively discouraged their own use, but again, the application of the prevailing pay doctrine has also played an important role in providing common ground for the parties to reach agreement on their own.

Contract Administration

TVA's grievance adjustment machinery for trades and labor and for non-management salary policy employees places primary emphasis on communication and on resolving employee complaints without resort to outside third parties. The relatively few grievances appealed to arbitration indicates that the central labor bodies have been successful in keeping grievances in-house. However, the inability of Council or Panel member unions to individually appeal employee grievances to arbitration does understate the number of appeals that otherwise would probably have been made. This is particularly true for trades and labor grievances because of the highly centralized nature of the Council and because of the inability of local union business agents to effectively utilize the grievance procedures without the support of their international representative—an individual who is much further removed from the day-to-day work environment. The more democratic structure of the Panel and of its member unions gives salary policy employees better representation, and, not surprisingly, more grievances are appealed to arbitration than on the trades and labor side.

An evaluation of how the grievance machinery serves the parties cannot be made solely on the basis of the number of grievances processed. Too few grievances filed could mean that employees have little faith in the adjustment procedure or that employees have no effective third-party recourse to arbitrary or capricious management action. On the other hand, a large number of grievances processed to arbitration could indicate that the procedure is not effectively screening out frivolous grievances. On the whole, the TVA experience indicates that the trades and labor machinery is perhaps too centralized and not adequately responsive to individual employee complaints. The salary policy machinery and union structure appears more able to protect individual rights while at the same time maintaining the integrity of the collective bargaining relationship. Both procedures would better protect individual employee rights if member unions of the central labor organizations could individually appeal grievances to arbitration.

The lack of adequate rank-and-file protection is by no means peculiar to the TVA-Council grievance machinery, and the effects of most proposed solutions to such a problem generally contain disadvantages which outweigh any increased protection to individual employees. Such proposals often present serious risks to the collective bargaining relationship between the employer and union. Increased protection of the rights of individual employees might seriously undermine the labor contract, and could even adversely affect the rights of majority employees in the bargaining unit. For example, to permit an aggrieved employee the right to appeal any case he wishes to arbitration could destroy the collective bargaining relationship. Such destruction could also occur as a result of overuse of alternative grievance/complaint procedures which function either in lieu of, or in addition to, contractual grievance adjustment procedures. Granting individual member unions of the Council and Panel the authority to appeal grievances to arbitration must also be weighed against the possible loss of control of the central labor organizations which are responsible for maintaining the integrity of the labor contracts with TVA.

Union Security

Union security for the Council and its member unions is guaranteed by official TVA policy and by the *General Agreements* between TVA and the Council. Membership in a union affiliated with the Council is considered a positive factor of merit and efficiency both for appointments to positions represented by the Council unions and for promotions, transfers, and retention in trades and labor positions. Union security for the Panel and its member unions is also assured by official TVA policy and by the *Articles of Agreement* between TVA and the Panel. Membership in a union affiliated with the Panel is considered a positive factor of merit and efficiency for promotion, transfer, and retention in positions represented by the Panel unions. Employees who become and remain members of TVA unions therefore receive preference over nonunion employees. Such preference is based on the rationale that union membership contributes to harmonious labor-management relations and thereby to the accomplishment of TVA's objectives.

Employment in TVA is governed by the TVA Act and other applicable federal law. The TVA Act provides that all appointments and promotions should be given and made on the basis of merit and efficiency and further that the TVA Board should provide a system of organization to fix responsibility and promote efficiency. Under this statutory authority, TVA has formal labor agreements covering virtually all nonmanagement employees. While union membership is not a requisite to TVA employment, these agreements provide that membership and participation in unions party to the agreements are recognized as advantageous to employees and management in promoting employee efficiency and understanding of TVA policy. Therefore, such membership and such participation are among the positive factors of merit and efficiency to be considered in selecting employees for promotion, transfer, and retention. The basis of this policy is the belief that TVA will be more efficient if its employees have an opportunity to participate in determining the conditions under which they work, and the further belief that this opportunity can be provided most effectively through unions which represent them.[13]

Including union membership as a positive factor of merit and efficiency in selections for promotions and transfers and for appointments for trades and labor positions is an expedient measure created by TVA, the Council, and the Panel to provide union security. Such a measure has in fact resulted in substantial security for the central labor bodies and their affiliated unions. Nearly 99 percent of all eligible trades and labor employees are members of Council unions and almost 87 percent of eligible salary policy employees are members of unions affiliated with the Panel. The arrangement has indeed served the interests of the unions and the Council and Panel and also has met management needs at TVA by providing stability to the Panel and Council organizations and their member unions. But what about the rights of individual applicants and employees as well as the interests of the public in general?

The public certainly benefits from harmonious labor-management relations, and the TVA union security mechanism contributes toward this end. A more traditional approach to union security, such as the agency or union shop, would insure membership and/or financial support for the union from those workers hired by management. Neither of these two union security devices would insert union membership as a factor in appointment or promotion decisions or presume that union membership was a job-related criterion for such decisions. Certainly, TVA could not statistically validate union membership as a criterion for determining merit and efficiency, and, thus, for making appointment, promotion, or other personnel decisions.

Cooperative Programs

TVA's union-management cooperative programs supplement collective bargaining
and in fact reinforce that relationship. Rank-and-file employees, particularly
salary policy and operating and maintenance employees, actively participate
through job stewards and other elected officials in communicating with management officials in a nonadversary atmosphere.

Improved communications is the underlying purpose of the cooperative
programs, and success in achieving such an objective varies according to the
particular organization. The majority of cooperative programs do in fact promote communication between management and nonmanagement employees.
Through such communication employees learn about personnel and other actions
occurring in their particular TVA organization and can better understand the
basis for many of these decisions. Management can also learn about employee
concerns and take steps to improve relationships.

Admittedly, the cooperative programs are costly to TVA and to the public
in terms of employee time away from regularly assigned duties. The benefits
are often extremely difficult to measure although the suggestion system has generated significant improvements in efficiency and cost savings. If a comparison
of the benefits versus the costs of such programs is made, the time spent communicating through the cooperative programs appears to be worth the costs
involved. This is particularly true since the collective bargaining structure is
highly centralized and minimizes employee participation. Indeed, the centralized structure may only be workable if the cooperative programs are used as
vehicles to gain employee participation or union-management relations.

Whether the TVA approach to union-management cooperation is transferrable to other settings depends upon the maturity of those particular bargaining relationships. We doubt that machinery designed to promote communication and cooperation can be successful when unions are fighting for recognition
or for security and when the relationship has not yet become stabilized. We also
doubt that a transfer will be successful if bargainers in another setting attempt
to use the cooperative machinery as a substitute for collective bargaining, rather
than as a vehicle for communications and employee input.

Notes

1. "Statement of David Lilienthal to Board-Staff Conference on Authority's
Labor Relations Policy," December 28, 1943 (included in unpublished TVA
document, *TVA Labor Relations Policy: 1933-1953,* pp. 1-2).

2. Ibid., p. 2.

3. One primary example of this is the TVA policy of encouraging union
membership which is contrary to national labor legislation and to Executive
Order 11491 but which is legal under the TVA Act.

4. Nonpower programs which are not self-supporting include navigation, flood control, recreation, and fertilizer production. The latter produces some revenue.

5. U.S. Bureau of Labor Statistics, *Handbook of Labor Statistics 1975– Reference Edition* (Washington, D.C.: U.S. Government Printing Office, 1975), pp. 229-230.

6. U.S. Bureau of Labor Statistics, *National Survey of Professional, Administrative, Technical, and Clerical Pay* (Washington, D.C.: U.S. Government Printing Office, March 1975), p. 2.

7. Michael L. Brookshire, "Bargaining Structure in the Public Sector: The TVA Model," *Journal of Collective Negotiations in the Public Sector,* Volume 5, Number 3 (1976).

8. See Sharon P. Smith, "The Principle of Comparability in Federal Pay Determination," (Paper presented to the Society of Government Economics, Atlantic City, New Jersey, September 17, 1976), pp. 9-10.

9. Donald A. Wollett, "Collective Bargaining in the Public Sector: State Government—Strategies for Negotiations in an Austere Environment," Industrial Relations Research Association, Proceedings of the 1976 Spring Meeting, May 6-8, 1976, Denver, Colorado, p. 505.

10. Ibid.

11. Ibid.

12. Raising wages above the competitive level in one industry might cause unemployment or a reduction of the rate of hiring for that industry which in turn would result in more applicants to other industries. The increase in the supply of labor to the lower wage industry would cause lower wages and higher employment and an under-utilization of human capital forced to take jobs where their productivity is lower.

13. Letter from Aubrey J. Wagner, Chairman, TVA Board of Directors, to Howard H. Baker, Jr., U.S. Senator, March 26, 1976.

Appendix A: Schedule A Prevailing Wage Survey

Fortieth Annual Wage Conference
International Association of Heat and Frost Insulators and Asbestos Workers

1	2	3	4	5 TVA Survey[a]		6
Location and Source	Classification	Effective Date of Contract	Coordinated Survey All Sources	Local Union	Association of Employers	International Union Survey[a]
Tri-Cities, Tennessee	Asbestos Worker	1/75	$8.390[b]			
Local Union 46						
International Union Exhibit 08						
Muscle Shoals, Alabama	Asbestos Worker	9/73	$7.710			
Local Union 78						
International Union Exhibit 08						

[a] If the wage rate surveyed by TVA is different from that collected by the International Union, the TVA rate is recorded in column 5 and the union rate is shown in column 6. Also, the TVA-surveyed rate may be shown under the column of Association of Employers to reflect the fact that rate had been validated as accurate by an employer.

[b] Basic hourly wage rate obtained by both TVA and the Union, effective 1/75.

Appendix B: Schedule B Prevailing Wage Survey

Fortieth Annual Wage Conference
International Union Making Request:　International Union of Operating Engineers

	TVA Survey Data			International Union Survey Data		
Remarks	Company Number	TVA Rate[a]	Effective Date	Union Rate[a]	Exhibit Number	Remarks
Birmingham	13	5.775	08/75	5.775	B-03	Birmingham
	17	4.825	10/73	4.825	B-08	
Chattanooga	18	5.580	04/74	5.580	C-01	Chattanooga
	19	5.810	04/74	5.810	C-02	
	19	6.170	07/75	6.170	C-02	
	22	5.580	04/75	5.580	C-05	
	23	5.895	05/74	5.895	C-07	
Johnson City Asheville Clinch River	29	5.250	04/74		J-05	Johnson City Asheville
Knoxville	30	5.790	08/74	5.790	K-01	Knoxville
	31	5.790	06/74	5.793	K-02	X-10 and Y-12
	34	6.032	06/74	5.970	K-05	Job Code 18
Louisville	37	5.140	07/74	5.140	L-02	Louisville
	38	6.470	09/74	6.470	L-03	
	49	5.250	11/74		L-16	
Memphis	50	5.970	10/75		M-01	Memphis

[a] These basic hourly rates surveyed by TVA and the union apply to certain job classifications within Schedule B (crane operator, pan scraper, and power shovel operator).

Appendix C: Average Wage and Fringe Benefits—TVA and Major Area Cities

Year	Month	Area				
		Chattanooga	Knoxville	Memphis	Nashville	TVA
1975	January	$7.84	$7.67	$8.55	$7.60	$7.98
	February	7.84	7.70	8.56	7.60	7.98
	March	7.88	7.70	8.59	7.60	7.98
	April	7.88	7.70	8.65	7.68	7.98
	May	8.20	8.02	8.91	8.04	7.98
	June	8.20	8.02	8.95	8.04	7.98
	July	8.24	8.07	9.21	8.17	7.98
	August	8.28	8.10	9.21	8.17	7.98
	September	8.28	8.10	9.21	8.17	7.98
	October	8.28	8.10	9.30	8.17	7.98
	November	8.48	8.18	9.30	8.31	7.98
	December	8.49	8.18	9.40	8.31	7.98
1976	January		8.20	9.44	8.31	
	February		8.28	9.44	8.31	
	March		8.28	9.48	8.31	
	April		8.28	9.50	8.31	

Source: Adopted from material in personnel correspondence files of the Tennessee Valley Authority.

Appendix D: Analysis of Survey Data

Asbestos Worker

Location	Total Rate by Rank Order[a]	Basic Hourly Rate	Additional Employer Contributions[b]			Daily Travel Per Hour	Grand Total[c]
			Health and Welfare	Pension	Vacation		
			Craft Request				
	$10.550	$9.900	$0.350	$0.300		$0.850	$11.400
			Survey Data				
Louisville	$10.460	$9.860	$0.400	$0.200	$1.000 W	$0.875	$11.335
Paducah	10.450	9.800	0.350	0.300	0.500 W	0.940	11.390
Memphis	9.950	9.100	0.350	0.500	0.560 W	1.170	11.120
Jackson	9.950	9.100	0.350	0.500	0.560 W	1.750	11.700
Nashville	9.250	8.650	0.350	0.250	0.850 W	1.080	10.330
Tri-Cities	8.890	8.390	0.300	0.200	1.000 W	0.900	9.790
Knoxville	8.890	8.390	0.300	0.200	1.000 W	0.900	9.970
Chattanooga	8.890	8.390	0.300	0.200	1.000 W	0.900	9.970
Atlanta	8.800	8.100	0.350	0.350	0.500 W	0.875	9.675
Huntsville	8.310	7.710	0.300	0.300	0.500 W	0.625	8.935
Gadsden	8.310	7.710	0.300	0.300	0.500 W	0.625	8.935
Birmingham	8.310	7.710	0.300	0.300	0.500 W	0.625	8.935
Shoals Area	8.310	7.710	0.300	0.300	0.500 W	0.625	8.935
TVA	8.150	7.650	0.300	0.200		0.850	9.000
Asheville	7.650	7.050	0.350	0.250	0.250 W	1.000	8.650
1974 Average	9.030	8.405	0.329	0.296			9.950
1973 Average	8.149	7.660					9.090
Increase	0.881	0.745					0.860
% Increase	10.80%	9.70%					9.46%

Source: TVA Wage Analysis Book, Fortieth Annual Wage Conference.

[a]Includes base rate, health and welfare, pension, and vacation as of April 1975.
[b]Unless noted, W = withheld.

Appendix E: Salary Rate Data

Firm's Code No._____   Surveyors_____   Date_____

Legend

Rates: Minimum—Minimum or hiring rate, whichever is higher, established for class of work; and F for flat rates.

        Maximum—Maximum rate established for class of work.

Time Period: Hour (H), Week (W), Bi-weekly (B), Semi-monthly (S), One Year (Y), Other (Explain).

Type Plan: Merit Plan (M), Satisfactory Service (S), Combination (C), Other (Explain).

Total Steps: Total steps from minimum (as listed in rate column) to maximum, not counting the minimum rate.

Total Time: Total time in years from minimum (as listed in rate column) to maximum rate.

Firm No._____

Title	TVA Grade	Firm's Title	Rate Minimum	Rate Maximum	Time Period	Current Average Salary	Total Positions	With-in Grade Progression Type Plan	With-in Grade Progression Total Steps	With-in Grade Progression Total Time
Schedule SA										
Accountant	SA-1									
Accountant	SA-2									
Accountant	SA-3									
Accountant	SA-4									
Accounting Officer	SA-1									
Accounting Officer	SA-2									
Accounting Officer	SA-3									
Accounting Officer	SA-4									
Administrative Officer	SA-1									
Administrative Officer	SA-2									
Administrative Officer	SA-3									
Administrative Officer	SA-4									
Cost Accounting Officer	SA-1									
Cost Accounting Officer	SA-2									
Cost Accounting Officer	SA-3									
Cost Accounting Officer	SA-4									
Data Processing Analyst	SA-1									
Data Processing Analyst	SA-2									
Data Processing Analyst	SA-3									
Data Processing Analyst	SA-4									

Payroll Officer	SA-1									
Payroll Officer	SA-2									
Payroll Officer	SA-3									
Property & Supply Officer	SA-1									
Property & Supply Officer	SA-2									
Property & Supply Officer	SA-3									
Property & Supply Officer	SA-4									
Purchasing Agent	SA-1									
Purchasing Agent	SA-2									
Purchasing Agent	SA-3									
Purchasing Agent	SA-4									

Source: Adopted from TVA survey questionnaire used in salary surveys.

About the Authors

Michael L. Brookshire received the Ph.D. in economics from The University of Tennessee in 1975. He is director of personnel services for the statewide University of Tennessee system and a former professor of industrial relations at the West Virginia College of Graduate Studies, Charleston, West Virginia. Dr. Brookshire has published journal articles in economics and labor relations and has served as a consultant to public agencies and private sector firms.

Michael D. Rogers received the Ph.D. in economics from The University of Tennessee in 1973. Since 1969, Dr. Rogers has been employed with the Tennessee Valley Authority where he has been actively engaged in the fields of union-management relations, grievance analyses and arbitration, negotiations, and special projects involving pay determination, collective bargaining, and personnel management. He is project manager, Compensation and Standards Branch, in the Division of Personnel. Dr. Rogers also teaches economics and industrial relations on a part-time basis at The University of Tennessee.